In the Midst of Chaos

My 30 Days at Ground Zero

David W. Ausmus

Note for Librarians: a cataloguing record for this book that includes
Dewey Decimal Classification and US Library of Congress numbers is
available from the National Library of Canada. The complete cataloguing
record can be obtained from the National Library's online database at:
www.nlc-bnc.ca/amicus/index-e.html
ISBN 1-4120-1000-4
Printed in Victoria, BC, Canada

TRAFFORD

Offices in Canada, USA, Ireland, UK and Spain
This book was published *on-demand* in cooperation with Trafford
Publishing. On-demand publishing is a unique process and service of
making a book available for retail sale to the public taking advantage
of on-demand manufacturing and Internet marketing. On-demand
publishing includes promotions, retail sales, manufacturing, order
fulfilment, accounting and collecting
royalties on behalf of the author.
Book sales in Europe:
Trafford Publishing (UK) Ltd., Enterprise House, Wistaston Road
Business Centre, Wistaston Road, Crewe CW2 7RP UNITED KINGDOM
phone 01270 251 396 (local rate 0845 230 9601)
facsimile 01270 254 983; info.uk@trafford.com
Book sales for North America and international:
Trafford Publishing, 6E–2333 Government St.,
Victoria, BC V8T 4P4 CANADA
phone 250 383 6864 (toll-free 1 888 232 4444)
fax 250 383 6804; email to bookstore@trafford.com

www.trafford.com/robots/03-1369.html

10 9 8 7 6 5 4 3

For my wife Janice,

Without you by my side, I would never have been able to travel this far, nor enjoyed the journey as much.

For our children, Jeremy, Jennifer, and Sara Ausmus and Jennifer, John (wife Brandee), and Julie Bellestri, Grandchildren Ethan Reed, Johnathan and Brenden Bellestri, and Devon Chapman.

This so you will always know and never forget what happened in New York City in the days following September 11, 2001.

For Mom,

Thank you and Dad for the sacrifices, love, and guidance throughout my life. You made it all possible.

May all of you live your lives with love,
peace, freedom, and happiness in your hearts.
Always know how much we love you.

Richard & Madonna,

I HOPE MY ACCOUNT OF THE
TIME I SPENT AT THE WORLD
TRADE CENTER ATROCITY IN THE
DAYS AFTER 09/11/2001 GIVES
YOU A VIEW OF 'GROUND ZERO'
THAT YOU MAY NOT HAVE KNOWN.
ALTHOUGH THE TRAGIC RESULTS OF
THE ATTACK ARE AN IMPORTANT PART
OF THE BOOK, I HOPE THAT THE
INCREDIBLE COURAGE, STRENGTH AND
COMPASSION OF THE AMERICAN SPIRIT
SHINES THROUGH.

BEST WISHES,

Dave

09/11/2006

Acknowledgements

I would like to acknowledge and thank the following people for their contributions towards my incredible 30 day journey to the World Trade Center and their efforts in this book.

Dennis Stevenson Ph. D, thanks for juggling the work load and making do without Randy, Mark, and I. The support and efforts in getting us to New York were greatly appreciated.

Garry Suenkel, thanks for having the confidence in Randy, Mark and my abilities and character to recommend us to be part of the WTC Emergency Response Team. Thanks for everything else you have done for my career and me over the last 13 years. I could not ask for a better boss or friend.

My wife Janice, my sister-in law-Linda Hammac, and countless others for their much needed assistance in wading through my butchered version of the English language and making it readable. Without your efforts, it would not have made it to a book.

Jamie Bailey (Randy's son) owner of Tiki Graphicz for the professional assistance on the book cover. To contact Jamie's website, go to **www.tiki-graphics.com** or to contact Jamie directly with questions about his services, **tikigraphicz@aol.com.**

Stew Burkhammer, thanks for giving me the opportunity to be a part of history and the World Trade Center Disaster Emergency Response ES&H Team. To say it changed my life would be an understatement. It was a pleasure working directly for the 'Boss' those several weeks. We miss you, but know that you are still making a difference in the safety of workers in this country and others.

The entire ES&H WTC Team. We will forever share a unique bond that only those of us that were there will ever understand. We walked through the Gates of Hell everyday and witnessed things that even the devil himself had not imagined. We walked back in everyday and did our jobs in spite of it. We volunteered to help our neighbors and fellow Americans. In the process, we became a part of history that no one can ever take away from us. Every one of you should be proud of your actions at the site of the worst terrorist attack the world has ever witnessed. You did it day after day with courage, compassion, perseverance, and a deep rooted concern for your fellow man. I will never forget you.

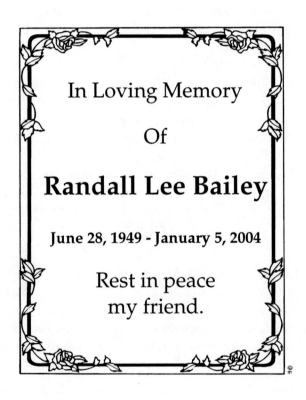

In Loving Memory

Of

Randall Lee Bailey

June 28, 1949 - January 5, 2004

Rest in peace
my friend.

Table of Contents

Introduction

As with the Kennedy assassination, Pearl Harbor, and other catastrophic events in our modern history, every American will always remember where they were and what they doing the moment they heard the unfathomable news that the World Trade Center was under attack. It was an event so profound, tragic, and earth shattering that it instantly became unforgettable.

The first moment I heard of the World Trade Center attack on September 11, I was at work in Oak Ridge, Tennessee. My friend and boss, Randy Bailey and I were standing outside of the construction office trailers discussing a subcontractor's hoisting and rigging plan. As we went through the plan, we were enjoying the beautiful Tennessee fall day. The weather was sunny, warm, and gorgeous. We had just commented how much we loved being in Tennessee when one of our coworkers, Tom Warnick, opened the office trailer door. Tom told us his wife Judy had just called and told him that "someone is flying Kamikaze planes into the World Trade Center, it is all over the news".

Initially, I thought that I must not have understood what Tom had said. It was just too unbelievable to comprehend. As most of America did, we stopped what we were doing and went to the nearest news source to get up to the minute information. We listened to the reports on Tom's radio for about 15 minutes until we heard that someone had a small TV in one of the other construction trailers. Randy, Tom, and I went over there to watch. As we were absorbing the fuzzy pictures of the towers burning, they switched to another scene of fire and chaos. It was the Pentagon in Washington DC that had also been attacked by a plane.

It was at that time that shock began to set in, the feeling of uncertainty, and trying to digest the implications of what was happening. Was this the start of World War III? Who is attacking us, the Russians, Chinese, Iraq, who? Were there other attacks we had not heard about yet, were more planes coming? With our minds and hearts racing, Randy and my thoughts turned to calling our families here and in other states to make sure they were all right and knew what was happening. I called my wife and told her the news and to turn on the TV. She began calling our children.

We also suddenly became very aware of where we were, on the site of a National Nuclear Security Complex, a facility that could be a prime target and for all we knew was on the unknown foe's list.

All of our focus was on what was happening and work was not even a consideration for most of us. All we could manage to do was watch it unfold before our eyes and wonder what was going to happen next. It did not take long to find out. Another plane had crashed in Pennsylvania, there was speculation that another was unaccounted for, and the President was heading for places unknown. The World Trade Center towers began collapsing and the world, as we knew it, was turning upside down. The whole world was watching our lives change forever on live television.

While we were glued to the television reports, a young contractor came in and asked Randy and I if we were finished reviewing his hoisting and rigging plan. He said that he had work to do. Everyone on the site including him had already heard that the World Trade Center had been attacked. I turned to him, incredulous that he could even think about work at a time like this and told him "no, someone has just attacked the Pentagon too". He looked at me with disgust and hurriedly left the trailer, mumbling something about 'life goes on', and slamming the door on his way out. Outrage is an understatement to describe my feelings at that moment. I could have slapped that soulless bastard right then. While our citizens were jumping to their deaths in our largest city, our country's military nerve center in our capitol was in flames, no one knew what was coming next, and he was upset that he could not lift a water tank. I still relive that brief, disturbing conversation in my mind every time I see him. This callous individual will never have one iota of respect from me. His lifting plan never did get approved that day as we were ordered to evacuate the Y-12 complex at noon. Although he probably suspects it, he was not going to get his plan approved by me that day one way or the other.

Into the wee hours of the night, my wife Janice and I stayed in front of the television, watching Hell unfold repeatedly in living color. The next day we were back at work as usual, however the security was now very strict, as it had to be. Armed guards were at all the entrances, the road going through the complex was closed, and no one was taking any chances. We listened to a radio every chance we had during the day. Everyone tried to actually perform work but invariably we ended up in small groups discussing the magnitude of it all and what the future may hold.

At the beginning of the next week, my supervisor and friend Garry Suenkel told me that the corporate safety manager, Stew Burkhammer, had called inquiring about who Garry had on staff here. He told Garry he was looking for experienced demolition and construction safety specialists that he may need to deploy to the World Trade Center. Garry told him that besides himself, there were Randy Bailey, Mark Spitzer, and myself. Stew said they were compiling a list of potential candidates in case they needed them. He said that he already had five or six people there trying to assist the rescue operations. Garry told Stew to let him know when he needed us. I told my wife that night about what was going on and then called my Mom. My Mom and sister Sue were coming from Michigan to visit beginning on September 20 and staying to celebrate my and Sue's shared birthday on September 22. I wanted them to know I would go if needed and may not be there for their visit. Mom said they were still coming down. She knew I would go if asked and I should not worry about her visit. She did not want me to decline on her account.

Nothing more was said about any of us going until Thursday, September 20 when I received an urgent page to call a man that I did not know. I called and reached him at the company's Maryland office. He said I was on a list of standby candidates to go to the World Trade Center and he was refining his list. He began asking me some detailed and gruesome questions that were difficult to actually give an informed answer. Questions such as would I be able to emotionally endure seeing body parts lying all over the ground or would it disturb me to see dead bodies removed. Would seeing pictures of victims or dealing with their families be something I could handle. There were a host of other less disturbing questions as well.

How do you answer those questions if you never have experienced those things before? I answered the best I knew how, that I thought I could handle it, yes, it was going to bother me, however I thought I could still do what was necessary for the job. He apologized for having to ask me questions like these but said he did not want me to walk into something I could not handle. He then said for me to be on a plane to New York City the morning of Wednesday, September 26 and bring the clothing I would need for fall and winter weather. My assignment was to last a minimum of ninety days as far as he knew at the time.

Later on that afternoon, I received a call from the Safety Manager in Oak Ridge, Dennis Stevenson Ph D. Dennis and I talked awhile about what I was getting into and whether or not I was sure I wanted to go. I told him I felt that I had to go whether I wanted to or not. I felt that this was a call to duty to me. Dennis said he felt the same way and he would support me in any way he could. He also told me to be careful; the first of a hundred times I was to hear that over the next few days.

Later that day Randy Bailey got the call to go too and Mark Spitzer was placed on standby. Garry could not go, as he was needed to keep our jobs running while we were gone. I went home that evening and told my Mom, sister Sue, and my wife Janice that I was going to New York. I do not think any of them were too happy about it because of the unknown dangers I could be facing, nevertheless they knew I had to go for personal reasons and that it was the right thing to do. We spent a great weekend together in the Smoky Mountains and Mom and Sue left for home on Monday.

Tuesday the 25th was spent packing everything I thought I would need and taking care of last minute details. Janice and I talked a lot and tried to ease each others fears of this trip. At 3:30 AM Wednesday, September 26, I left the safety of my life and home to embark on a journey that I knew would be at the least painful and sad.

What I did not expect was that this incredible journey would alter me forever, in ways that I never imagined. I went there expecting to visit Hell and I definitely found it. However, I unexpectedly found mankind, America, and myself. I witnessed the worst mankind has to offer and then I saw the best. I saw the results of cruelty, hatred, and selfishness laid out in plain view to the world and myself. However, as if to balance the terrible equation, compassion, love, and selflessness leapt out of every nook and cranny. I walked among the dead, heroes whose lives ended as the result of cowardice. I walked side by side with living heroes who rose to greatness in spite of those cowards. I spent 30 days in New York City and in that, short time I experienced more than I had in my lifetime.

I worked at the World Trade Center disaster in New York City from September 26, through October 27, 2001. This is a diary of my experiences, innermost thoughts, and emotions of the time I spent at the site of the worst atrocity in modern history. Ground Zero.

1

Destination: New York City

September 26, 2001

I left for New York City early this morning. My wife Janice drove me to the Knoxville, Tennessee airport to begin this journey into tragedy. She did very well with her emotions considering I am leaving her alone again a long distance away from our children. She was quiet but did not cry even when she dropped me off at the gate. I wonder if she knew that I was fighting off a display of a whole range of emotions. So many thoughts and concerns have been running through my head these last few days. It has crossed my mind more than once whether I will survive this and see my family again. I am going to walk into a war zone, devastation so terrible its now known world wide as Ground Zero. God only knows what might happen to me there. I cannot help wondering what terrible things I am going to see and whether or not I will be able to emotionally handle them. I know I am going to miss her and our happy comfortable life while I am in New York. I can only hope that I will return to that life when this is over.

As I expected, it took longer than usual to get through the airport security checks. The ticket agent at the counter double-checked my identification and there seemed to be extra guards all around. I had brought a small carry-on bag with some reading material, snacks, and incidentals. The scanner attendant stopped my bag and looked it over carefully on his view screen. I would guess that the airport personnel are just as nervous about a terrorist incident as we passengers are.

My apprehension about getting on the plane and making this trip is high. I do not like to fly much as it is. With the events of September 11 still fresh in my mind, I was unsure about going by plane. I would have rather taken a train or driven myself. Randy said his sons Jamie and Michael had told him they wanted to drive him there instead of this flight.

I found Randy sitting at the boarding gate area and we talked for over an hour while waiting for our flight. The short notice to go to New York and the reduction in commercial flights resulted in some difficulty getting our normal coach tickets and we ended up with first-class seats together. We were in the first two seats, making us the last lines of defense for the pilots in case someone rushed the cockpit. Waiting for the boarding on my flight to finish was nerve wracking for me. I seriously and thoroughly looked over any passenger I thought was suspicious looking, Arab or not, wondering if they could be one of 'them'. I looked for bulges in their clothing or if they appeared nervous. I also had a pen in my shirt pocket I thought I could use as a weapon if someone rushed the cockpit. It seems I was a little paranoid but it had to be a consideration in this dangerous time. I also tried to determine if an air marshal was on board and who and where he or she might be sitting. If we did have one on the flight, they blended in well with the rest of the passengers.

I feel bad that all of a sudden people of Middle Eastern persuasion should make me suspicious. Millions of Arabic people in the world have never bothered a soul. Now after the attacks, people are afraid and suspicious. Sometimes it is hard to put blame where it belongs I guess. We should blame the individuals instead of the whole group.

Randy and I talked very little on the flight, both lost in thought about what we were going to walk into in a few hours. I had many discomforting images playing through my mind. Based on the hell I have seen on television and the graphic questions asked by our company, I know this is going to test me to my very core. It will be unlike anything I have experienced and I do not know how I will react. That fear and uncertainty made for a very long flight.

We had heard that the airlines had stopped issuing metal eating utensils with onboard meals due to the safety concerns. When they brought our breakfast, they gave us a plastic knife, but a real metal fork. Randy and I talked about how ridiculous that was, as a fork could be used as a dangerous weapon as well. I hope they correct that on future flights.

Thankfully, no one caused any trouble and it was a quiet and uneventful flight. However, I remained skittish until those wheels touched the New York ground. The first step of this journey is accomplished. I am sure that this was the easiest step. It probably can only get worse from here.

Our arrival in New York City was interesting. It is my first time here, so I was naturally looking at everything on the drive from the airport. The first place I saw was Shea Stadium where the New York Mets play baseball. We went past Central Park and some other places I had heard of, but those were just quick glimpses out of the taxi window. We drove past many large apartment buildings and I wondered if they were the homes of some of the famous people that live here. I looked for the Dakota Building where John Lennon had lived and died, however I did not see a sign or anything designating its location.

We arrived at the Marriott Marquis Hotel, located right at the intersection of Times Square and Broadway. I cannot believe that we are actually staying in this luxury hotel. It is impressive and they tell us that it usually would cost $300 - $400 a night for a room here. Our company reserved the rooms here because it was the only hotel that could provide the twenty five to thirty rooms they needed anywhere near Ground Zero due to the thousands of people here to help the efforts. My room is located on the fortieth floor, room 4047. I am not sure that I am comfortable being this high in a New York City building under the present circumstances.

Outside on the street there were hundreds of people everywhere. All of the things that you see on television; Broadway show advertisements, Madam Toussad's Wax Museum, ABC television studios, taxis by the dozens, and the electronic signs broadcasting the world and stock market news are all right outside our hotel.

After we had checked in and unloaded our gear at our rooms, Randy and I went up to the room of our boss Stew Burkhammer and met with him. He filled us in on a few of the details and told us there would be a meeting this evening with the entire crew. Afterwards, Randy and I volunteered to spend most of the afternoon packing a few dozen backpacks with safety equipment for each of the safety representatives that will be arriving today. Flashlights, maps, waterproof notepads, gloves, respirators, safety glasses, and rain gear are all items we will need when we begin working at the disaster site.

Later in the evening, we attended the meeting with Stew and the rest of the crew, about 20 or so in number. We all introduced ourselves and told what area of the country we came here from. I know only one other person besides Stew and Randy and that is a guy named Denny Blackwell. Jeannette Walker, the medical professional for the crew, passed out the backpacks, hardhats, and information packets. Stew proceeded to explain the ground rules that we will have to follow. Anyone with beards or Fu Man Chu mustaches will have to shave so they can wear the respirator. Randy is going to shave the moustache he has had for over 20 years and several of the other men have beards. Stew had some fun with Randy, telling him he had to get a haircut too. Stew bantered back and forth with him quite a bit throughout the meeting. It is evident that Stew has a lot of respect for him.

Stew said that the city implemented a new rule today that prohibits the taking of any personal photographs at the site. I have brought my 35-millimeter camera with me; I guess I will not be using it much. The supervisors will have camera passes for work related photos though. We will work in 12-hour shifts, six days a week and they will let us know later in the week when our day off is. I will be on the day shift and assigned to Sector 2 or the Bovis Company area. Randy will be the night shift supervisor, in charge of about ten safety representatives.

Stew began describing the scope of our task, what the conditions are at the site, and what we should expect tomorrow morning. My God, it sounds so unbelievable! There are so many hazards that we will have to protect the workers from, as well as ourselves. Stew said that massive fires are burning under the debris piles and unknown amounts of chemicals and radioactive materials are buried somewhere in the pile. Explosive materials that were kept in the some of the federal offices are unaccounted for, holes up to 20 feet deep are in the streets, and buildings of questionable stability are all around the immediate area. Many of these buildings have severe damage, steel beams hanging from them, glass falling, and large holes in floors and walls. Worst of all, bodies and body parts are everywhere on the site, in buildings, and under the debris. He said that we are not to be involved in any body removals and under no circumstances are we to touch any remains.

Most of the workers on the site are not wearing any safety equipment such as hard hats, respirators, or work boots. So far, they have counted it as a victory if they can get them to wear long pants and footwear other than tennis shoes. Our job is to assess the situation, install safety procedures, and assist the rescuers and workforce with a safety mindset. In other words, we are to restore some semblance of safety order. This is not a small task in normal circumstances, let alone in the middle of chaos, death, and destruction.

Stew told us that he had the utmost confidence that we could accomplish this although there has never been any task so dangerous and challenging as this one. He said he picked each of us to be here because we were the 'best of the best' that our company has to offer.

That comment meant a lot to us coming from him. I hope we can live up to that belief.

After the evening meeting, Randy and I went to Times Square to get something to eat and look around the area. The first thing we saw was a tall guy wearing a cowboy hat, boots, and a pair of underwear with 'The Naked Cowboy' written on them. He had a guitar that he strummed and people were paying him money to get their picture taken with him! Unbelievable, but I have to say that he appears to be making an honest living no matter how ridiculous he looks. A few blocks down a guy was standing on the corner holding a sign that said 'need money for booze, drugs, and hookers. Why lie?' There were several people on the streets looking for handouts. No one approached us and they mostly just sat on the sidewalk or stood against a building with their signs for help or a coffee can to collect any donations. It was a zoo-like atmosphere, packed with people, but there were so many police officers on foot and horseback that it felt safe. Cleaning out the criminal element in Times Square so tourists would come back was one of Mayor Giuliani's projects. It seems to have been successful as the place is incredibly crowded with people.

We went into a place on the corner of Broadway and Times Square called Lundy's which is supposedly world famous. We grabbed a booth and began looking over the menu. After a few minutes we decided that the $15.00 they wanted for a sandwich was higher than we wanted to pay as it was over half of our daily meal allowance. I am not saying that Lundy's sandwich was not worth the money. We just were not willing to pay that price to find out. We ended up at Tad's Steaks a few doors down and ate a steak dinner for less than the sandwich price.

During dinner, we chatted about the incredible description of the site conditions we have heard tonight. Even though Stew tried to paint a realistic picture for us, I do not think either of us can actually comprehend or visualize what awaits us tomorrow.

I can only hope I am mentally ready for our first trip to the site tomorrow morning. I keep telling myself that I need to slip into my 'just do it' mindset. That mental game usually seems to work most of the time when I have to overcome one of my phobias that are standing in the way of doing my job. Suppressing my fear of heights this way so I can climb out on structural steel beams ten stories up or up into tower cranes to perform inspections is a common mental game for me.

Back in my hotel room and after I made my calls home to let everyone know I was safely in New York and the events of the day, I laid out the clothes and equipment I would need in the morning. I started my journal of this trip and wrote down most of the days' events. It is 11:30 PM already and I have set my alarm for 5:00 AM. This has been a 20-hour day and I am physically tired, but my mind is still racing with thoughts of tomorrow. I do not know if I will be able to sleep much tonight.

Notes

Randy became one of my good friends since I began working with him over twenty years ago in our hometown, Monroe, Michigan. Randy was a 1967 graduate of Monroe Catholic Central High School and I graduated from Monroe High School in 1971. I first met him when I took an Emergency Medical Technician class at the local college and he was the instructor. His full time profession was as a safety representative for the company that I was working for, however he worked at a different job site. Several months later, he was transferred to the Enrico Fermi Nuclear Power Plant, where I was working as a construction laborer and had also became a part-time safety assistant. Randy ultimately became my supervisor on the afternoon shift. We seemed to hit it off right away and became friends. After a few years there, Randy transferred out of state and we did not see each other for a few years. One day in 1990, he called me and said he needed a safety person on his job in Pennsylvania and wondered if I would be interested in applying for it. Janice and I had just married seven months before, I was between construction jobs, and had recently given up managing a local bar. I needed a job and even though I did not really want to leave my bride and family, I applied. I was hired and went off to Beaver Valley Power Station in Shippingport, Pennsylvania. It has proven to be the best career move I ever made. I have been with the company for twelve years now and have a job I am not only good at, but thoroughly enjoy. I owe that to Randy for believing in me, that I had what it took to make a good safety representative.

After the Pennsylvania job, I transferred back to Detroit, Michigan, forty miles from home. I was the safety representative for the building of scrubber/bag houses on the Greater Detroit Resource Recovery Facility or the 'Trash Burner' as natives of Motown called it. After four years there, my wife and I began moving with the company to wherever the next job was. We went to St. Louis, Missouri, Anniston, Alabama, and now are here in Oak Ridge, Tennessee, where I began working with Randy again.

On the day before we left for New York I called Randy's house in Tazewell, Tennessee to see what time he was going to the airport and his wife, Linda answered. Linda, (nee Shelton), was from our hometown also, a 1970 graduate of Monroe High School. Linda and I talked a while about our families while waiting for Randy to come in from the feeding their horses and she told me she was worried about Randy going to New York City. She was concerned for our safety there with such uncertainty about more terrorist attacks and the conditions in New York. I told her not to worry that I was going to keep an eye on him, we were sticking together. Linda said she knew I would look out for him and that she felt better about it knowing that we were going together. I never had inkling at the time that this would be the last time I was ever to speak with Linda. Tragically, she became suddenly ill and died on January 2, 2002, at the age of 49. She was a great lady and friend. Randy was lost without her.

On January 5, 2004, my wonderful friend of 23 years, coworker, and fellow World Trade Center responder, Randy Bailey, passed away after a valiant battle with cancer. He died almost two years to the day after his beloved wife Linda. He faced this last tribulation with the same courage, strength, and positive outlook that he had during everything else throughout his life. I greatly admired and loved him. I am thankful that I was able to spend many hours with him during his final days and that he was able to see this book published shortly a few short weeks before he died. He knew that as long as a copy of this book existed, a part of him would exist beyond his short lifetime. Surviving Randy are his sons Jamie (and wife Adrienne) and Michael Bailey. Randy also left many friends, relatives, and coworkers throughout the country with a void that will remain unfilled.

2

My God, What These
Madmen Have Done

September 27

This day was so incredible, tragic, and intense that I will never be able to describe it adequately enough. I do not know enough words. My God, what these mad men have done.

I slept all right once I fell asleep after midnight. I got up at 5:00 this morning and I was very nervous. The thoughts of what horrors awaited me just would not go away. After showering, dressing, gathering all my gear, and picking up a radio at the storage room, I went down to the lobby and met with the rest of the crew. There were about 25 of us and most were making our first trip to the site. At 6:15 AM we loaded up in vans that they have rented and took the ride down to Ground Zero which is about four or five miles away from the hotel.

About two miles or so into the trip, the security checkpoints started. The first several were manned by the NYPD, the ones closer to Ground Zero had the U.S. Marines, Army and National Guard stationed at them as well. At every checkpoint, we had to stop and explain who we were and where we were going. As most of us did not have our badges yet, our boss and driver had to answer many questions before we could proceed to the next checkpoint.

It seemed as if it took a very long time to get down to the site but I think it only felt that way because I was so nervous about what we were walking into. Once we made it close to the site and finally found a place to park, we had to walk a few blocks to the 'Command Center'. The city has taken over a grade school, PS 89, which was several blocks north of the World Trade Center site and turned it into the Emergency Command Center. Everyone that will be working at the site and needs an access badge has to report here. It was very crowded with construction workers, volunteers, military personnel, and others reporting for their first day of work as we were. Security, provided by the NYPD and branches of the US Military is extremely tight here. You have to show picture identification and stay at the badge area until they finish recording all of the required information you have provided. Some of the people around our group became inpatient with the slow process and grumbled about the hassle, but I felt secure because they were being thorough to keep the terrorists from getting in here.

Once we had our badges, we had an internal meeting to discuss some of the important information we needed to know. Details such as work areas, contacts, and dos and don'ts that will assist us in doing our job. Afterwards, we all attended the daily morning meeting held in a classroom on the second floor of the school. A representative of the New York Department of Design and Construction (DDC) led the meeting but many agencies participated. Our company is working directly for the DDC. They are in charge of the safety of the site operations. The meeting was quite informative on the status of the operations, fires, changing conditions, and safety concerns. We met many of the city, state, federal officials, and contractor representatives that we will be interfacing with on a daily basis. After this meeting, we began our tour of Ground Zero.

Stew and the day shift supervisor, Jeff Vincoli, led the tour. They have been on site since September 12 and know their way around. The tour was thorough and incredible. We started at the perimeter of the damaged area, starting at the corner of West and Chambers Streets. We worked our way around the area, circling the blocks and moving closer to the World Trade Center. We went just about everyplace in the damaged area that we could access. The destruction zone encompasses a few blocks in every direction, all the way around the World Trade Center. There were so many things happening everywhere that I looked, many of which I have never imagined I would see, all mixed together with a cast of thousands.

Temporary morgues, I believe there are four, (just tent complexes), are set up in each corner or section of the site. Stretchers and body bags are stacked outside of them. Reading the morgue sign and seeing those bags caused an awful, morbid sensation in the pit of my stomach. Just knowing that those bags will be used frequently and probably right in front of me is so disturbing to contemplate. We went into several first aid/triage stations that are set-up in abandoned and heavily damaged buildings. These buildings are cleaned-up and stabilized enough to accommodate these needed services. Some of the stations are temporary tents set in strategic locations throughout the site. Most have tables and boxes full of emergency equipment, bandages, stretchers, medicines, and even some advanced life support gear. Volunteer nurses, paramedics, and even doctors are staffing them. Others have stocks of only the basic supplies but also appear well staffed by volunteer medical personnel.

About a block away from WTC Building Five stands Trinity Church that has a small cemetery buried in 12 to 20 inches of papers and dust. Hanging in the trees around it are window blinds, clothing, computer wire, and other office paraphernalia. They were all pieces of a life that ceased to exist on September 11. It looked so surreal, like it was something Hollywood had dreamed up for a movie about Armageddon. Trinity Church has a well-documented history. Apparently, George Washington once worshipped at this church. The recovery workers are calling it the *'Little church that stood'* because it did not suffer a single broken window in the attack although the buildings all around it did.

The amount of dust covering the several square blocks is staggering. It covers absolutely everything. There are also vast amounts of paper mixed in with the dust. The papers are from files or desktops sitting in the towers before they collapsed. Any place you look there is a thick layer of this gray concrete dust. On the dust

covered windows and vehicles people have written the names of
missing friends, fire department numbers, cities and towns they came
from, messages to Osama Bin Laden, and to the world.

Occupying every available space it seems, on the sides of
buildings, signposts, and windows are signs written in fluorescent
paint directing you to the locations of the morgues, first aid, food, and
anything else you need to know. Intermixed with these signs are
hundreds of posters of the missing people. Their families and friends
have put them up in hopes their loved ones survived, but so far are
unable to call home. The faces in the pictures seem to stare out at you.
These are so difficult for me to look at. I know that these people are
under that pile and never going home again. Reading some of them
was too much for me to take. Families have put any information on
them that they think will assist in finding them. The clothes they
were wearing that day, height and weight, what floor they worked
on, and the ever-present plea for someone to call with information.
Others have personal messages such as 'please come home Dad' that
made me cry for the first of many times today.

Makeshift memorials have sprung up in several locations.
One, located at Battery Park has hundreds of flower bouquets, teddy
bears, and cards and letters. Others have candles, cards, and banners
from children and people from all around the world. Some are just
simply a cross with a message; 'We will never forget' and 'Our
heroes' are a few that I saw. Viewing these triggered sadness, pain,
and anger for the senseless loss of life.

Dozens and dozens of destroyed vehicles of all kinds, taxies,
fire department, police, and privately owned are located all over the
streets or already loaded onto the backs of trucks. Some are just
flattened to their wheels and others are in various stages of ruin,
whether it is broken windows, debris stuck into them, completely
burned out, or just filled with dust. One vehicle appeared smashed
into the pavement a few feet deep and could not have been more than

a foot thick in spots. It is so badly damaged that I have no idea if it was an automobile or a truck.

The surrounding blocks have dozens of damaged buildings. Most have the majority of their windows blown out with the remaining dangling glass falling to the street when the wind blows. On several occasions, I heard the tinkling of glass breaking on the street within feet of our location. Many of these buildings have safety netting in place or boarded windows to keep the glass and debris from falling onto people below. However, many do not have anything up to prevent the debris falling and do not have barriers to keep people from unknowingly wandering into these dangerous areas.

Two or three buildings have large sections of beams from the towers embedded into gaping holes in their sides that seem to dangle precariously over the work areas. I saw one building that has multiple large holes in the side facing the World Trade Center and fires or explosions have blackened the area around them. It appears these holes resulted from falling debris slamming into the side of the building. Several floors appear to have suffered severe fire or explosion damage. This building and a few others appear they could collapse at any moment.

There are places in the streets, around the perimeter, and in the debris field that you could fall twenty feet or farther into a mess of jagged steel. No barricades or covers are in place to stop you from walking right into one of them. At any given moment, there is so much dangerous activity in every direction to watch out for that it would be easy not to notice a gaping hole in the street.

Eventually our tour group made it right up to the World Trade Center complex. The damage done here is just unbelievable. The two, 110-story towers, are now just a pile of smoldering rubble. It is almost unfathomable that buildings of this tremendous size are now the piles of debris laying here. No matter how you look at it, there does not seem to be enough rubble to equal what had been here before September 11. The tower façade columns look like some giant threw a box of his giant matchsticks on the ground. They are lying on or stuck into the pile in every position imaginable. The remainder of the debris pile looks to be just dust, paper, piping, wire, and pebble sized concrete pieces. The façade portions that are still standing uncannily resemble the Roman coliseum ruins. Thoughts of comparison to the fall of that ancient empire fluttered briefly through my mind. Could this be the beginning of the fall of another empire?

Search and rescue teams are almost everywhere around the perimeter of the debris pile, sitting on the ground, or just standing and watching the many other teams work. These teams, their personnel laden with equipment such as ropes, hooks, radios, and more, are crawling all over the debris pile following all different types of dogs in, out, up and down hills, holes and valleys of destruction. Some of the dogs are wearing what look to be booties or socks to protect their feet from sharp objects and the heat coming from the pile. Other dogs seem exhausted from their search and are sleeping around the perimeter in anything that looks halfway comfortable. They sleep in stretchers, beds of trucks, or on a pile of firefighter's gear. They never flinched or woke at the ground-shaking roar of the semi-trucks and massive construction machines passing a few yards away. These Search and Rescue teams have their home cities and states printed on the backs of their shirts. They have come from everywhere, California, Florida, and Britain, to name just a few.

Armed police officers and U.S. Army soldiers stationed at intervals of what seems is every couple of yards, are stark reminders that I am in the middle of a war zone. These sentries have a searching, serious look on their faces as if they are expecting trouble at any given second. They intently scan our faces and check to verify that we have the proper badge to be here. Our badges are a new type recently issued and we have been stopped and questioned a few times. Our supervisor clears it up so we can continue.

Cruising continually back and forth on the streets are Humvees, jeeps, and troop transport trucks. Army helicopters are flying overhead, some transporting more troops and equipment to temporary bases nearby, others circling to protect us from enemies. Army vehicles equipped with large machine guns are blocking intersections around the perimeter. A soldier gazing intently down the barrel of their machine gun staffs each of these, and their finger is on the trigger. It is a heavily armed and protected area. New York City is prepared for a war on the streets of Manhattan. It is almost beyond my comprehension.

A constant stream of semi and dump trucks, four-wheel drive vehicles, police cars, and fire equipment are intermixed with the military vehicles on the streets. All of these people seem to have some important mission at hand. The semi and dump trucks are here to get loaded with debris. After being loaded, they haul the debris down to a pier for loading onto a barge. These large trucks are moving and backing up helter-skelter all over the place. Some workers assigned to direct the traffic and attempt to keep it organized are overwhelmed and they cannot keep up with it. I find myself continually scanning the scene in every direction to keep out of their way.

Firefighters appeared to be everywhere and involved some way or another in just about every activity. Their emotional and physical conditions seem to differ with each one you see. Some are just sitting on the ground with their heads in their hands and still in shock, others seem to be dead on their feet, as if they have not slept for days. Many just stand by themselves in the debris field watching the activities and others just sit in small groups quietly talking. After we met some of the fire department chiefs in our sectors, we talked to a few of the other firefighters that were with them while our bosses and the chiefs discussed the day's activities. All of these firefighters seem to be on the edge, some on the brink of crying at any moment, and all of them know someone who was lost. They told us that a few of these firefighters are looking for missing sons. I cannot even imagine what they must be going through. To lose a child is what every parent fears and is the worst thing that can happen. To lose them in front of your eyes and have to desperately search for them for days on end in this rubble has to be Hell on earth. You can feel and see the glimmer of hope that they cling to for their children's survival fading with each stroke of the clock. I get the feeling they just have to do something, even if it is just being here.

Something that stands out so clearly in my mind is the desperation on everyone's faces as they try to find survivors, knowing that time is running out. It has been two weeks since the attack and the limit of human survival without food and water is at the point of requiring a miracle now. I cannot explain it other than to say you do not need any of your five senses to know that desperation is here. It seems to hang over the site like a fog, blanketing everyone and seeping into your consciousness. It is the most important race they will ever run and they are losing.

One of the saddest places I saw today is Fire Department-New York (FDNY) Station Number 10. It is located right across Liberty Street from the WTC Building Four. Taped to the outside walls are hundreds of cards, letters, photos, and posters. All of them sent from people all across America and around the world, offering their sympathy and sorrow. Firefighters from this station were the first to rush in and begin evacuating people. When they first ran in, like everyone else, they believed it was an accidental plane crash. This station lost several of their firefighters in the subsequent attack and collapse of the towers. Firefighters sit in front of this station just watching until they are ready to go back into the mayhem and continue searching for victims. I have the feeling that they will work twenty-four hours a day until forever to find their firefighter brothers and sisters. They do not want to quit searching until they find every single one of them.

At the end of the tour, the night shift crew left to get a few hours sleep before they come back at 7:00 PM. Randy is the supervisor of that group. They are going to be exhausted by the time the end of their shift tomorrow morning. After the night shift left, our supervisor took the rest of us to our work areas and told us to become familiar with them. He said not to worry about taking official notes until tomorrow. My work zone is Area 2 or the Bovis sector and encompasses most of World Trade Center Towers and the Vista (Marriott) Hotel. I also have several perimeter buildings that fall into my footprint of responsibility. The World Financial Center complex, consisting of three, multi-story buildings and 90 West Street, a 25-30 story building are my responsibility. All appear heavily damaged in some areas. I have not entered inside them yet to assess their interior damage.

I attempted to get orientated using the map we had been issued as I wandered around my designated area. As this is my first time here, I was having difficulty figuring out what street I actually was standing on. I ended up recruiting two NYPD officers to help me. They showed me the limits of my area, and pointed out on the map all of the places I needed to know about. One of those was how to get back to the Command Center at the end of the shift. I had no idea where I was at and they helped me a lot. It was not that easy figuring out the map for them either at first. Many of the landmarks and street signs are gone, destroyed in the attack. These officers live and work here, however it is now a foreign landscape to them too. The massive extent of this devastation caused them to pause and contemplate the directions they were probably used to rattling off without a thought before now.

Multiple agencies are involved in this effort. I have seen personnel from the Occupational Safety and Health Agency (OSHA), Federal Bureau of Investigation (FBI), National Transportation Safety Board (NSTB), and the Secret Service. US Customs, Federal Emergency Management Agency (FEMA), and Alcohol, Tobacco, and Firearms (ATF) are here as well. Some of the officials told us that the Central Intelligence Agency (CIA) and National Security Agency (NSA) are here also. Of course, they are not wearing anything that could identify them. All of us are here in New York City, standing in the aftermath of the worst terrorist attack in history. Every one of us has a mission to fulfill, different goals, but important all the same.

I had my first experience with the terrible reality of this atrocity this afternoon. As I stood on the edge of the debris field in front of WTC Tower Two, I watched as a dog and its handler from one of the Search and Rescue teams made their way back and forth over an area of the debris. During this crisscrossing of the rubble, the dog stopped to intently sniff a three-foot square area for a few seconds until it started pawing the ground and looking at its handler. The man with the dog signaled to the nearby firefighters and they began digging with shovels, picks, and their hands at that spot. They slowly, but intently worked to remove metal, wire, piping, and concrete for approximately 45 minutes until they located and finished uncovering what only the dog had been able to sense, the body of a victim. Although I was at least 30 yards away, I could tell when they had found the remains because the firefighters and others around them stopped and formed a circle around the hole they had been opening up. They waited a few minutes until a firefighter chaplain or priest arrived before they took off their helmets, bowed their heads, and he led in prayer. After this prayer service, they placed the body into a black body bag and placed it onto an orange plastic stretcher. Six firefighters carried the stretcher over to one of the four-wheel drive All Terrain Vehicles (ATV) that the FDNY uses. The stretcher was loaded into the bed of the ATV and a firefighter began to drive away. The entire event did not seem real to me up to that point. I do not know if it was because it was the first time I have witnessed anything like this or it was shock. Oddly, whatever the reason, the sad scene, emotions, and the thoughts that would normally race through my mind, did not overtake me and I returned my thoughts and attention to observing the machines performing the work activities.

A minute or so later, I was startled when the ATV drove right up next to me and stopped. I was neither expecting nor prepared for it. Although the ATV was there only briefly as the firefighter driving spoke to a colleague, those several seconds of staring at that body bag brought the flood of emotions and thoughts that I had briefly restrained. I could not help but to think of who the person had been. Have I seen their face on one of the hundreds of missing posters today? Was he or she a stockbroker, insurance agent, or janitor? Who is waiting for them to come home? Someone's child, a parent, a brother or sister is now wrapped in a plain, black plastic bag and being carted away to a tent for dead people in the middle of what can only be adequately described as Hell on earth. With these thoughts parading through my mind, the inevitable emotions and pain began. Stinging tears and an Adam's apple that felt it had swollen beyond the limits of my throat. It became hard to breathe with that hollow and aching feeling in my chest. I have not had the awful feelings with such intensity since my father, Kenneth, died almost ten years ago. I never expected that I would react this intensely to the death of a stranger. I had to walk around for quite some time and find other matters to occupy my thoughts until I could swallow and breathe without pain again. This is how my first encounter with the recovery of a victim's body took place. It was such a strange, painful, sad experience and feeling. I know that this was just the first one of too many more people I will witness dug out of this rubble before I leave this place. I wonder if they all will hurt as bad as this one.

New York City officials began bringing family members of the victims to the site today. I inadvertently ended up in the middle of a group totaling perhaps a hundred. I did not see them coming. By the time, I noticed that the people standing next to me were holding flowers, photos, and Teddy bears and were distraught and crying, they had surrounded me. I managed to work my way out of the middle and off to the side of the group, finding myself between them and a wall built around a portion of the World Financial Center. Without wading back through the group, I had nowhere else to go. In hindsight, I should have left there any way I could have. We were on the corner of West and Liberty Streets, which is directly across from WTC Tower Two, and Building Three or the Marriott hotel. This location is less than two hundred feet away from the location of the earlier removal of the victim's remains. They stood on the corner of Horror and Hell and witnessed it all first hand. I can understand the victims' families wanting to see where their loved ones died, but this sight of the search dogs, rescue personnel, and machines looking and digging for their family members and friends overwhelmed so many of them. Some held onto each other, others cried into the Teddy bears they held, and a few just could not withstand it and were helped away by counselors. I sensed that many of them had still been clinging to a thread of hope that their loved ones had survived and were moments or hours away from rescue until they saw this devastation first hand. I feel that I witnessed the moments that their desperate hope deflated like a balloon and grief, loneliness, and defeat rushed into the void. It was terrible to see, I cannot even begin to imagine how much worse it was for them.

I could not continue to watch them any longer in their grief; I found an opening and walked down the street. It just hurt too much, my throat felt as if it would explode. I hope that my family or anyone else never has to go through something like this. I do not have much hope it will not happen again and I am afraid that this is only the beginning of sadness and pain for our country.

They escorted two more large groups of family in this afternoon. When I noticed the groups walking down Liberty Street, I went out into the pile and stayed away as far as possible. I do not think I can handle that again. I understand that these visits will be a daily activity for the weeks to come.

Now, after two weeks since the attack, a faint but pungent, odor of death seems to hang throughout the site. It is not as strong and overwhelming as I had expected or prepared for. The smoke, dust, and machine exhaust swirling around the site seems to dilute it somewhat, however it always seems to be there in the background as a reminder of human toll that lies beneath our feet. I have brought a stick of deodorant in my backpack to rub onto my respirator if it becomes worse and more than I can handle.

It feels so odd and unnatural to write about these morbid things, but I want to tell the whole story so my family and future descendants may know what it was really like. The information and pictures I have seen broadcasted on CNN and other news media cannot begin to capture what I am experiencing here each minute. Terrible and unthinkable sights in every direction, the rumbling sound and ground vibration from the dozens of machines and trucks, and this permeating smell of tragedy and death. These and the encompassing, to the bone sorrow, grief, and desperation here could never be captured on film.

Although our supervisor had told us we did not need to take notes this day, I wrote two pages worth of all the things I saw that were dangerous and I felt need to be changed. I saw a so much more than two pages worth but I concentrated only on the most serious. One of the major problems that I think correcting will lead to the improvement of many of the other things on my list was to gain control of the work zone. There are the checkpoints all the way up to the site to control entry, but if you are a friend of a policeman, firefighter, or city official it is easy for you to gain entry. Once they make it past that point, they can go anywhere on Ground Zero they wish to. The result is chaos. People are blindly walking into harms way and everywhere else whether they belong there or not. They wander in front of the massive, moving machines, under thousands of pounds of dangling steel, and into any area that looks interesting to them. They do not have a clue what dangerous situations they are placing themselves. It seems that many of them want their photograph taken with debris and 50-ton machines looming over them. I am not talking about a few looky-loos either; there are hundreds of them.

I finished my first shift exploring my area, taking notes and talking to people that look like they know what is going on, trying to get the feel of this task. It is going to be formidable to say the least. The extent of the damages are more than I had ever envisioned and it seems the mindset that is driving the thousands of people here is safety be damned - it is rescue and recovery at all costs.

Several times throughout the day, I have told myself to keep my focus on the job I have to do and I will be able to get through it. When unexpected things happen that are way outside of my experience, I have to keep my emotions in check. What else can I do when a firefighter stops within five feet of me with a body inside of a bag? When suddenly realizing that I am in the midst of dozens of sobbing, distraught relatives of the missing and dead holding onto flowers, Teddy bears, and each other? It tore my heart out, but if I lose control at these times, I will be emotionally finished before my first day or two is over. I just did my best to try to maintain some semblance of mental balance and composure. I am on new, personal, and emotional ground here. I have no idea how I am going to cope, assuming I even can.

Around 6:00 PM, I started heading toward the Command Center to meet the night shift crew and have a turnover of what I have seen today that they need to know. Walking up West Street, I stopped and looked over WTC Building Six. It is nothing more than a burned out hulk now. I took a short detour and observed the crews working on the clean up of WTC Building Seven. This building is only a pile of smoldering debris as the towers are. It burned and collapsed because of the attack as well. The buildings behind and on either side of where it once stood have suffered heavy damaged. Debris blown into these buildings has created gaping holes and portions of them have extensive fire damage as well. Collapsed sections are intermingled with debris from WTC Building Seven. It is difficult to tell where one building started and another stopped. One of these structures is the Verizon Building. It seems to have faired the best out of all of them in this area. It has a few holes and some noticeable internal damage, but appears to have held up well considering its close proximity to WTC Tower One and Buildings Six and Seven.

Continuing my trip down West Street I saw many trailers and tents of the groups that have responded. There is even a hospital trailer for the rescue dogs. The Coast Guard, Army Corps of Engineers, Salvation Army, and many more agencies are set up along this street. A few blocks farther down, I passed many media trailers. I noticed a lady interviewing a man in front of a large van type truck. On the side was WTOL 11, Toledo, Ohio. I have watched that station practically my whole life back in Michigan. If we were not under strict orders not to talk to the media I would have tried to at least get on the air long enough to let everyone at home know I am alright. The newscaster was doing an interview as I walked past; maybe I made it into the background shot.

We met the night crew, who were 45 minutes late due to parking and traffic problems and gave them a turnover of our observations. Everyone was mostly curious about how bad it was and what dangers did we find lurking in his or her particular area. Afterwards we headed back to the hotel for some much needed rest. I am exhausted but wide-awake.

I really do not have anything in my life experience with which to compare this day. It seemed like time was moving so slow on the one hand, but on the other my brain was operating at lightning speed trying to catch up with the tremendous amount of visual information I found myself bombarded with continually. It feels like I spent a week there in one day. I do not even remember eating or drinking anything at the site today.

This day was extremely difficult and painful for me. I rarely cry in private let alone in a position where others can see me. So many sights and experiences caused tears to flow freely and often today. I cried more today than I have in total for at least 10 years, probably more. I also do not usually discuss my emotions with anyone other than my wife and in what seems to be the male nature I try to keep some of them hidden from her as well. Writing these private emotions down is difficult as well, knowing that someone will read them someday.

In addition, to the death, destruction, and pain that so many families are going through, many other things affected me deeply today. The hundreds of tireless volunteers continually were approaching me, asking if I needed anything and if I was doing all right. They are hauling water, food, kind words, and more throughout the site. They smiled, squeezed my hand, or laid their hand on my shoulder and unexpectedly touched my heart. I would never have believed that a brief encounter with a total stranger, their few words, questions, or gentle touch of compassion could stir such emotion in me. The tears they brought were unexpected, welcomed, and an incredible feeling that I will never forget. To experience so many people genuinely caring about strangers and one another is an incredible feeling.

Standing at Battery Park and looking out across the Hudson River, seeing Ellis Island and the Statue of Liberty for the first time in my life was another emotional moment. The lady is still standing.

To sum this day up in a few words: Today I stood in the midst of mayhem, chaos, and devastation. All of it is the result of insanity and evil. Today, I stood at Ground Zero.

Notes/Facts

To understand the incredible size of the debris pile, here are a few facts about the World Trade Center Towers:

1. *There were 68 miles of steel beams used in the construction. Enough to build three more Brooklyn bridges.*

2. *Over 43,600 windows or 600,000 square feet of glass.*

3. *239 banks of elevators with 20,000 elevator doors.*

4. *Over 75,000 telephones with 19,600 miles of telephone cable.*

5. *16 miles of staircases.*

6. *12,000 miles of electrical cable.*

7. *Enough concrete to build a road from New York City to Washington DC. A distance of 235 miles.*

8. *49,000 tons of air conditioning equipment.*

9. *23,000 fluorescent lights.*

10. *87 tons of food was delivered there each day.*

11. *All of the building material added up to 1.5 million tons or 3 billion (3,000,000,000) pounds.*

I was in awe and shock of this devastation everyday that I saw it. It did not seem to matter that I saw it for twelve hours the day before. Unless you stand in the midst of it, you just cannot imagine the enormity of it. I thought I had an idea from the pictures on television. I did not. I was tremendously stunned as it was unbelievable.

That fast forward but in slow motion time warp sensation continued the entire time I was there, and it took me several weeks after returning home to shake that feeling and begin feeling normal again. Well, at least to get my body and brain back into the same time zone again. What I considered normal before is just a memory now. I will never be the man I was before this experience.

The experiences from this day are still vivid enough to make me cry. It usually happens when I am least expecting it. I do not consciously try to remember some of these awful things, however occasionally a memory just pops back up as if something pulled the trigger to remind me of it. I begin to think about it and it pushes its way to the surface. I guess it is our way of protecting our sanity and releasing the pain in small increments. I am afraid that to take away the pain, this process is going to take a very long time.

3

Mayhem and Chaos

September 28

I was wide-awake before the alarm went off this morning. I guess it was either anticipation or fear. After my shower and gathering up my gear, I walked across the street to the Times Square McDonalds and got a cup of coffee and a sandwich before climbing aboard the van for my second trip to the site.

The morning turnover in the Command Center was short as the night crew spent their shift trying to get familiar with the area as we had yesterday. We had some time to wait until the Department of Design and Construction (DDC) meeting so I ate a full breakfast on top of the Egg McMuffin® I already had eaten. The area where we meet each shift change is in the elementary school's cafeteria. The kitchen is open and operated by volunteers from the Red Cross or Salvation Army. The breakfast they provided today gave a choice of eggs, bacon or sausage, potatoes, French toast, cereal, fruit, donuts, cookies, and more. You can eat as much as you like and they even have items such as candy and energy bars that you can take with you.

After the meeting, we walked the four or five blocks to the site. On the walk, I noticed that the smoke and airborne dust seem heavier than yesterday. I surveyed the damage to the outlying buildings again on my way through. Still an unfathomable sight and I noticed many areas of damage that I did not see yesterday. Twisted at odd angles are street sign poles and one of the street name pieces is folded in half, in the direction away from the towers. It appears that debris hurled by the force generated by the towers collapsing caused it. There are many small chunks of brick or concrete knocked out of building's façades, streets, and retaining walls around subway or building entrances. Building awnings are in tatters, stair handrails bent or broken off, and even decorative trees and bushes broken and dying.

I went straight into my work area and spent most of the morning just observing the work and the immediate surroundings. I spoke to some of the construction supervisors about their plans for the day. For the most part, the plan depends on the desires of the FDNY. Based on the latest information provided from the night shift on where the search dogs have indicated potential victims, they direct the crews accordingly. Other than cutting and loading of steel on the periphery of the pile and work in other buildings, all work depends on the firefighter activities.

I wrote three or four pages of notes to document the safety concerns I observed this morning. It is going to take a few days to get the familiarity with the ebb and flow of the site. Once I reach my 'comfort zone', I can be much more effective in getting safety problems corrected and things accomplished. Until I actually feel safe here, my attention will always be distracted in trying to keep alive or in one piece. There are so many activities happening all around me that I do not know which way to look. My head is constantly turning towards sounds or blurry, corner of the eye glimpses of movement.

I think it will be a long time before I notice the rubble pile getting smaller as it is still a huge burning, smoldering mess. We have so many significant safety problems to deal with here. There is debris and glass falling from the damaged buildings, equipment running everywhere, cranes lifting tons of material overhead, and grapplers picking up rubble and loading the trucks. Tour groups and individuals are just walking into the demolition zones without a clue of the danger. In addition to all of this, you have multiple contractors working their portions and areas without any one group actually being in charge. It is just chaos, an uncontrolled free for all.

Most of the workers are not wearing proper protective equipment while doing just about anything to help the firefighters find their comrades. I saw trash dumpsters lifted eighty to one hundred feet in the air, loaded with over two dozen workers, not one of them wearing fall protection. Riding inside with them were several acetylene and oxygen gas cylinders that they used for torch cutting. Combined together, these gases are highly explosive. Believe it or not, they lower this dumpster full of people and cylinders into a smoldering, red hot mess of carnage that is generating heat up to a 1,500 degrees in places. Simply put, I compare this to riding a bomb into Hades. Other people are in tangled masses of steel working over top of each other with torches, dropping hot slag and beam parts. Firefighters are working under thousands of tons of steel that dangles over the sides of what little remains of these buildings. You can pick a safety concern and someone here is doing it. It is not an easy task turning around these practices and mindset to basic safety principals. However, that is why we have come here, to assist in keeping anyone else from injury or death.

I watched the firefighters recover a few more bodies today. I noticed that one of the recovery efforts and ceremony afterwards was very different from the others. I found out that was because it was a firefighter. Earlier I observed that an air tank, part of the self-contained breathing apparatus firefighters use to enter smoke filled areas had been located. This tank was an indicator that a firefighter's body was more than likely close to this location. They called one of the canine search and rescue teams to the area and had the dog search in circles around the tank. After several minutes, the dog began pawing at a spot in the debris, indicating that either a body or part of one was present. It was at this point that the firefighters actions began to differ from the previous recoveries I have witnessed.

Somehow, the news of this discovery traveled throughout the site in what seemed a matter of minutes. Firefighters and rescue team members began to gather around the area by the dozens. Many began to quickly use their shovels, picks, and rakes to unearth whoever the dog had indicated was there. The majority of them formed a loose circle around the others and waited. As they dug and removed material for close to three hours, the circle of workers only grew larger and no one left. They stoically stood there hour after hour, breathing in the dust, smoke, and fumes as the efforts continued.

When they finally located and were able to free the body from the debris, their suspicions proved correct. The body was that of a firefighter. The protective, fire resistant coat that all firefighters wear had survived the collapse and ensuing fires. They placed the firefighter into a body bag and onto a fluorescent orange plastic stretcher and waited while someone brought an American flag to the scene. They only cover firefighter and police victims with the flag; civilians are not included in that distinction. Once they had covered the body with the flag, with bowed heads a chaplain led them in prayer. Following the prayer service, they all snapped to attention and saluted their fallen comrade.

After the recovery of the civilian yesterday, they drove the body to the temporary morgue in an ATV. This is not the protocol for firefighters. Six firefighters hand carry the stretcher the entire way to the morgue, a few blocks from this location. A worker, who has been here since the second day after the attacks, explained the process to me today. He said that they carry all of the firefighters this way unless it is raining. When that is the case, they will put them onto a covered ATV to prevent the body bag from getting wet. They slowly drive the ATV to the morgue with a lone firefighter walking alongside with his hand on the stretcher for the entire trip.

As they began hand carrying the stretcher out of the debris, most everyone in the vicinity stopped their activities and took off their hard hats to show respect. I stood with hat in hand for what seemed like an eternity, watching this solemn procession slowly walk down West Street until they were out of sight. My feelings during yesterday's experience with the body recovery were very different from those I felt after the one I witnessed today.

Although it is always very sad to see the life story of a person end by being dug out from a pile of smoking building debris and carted away in a plastic bag, today the sadness felt bone deep. Maybe it was the flag or the slow walk past me that struck me so much harder today. Whatever it was has resulted in a memory I do not believe I will ever forget no matter how hard I may try.

Listening to firefighters and others in conversation these past two days, I believe that the firefighters and police are getting a sense of completing their job with each person they find. I have heard that firefighters have an unwritten code that they will never leave a fallen comrade. They have vowed to find every lost firefighter and 'bring them home'. The determination I am witnessing in the hunt for their friends and loved ones leads me to believe that they are men and women of extraordinary honor.

I went into the World Financial Center Buildings for the first time today. The buildings are called WFC One and Two and are on opposite corners of West and Liberty Streets, just across from the World Trade Center Towers. They are connected by a pedestrian walkway that is on the second floor and spans Liberty Street. Generally known here as the American Express Building, WFC Three is further to the north on West Street. These buildings are approximately 40 to 50 stories tall and are quite distinctive with their domes on some roof sections. There is also a very large glass structure between WFC Two and Three. Called the Winter Garden, it appears to have been a plaza and mall type area with palm trees, flowers, benches, and tables inside. The entire front section of this glass structure was destroyed, however the portion furthest from the WTC appears in much better condition. The Winter Garden and American Express Building are in the AMEC contractor area and are not my responsibility. A coworker named Joel is in charge of this area. The American Express Building has extensive damage. A large section of the WTC Tower Two façade imbedded itself into the side of the building, at approximately the 25th floor level. It is jutting out over the work zone 20 to 40 feet. It seems that it is barely hanging there, but engineers have told me that it is solidly imbedded into the structure. You can see into the offices through the hole it created. In addition, a small lower section of the building has collapsed.

The damage visible from the outside of WFC Two and Three appears to be hundreds of broken windows and a few areas of significant structural damage but mostly superficial. A thick layer of concrete dust covers those few windows that survived the onslaught intact. Today I have observed dozens of workers walk past the broken windows or come out onto a roof area about 12 floors up. I needed to see exactly what the inside conditions are and what contractors are working in here.

It took me several minutes to locate an unlocked or un-boarded door to either building. I finally found one I could get through in WFC Building Two. I went into the first floor lobby. It has been cleaned up in a few spots, just enough to set up a small storage area that contains stretchers and body bags. It also appears that some of the rescuers have been sleeping in here as there are a few sleeping bags stretched out in some corners. The other portions of the lobby remain covered in half a foot of paper, debris, and dust. It is amazing how the papers from the World Trade Center ended up inside of these buildings. I walked up to the second floor on what had been an escalator. Also covered with paper, dust, chunks of plaster, and glass, I had to carefully navigate my way through the debris. The Plexiglas half walls around the stairway and on the second floor have holes through them and the flying debris has broken off sections. You could fall through these openings to the first floor, a drop of 20 feet.

There is a shopping area with several expensive looking stores on the second floor. It is almost surreal to look into them through the dusty windows. In a Kids Gap store, several kids sized and clothed mannequins stand covered with dust an inch thick. The floor is debris littered like every place else for blocks around. In other stores, you can see mannequins displaying expensive dresses and furs, all standing just as they were on September 11, frozen in time and totally encased in that thick blanket of concrete dust.

I went onto a few other floors in WFC Building Two. One has a bank as a tenant and the vault is wide open and empty. I assume that the bank employees returned and took everything of importance from here after the attack to keep it secure. I did not go into the bank area just in case its empty condition was due to looters though. I did not want any question of my presence there being anything but job related. On the other floors are offices of various companies. Heavily damaged offices run along the side facing West Street, their empty window casings facing the now missing WTC towers. Although the windows were shattered and the offices are a mess, there are not many holes in the walls or structural damage. Tipped over furniture is everywhere and some have slid from their original positions in a direction away from the WTC Towers. Computers, photos, and other desktop items and mementos litter the floor, thrown and broken from the force. The forces that came through these windows and caused this much damage had to be incredible. I do not know if anyone was still in these offices when the towers collapsed. On some walls, words such as 'searched 9/12' faintly glow from the orange fluorescent paint. I have heard that many body parts and pieces of the planes ended up on the roofs of these buildings, most found in those first few days.

I crossed through the pedestrian walkway to get to WFC Building One or the Dow Jones Building. Heavily damaged, this walkway does not have a single window left intact nor did the window frames survive unbroken or bent. The siding of the structure is completely gone; the metal peeled right off, exposing the insulation underneath. Metal pieces, glass, insulation, and other materials that appear they came from WTC Tower Two across the street litter the floor. Tied to some windowpane struts is one of the many flags hanging throughout the site. It is slowly flapping in the breeze, smoke, and dust today. The view from this walkway is of destruction on the east side and some of Battery Park and the Hudson River on the west side.

The Damage in the Dow Jones Building is nearly identical to WFC Building Two. I went through several floors, surveying the damage and speaking with work crews that I ran into here and there. Most are working directly for the owners of the building and I do not have responsibility for them. However, I gave a gentleman hanging out of a window several stories up some unsolicited fall protection advice. I worked my way up approximately 12 floors to the first roof level where I had observed a work crew. I had to climb through a large broken window to get onto the roof as a large pile of debris blocked the door. This level has a dome structure on it that is around 20 to 30 feet higher than the roof. The locked dome door prevented my investigating what was inside. The work crew had disappeared by this time so I was free to look around.

The view of the damaged area from this roof is staggering, as the entire WTC complex is visible. This is the first time I have seen this tragedy from this perspective. I stood up there and was in complete awe of this sight for several minutes, absorbing for the first time just how massive the damaged area is. Although I was given a complete tour yesterday, seeing it up close and personal in sections like that did not come close to adding up to this sight. It just did not seem this extensive at eye level. The huge grappler machines, trucks, and people appear so small and insignificant on this giant debris pile. What an incredible sight.

As I began to look around this roof area, the sounds of breaking glass caught my attention. I looked in the general direction of the sound in time to see a large piece of glass hit the deck. Glass was falling from the upper floors onto the roof, some from as high as 20 stories above my location. What is worse, it was falling in the area of the window that I needed to get back inside the building. I watched for a few minutes and it only seemed to fall heavily when the wind gusted. I waited until the first lull in the breeze and made a run for the window. I made it back in safely, thankfully. I am going to assess this hazard closely before I venture into some of these places again. I could easily get myself killed if I am not more careful.

When I got time to take a short break, I went to look around a little bit more in the surrounding blocks. There is lots of dust, papers, and broken windows in these areas as well. One little park area is covered in business papers about six inches deep and areas that don't get the wind or rain are covered with six to ten inches of dust. The dust was so bad on September 11 that it affected buildings five and six blocks away. The *insides* of the windows that were facing away from the World Trade Center are plastered with dust so thick that you cannot see out of them. The dust went into every nook and cranny it contacted or passed by.

I saw one business a block away from the WTC that had a fire escape four stories high. This fire escape was packed from the steps to the top of the handrails, a good three feet deep, with debris from the collapse. Such an incredible force was at work to create these bizarre scenes. I cannot imagine anyone being able to keep on his or her feet anywhere near this tornado of debris and dust.

A few blocks further down there is a huge stack of vehicle parts, mostly doors, wheels, hose reels, and fenders. The parts are the remnants of fire trucks, police cars, taxis, and ambulances destroyed in the buildings collapse. They have been pulling these pieces out of the rubble and hauling them down here to sort them out later. For now, it is just important to get them out of the way of the recovery efforts. Separately kept in an area controlled by the FBI are some vehicle and airplane parts. The airplane parts are naturally evidence, but I am not sure what places certain car parts into the evidence category. I can only speculate that perhaps they have airplane pieces embedded into them.

The amount of businesses affected in the area runs into the hundreds I think. Delis, clothing stores, florists, lawyers' offices, restaurants, bars, clubs, and drug stores all affected in some fashion. All are closed and have varying degrees of damage. They all share one common problem though; their insides covered in the unrelenting dust. There are so many people out of work with their livelihood stopped for weeks. Some businesses that are close to the site may stay closed for months to come. As they pull the perimeter of Ground Zero into a smaller and smaller footprint over the coming weeks, I would think that many of these businesses could begin to clean up and re-open for business.

A parking garage about three blocks from the site is still full of the cars that parked there on September 11. Some have broken windows but most of the damage is just the heavy amount of concrete dust that permeated the insides of them. I spoke to a police officer guarding the garage and he told me that his car was in there and he was unable to get it. Until the city allows insurance adjusters into the site to appraise the damages, these vehicles have to stay where they are. He put it into stark perspective when he told me, "I am not complaining because most of the people that owned these cars are never, ever coming back to get them".

East of the site, at Battery Park and the waterfront of the Hudson River, there is quite a bit of activity also. The US Coast Guard and Army, as well as the NYPD heavily guard the waterfront as well as the rest of the area. Armed police and US Coast Guard boats patrol up and down the river and soldiers are guarding the shoreline. The small Coast Guard boats have machine guns mounted on the bow and each crewmember carrying a weapon as well. At the entrance to the harbor is a large Coast Guard ship. Looking past the Statue of Liberty and seeing this ship brings forth the thought that we are definitely now at war. Security stops, inspects, and escorts every ship and small boat that enters this waterway. There are no chances taken here.

The USN Comfort, a very large hospital ship, is moored a few piers North of this location. The Comfort came here shortly after the attack to give the rescue workers some place to eat, sleep, get medical attention, and even call home if they wanted. It is an impressive sight, painted all white with red crosses on the sides. We received a flyer about it when we first arrived onto the site, but I have not visited it yet.

I walked the entire perimeter of the controlled area or the actual footprint of the site. Some of the area is fenced off but most has only the wooden police barricades and ever-present guards. Outside of this area, the public seems to be going about their business of everyday living. However, large crowds congregate in some of the areas that provide them a view of the damage, albeit a small distant snapshot. They seem to come just to glimpse what they can of the damage done by the attack. Some stand for a long time just staring in disbelief and others break down and cry at the enormity of it. I do not know how they would react if they could stand where I have, in the midst of it. The guards are not allowing pictures and are announcing it whenever they see a camera come into view, but many people are getting some photos anyway. It is the same way on the site, many pictures are being taken despite the orders not to.

This second day was almost as intense and disturbing as the first. The tragedy of it all just hits me in the face as soon as I walk onto Ground Zero. It seems just as unbelievable as yesterday. It is mayhem, death, pain, and chaos. I cannot describe it any better than that. Most of America punched in for work on a time clock this morning; we walked straight through the Gates of Hell.

4

Does America Really Know the Truth?

September 29

My calves and shins are very sore this morning. The stairs are testing my legs each day. I have climbed so many stairs that I have lost count, not to mention walking back, forth, up and down the 16-acre mountain of debris that makes up our area. I believe I am getting a little old for the physical exertion this requires. I definitely am not in shape. The pain is tolerable as long as I keep moving. It is when I sit down that I begin to get stiff and sore. Keep moving has always been my motto, if you stop, you seize up.

It was another extremely busy day. I saw so many dangerous situations and unsafe practices today. Every time I turned my head to look in another direction, someone else was in harm's way. Sometimes I discovered that I was the one who was in the line of fire because a truck or machine was barreling towards me, or a large steel beam lifted over my head. If I have a mental lapse at any given time, I may not make it out of here in one piece myself. It is so frustrating trying to get the rescuers and workers to do their tasks correctly and safely or to back off from a dangerous area until safety measures implemented. Most of the time, they just ignore me and continue working no matter how bad the conditions. We really do not have the authority to stop them as we would on our regular job sites because there are not any agreements in place to say that we are in charge of safety. I am giving it hell everyday, doing the best I can, and am actually winning a few battles here and there.

The smoke from the fires was brutal today. It hung low to the ground, was very thick, irritating, and pungent. I wore my respirator most of the day unless I was in a building, at lunch, or a few blocks away. I even wore it outside of the 'respirator required zone', the smoke was that bad. Although the smoke makes it difficult to breathe, the respirator use by the rescue crews and construction workers is mostly non-existent. It seems as if their attitude is that to wear them is a sign of weakness. I talked to several people that had tears in their eyes from the biting smoke and they still would not put a respirator on as I suggested or move out of the area. None of our safety crew has had much success yet in getting them to wear the proper equipment. Some people listen and do make an effort, however the majority appear to think we are an avoidable nuisance.

I went with several of our group to have lunch on a dinner cruise boat called the Spirit of New York, docked at Battery Park on the Hudson River, three or four blocks from the site. Some people in the long line told us that the owners had donated its use for the rescue effort. It is a very nice yacht and lunch was actually a relaxing and enjoyable experience. Volunteers from the American Red Cross staff it. Every one of them was so friendly and caring, from the minute we got up to the boat until we left. Two of them, a man, and a lady greeted every person as they approached the steps or gangplank. They asked where we came from, how we were feeling, told us to watch our step, and directed us to the boat deck that had the shortest line. The boat has three levels or decks as far as I could tell and there were hundreds of people eating on at least two of those levels. Once we made it up to the food bar, the volunteers loaded our plates with whatever food items we selected and asked us if it was enough. There was a wide selection of food laid out; roast beef, fish, Chinese, Italian, and all the trimmings. The places I have eaten at up to now have very good food, but a limited selection due to their small kitchens and space. The Salvation Army kitchens are modified trailers, towed to the location of the emergency, so they are limited in what they can cook at any given time.

I looked at the faces of the volunteers to see if any were celebrities. I have heard that Susan Sarandon and Timothy Robbins were serving lunch at the Command Center my first day here. Yesterday rumors circulated that Brooke Shields, Olivia Newton-John,

John Travolta, and a few other actors were doing the same at one of the respite centers. If any of these people serving the food on the boat were famous, I did not recognize them.

Once we wound our way through the food line and sat down at the long tables, more volunteers catered to us, hand and foot. Sitting at our table were FBI, Secret Service, Alcohol, Tobacco and Firearms agents, and the NYPD and FDNY. The food and the view out of the window were great. I could see the Statue of Liberty, Ellis Island, New Jersey, and a few large boats in the harbor. The river traffic was very limited due to the circumstances. I watched through the window as US Army helicopters flew back and forth across the river until landing somewhere out of my view.

No matter which direction I look, there are some ever-present reminders that the United States of America is at war in her own front yard. Our front door is a few thousand feet from where I sit. Ellis Island, where untold thousands of people fleeing dictators, oppression, war, famine, looking for freedom and a chance to live a better life, entered our homeland and adopted it as their own. The magnificent Statue of Liberty stands outside that door like a lamppost, welcoming them to freedom. Now it is a war zone and I am in the middle of it, the place where it has begun, where our enemies have struck the first blow. I am in the dead center of the bulls' eye, the place now called Ground Zero.

Firefighters found more bodies today, most were located in my area around WTC Tower Two. I am trying to go to other areas when I notice that a removal is about to take place, however sometimes it is unavoidable as I am in the middle of solving a problem. Today, as I walked out of the hotel area, I happened to intersect with firefighters carrying a stretcher down West Street towards the morgue. Another innocent person is finally going home from work, their crime nothing more than earning a living to take care of their family. Instead of walking out of the World Trade Center and getting in their car or boarding the subway on the afternoon of

September 11 to return to those families as they expected, they are being carried out by strangers. Although the strangers treat them with dignity and gentleness, the fact remains that encasement in cold, impersonal, and unremarkable plastic bags, only to be unceremoniously left at a makeshift tent morgue erected amidst the ruins of their lives and careers awaits them. This is only their first stop on this final journey; they will endure many other indignities and cold impersonal places before being allowed to rest.

Every time I observe any portion of this terrible task, I begin thinking of the victim's family and how so many people are suffering because of this act of fanatics. My thoughts always end with my family and how I would feel if that body were my wife, child, or any relative. I have not been successful in suppressing these thoughts, as they seem to automatically push the onslaught of sights and sounds of Ground Zero aside. The only recourse seems to be going elsewhere or busying myself with other things in an attempt to evade this cause of the emotions that well up and leave me with a lingering, painful ache of sadness. Occasionally the immediate situation I am dealing with prevents an early flight to a place away from the pain. Other times it seems something inside holds me there to experience it in spite of the emotional price. It is not morbid fascination, it is more a feeling that I am obligated to know. I cannot explain it other than that sometimes I just know I am not supposed to take the easy way out and walk away.

The official's best estimates report that there are 5,000 more people still missing. During the three days I have been here, I am aware of only four or five body recoveries a day. The slow pace of the recovery operations demonstrates the enormity and complexity of this destruction. It is such a tangled and compressed mess that the firefighters and construction workers frequently spend hours picking their way through a few feet of it in an attempt to locate what the search dogs have indicated is there. After this meticulous and backbreaking process, more often than not they uncover only a small body part. On the pile, I often observe them collecting these small human remnants in five-gallon plastic buckets, later to bag and transport them to the morgue. It is an all to common sight to see one of buckets emptied into these bags and carried through the site.

The dogs only detect decomposing flesh. They cannot differentiate size or even if it is human. That happened today according to my supervisor Jeff. He told us that the firefighters had spent several hours uncovering a side of beef that had been in one of the World Trade Center restaurants.

I wonder if the rest of America and the world really know what horrors are taking place here. Do they understand that men and women are collecting pieces of people, some of them their relatives, co-workers, and friends? Do they know that they spend hours in the middle of a scorching hot pile of destruction, inhaling smoldering, pungent chemicals, acrid smoke, and the constant smell of death? Aware that they are enduring heat that melts their shoes and suffering burns and cuts while meticulously dismantling a dangerous puzzle of tons of debris to find a family's loved one? Can the world comprehend that sometimes the body they uncover is their own brother or son? Do they know that after recovering and carrying a victim out of that hellish tomb with all the dignity and compassion they can muster that they walk right back in to do it again? Does America know the emotional roller coaster they ride several times a day?

I do not think that they know these things. I know I could not have comprehended or imagined it without standing here in the middle of it. In three days, I have learned about pure evil and other things that now seem to have so obviously escaped me during my 48 years of life. I now know the reasons that make this country so unique and great. It is courage, sense of duty, fortitude, compassion, kindness, and love of our people. America's best are demonstrating all of these on a minute-by-minute basis here.

Surprisingly, while witnessing the worst of man's inhumanity to man, things so awful that selfish thoughts of regret at having come here cross my mind, this most beautiful and incredible display of mankind at its best should be so evident. It is ironic that it has taken the worst for me to see the best.

5

90 West Street

September 30

It was another day with the same problems, sights, and horror.

The firefighters spent most of the day attempting to uncover a stairway in the WTC Tower Two area. They believe that a few hundred firefighters may have died in this area while evacuating the tower. They are very anxious to get in there to find out. There were dozens of firefighters gathered around this area all day. Some were directing the grapplers on where to dig, others busy digging by hand, but most were just silently watching. I was busy elsewhere most of the day and did not watch their progress, but I did see them remove one victim. The stretcher was flag draped, indicating a police officer or firefighter. I have heard that they found four firefighters altogether there today, but I do not know if that is accurate.

I am having many problems with a crew working inside of the 90 West building. There are about a dozen men working to install shoring in an attempt to support the heavily damaged floors and to close off the holes in the building facing. They are not following any safety rules whatsoever and I have observed them in serious danger of being killed on numerous occasions. These guys are either hanging out of the windows several stories up or standing underneath ceilings and upper floors that appear ready to fall at any given moment. They are scaring the hell out of me.

These workers are from Poland and apparently, only their supervisor speaks English, as well as Polish, and he translates my instructions. At least I believe he is telling them what I actually say. He could be telling them to push me out a window because I am an asshole for all I know. I do not know a single word of Polish so I am at his mercy. From my conversations with this supervisor, I have the impression that he does not seem too concerned for their safety at all. According to him, the crew works in this manner all the time in Poland. I am trying to get him to understand that they are not in Poland anymore and we do not risk our life needlessly in America. It has not sunk in yet as every time I turn around they are doing the same dangerous things again.

The 90 West Building is directly south of WTC Tower Two. A small church was in between the two buildings but the subsequent collapse of that tower destroyed it, the debris removed by the time I arrived.

I spent several hours going through this heavily damaged building today. The inside and outside skin took a beating. Many life threatening safety concerns are present inside, outside, and in the area surrounding the building. A nearly destroyed tavern occupies a portion of the ground floor. The bar, tables, and chairs are twisted and blackened by the ensuing fires that erupted as a result the attack. Blackened cases of imported beer are stacked six cases high on the floor and wineglasses still hang in a twisted rack over what is left of the bar. I had to barricade a very large hole in the floor here to keep anyone from falling through it and into the basement. A little further down the corridor is a bank of six or eight elevators. The elevator cars halted on whichever floor they were at when the power failed. A few of the elevator doors are stuck open, in some cases revealing nothing but an open shaft to the basement. I barricaded these door openings to keep anyone from walking in and falling the ten or twelve feet down these shafts. It has been three weeks since the attack and no one had yet bothered to protect people from these hazards. It is a wonder that no one has been injured or killed in here during that time.

I continued through the building, up to about the sixteenth floor but skipped some floors in between. Some of the floors have desks, computers, bookshelves, and everything else blown from the window side, facing WTC Tower Two, to the interior of the building. All of this ruined furniture and equipment ended up piled helter-skelter up against the inner walls, in hallways, and blocking doorways. Charred wooden beams, twisted pipes, and electrical wiring hang from the ceilings on other extensively burned floors. There are also very large portions of the floors missing or partially collapsed that are not always easy to see due to the twisted structural and office wreckage around them. On the sixth floor, one of these floor sections sloped at a 35 to 45 degree angle towards a large hole blown through the outer wall. Thankfully, I spotted the floor condition before inadvertently walking out onto it. If it did not collapse and drop me to the floor below, I could have slipped in the dust and debris and slid out the hole and fell sixty to eighty feet to the ground. Many destroyed windows and surrounding structures create dangerous openings like this one.

Flashlights are necessary to navigate through the darkness in places other than near the windows and holes in the outer walls where natural light shines through. The company provided us with small, but powerful flashlights and it sure was handy today. Wandering through this dangerous, blown apart and burned landscape by flashlight is eerily surreal. The dancing shadows created by the mixture of the sweeping light beam and hanging debris deceived my eyes in seeing the dangers and true landscape. My sixth sense was working on overdrive. I could 'feel' it as I was nearing a particularly bad spot, even though I could not see it. At those times, I just stopped and studied the area with my flashlight until I either found the safest way through or decided I should turn back.

The people that worked here left so fast on September 11, that their lunch boxes, purses, keys, and coats are still sitting there at their desks. Some offices are untouched by fire or structural damage other than broken windows. These offices are just as they were that day except are now blanketed in a few inches of gray dust. Others have file cabinets tipped over, broken light fixtures, or beams hanging from the ceiling. However, on the desk a framed picture of their family, a vase of flowers, or other common desk items sit undisturbed. On one of the floors, in a small office nook there is a plate of donuts stacked pyramid style, covered in this dust. Coffee, brewed that morning, remains in the pot next to the donut tray. It gives me the impression that time and matter have frozen here.

Add these inches of dust to every nook and cranny and you have a good idea what it looked like. The 90 West Building seems to be the most dangerous building in my area. Boarding it up temporarily and tearing it down later seems the solution in my mind. Regardless of my opinions, the owner plans to restore it. In fact, extensive renovations at the time of the attack were in progress. Scaffolding surrounds most of the building for that purpose. I have to say that the architecture is ornate and beautiful.

I am responsible for the work performed by the Bovis subcontractors in and around the building. The owner of the building also has crews working inside, but I am not responsible for them. However, their presence causes me a lot of confusion and many unnecessary trips up several flights of stairs to determine who is working where.

I discussed my observations of the 90 West Building with Ray Master, the Bovis company safety representative this afternoon. Ray is in 100% agreement with me about the safety mess in there. He said he is attempting to get control of his subcontractors working in and around the building. This building is very dangerous, not to mention it is such an eerie place too. Ray has many concerns on his plate. I do not see how he finds the time to juggle it all. He is working alone until the assistance he has requested arrives. I have to say that Ray is the most conscientious and knowledgeable contractor safety representative that I have met so far. A 'true' safety professional, not someone stuffed into a position for appearances.

We are having some problems getting home at a reasonable time at night. The security routes change continually and finding a place to park is an ordeal. We have the same problem in the morning and have been late relieving the night shift too. Nothing we can do but grin and bear it. We did not get back to the hotel until 8:00 PM tonight. That does not leave much time to do the necessary things like shower, get my gear ready for tomorrow, and make my telephone calls home. I have not been to bed before 11:00 PM since I got here and I am up before 5:00 AM every morning.

I am in some danger here as the buildings like 90 West are in such bad shape and I have to go in them all the time. However, this is what I do for a living and I am able to assess the status of a situation very quickly. I do not normally take any unnecessary chances and plan to follow that rule here too. However, this is such an extraordinary circumstance that I expect I will be breaking many of my rules because there is not another way.

I sure miss my wife and our home. Janice said she had a lonely weekend with my being gone and had all sorts of household things going wrong to boot. She seems to have snapped back to her normal self today. She handles everything that comes up and is keeping up my morale. I am so busy that I do not dwell on being alone, but she does. I feel guilty leaving her in this uncertain time. I just hope that she understands that I had to come here.

Whether to leave her and come here or not was not an option as I see it. I am sitting here struggling to put into words my thoughts and reasons I feel this way. I guess I feel that I have never actually measured up as a man and an American as so many others have in our history. Just in my lifetime so many have sacrificed everything in the Vietnam War, Gulf War, and other conflicts. It is doubtful that I will ever go to war at my age now, but I can do what I can to help in this, one of history's worst disasters.

I could never have lived with myself or looked my wife and children in the eye again if I did not come here for selfish reasons. We have sons and daughters that are of the age to volunteer, or drafted into the armed forces to protect our freedom by going to war. How can I say 'you have to go, it is your duty as an American' if I did not have the guts or integrity to answer my call when it came? How could I expect them to have a moral compass if I did not? At times, I do not feel I have always done enough to be that guiding compass for our children. I could and should have done a much better job. I admit that I made plenty of mistakes in those days when I was young and foolish. I have tried to lead by example since and I hope that I am now.

I guess that I want our children and grandchildren to be able to say that when Hell visited America on September 11, 2001 and help was desperately needed, I stood up and responded with the thousands of others. I hope that my coming here and helping my country and fellow citizens will be an example to remind them that if the time ever comes, they need to stand up and be counted as well.

I have seen several signs posted throughout the site with the saying, "Freedom is not free". I believe I am beginning to pay on this long overdue debt.

6

The Flag

October 1

The firefighters found and recovered sixteen of their lost heroes today. Watching them carry out the flag draped stretchers one by one throughout the day really hammered home the magnitude of this tragedy. One after another of these processions were gut wrenching to witness. I stood along with dozens of others to watch these solemn rituals no matter how much it bothers me. Showing my respect and compassion is the least that I can do. Hard hat in our hands, eyes clouded with tears, lumps in our throat, and thoughts of lives so senselessly taken away from their loved ones, we paid our respects to these American heroes several times today. I am sure I will see so many more of them taken from here in this manner. Over 300 firefighters are still missing and untold thousands of others.

Work crews removed enough debris so that they can gain entry into a few more areas where they believe victims congregated while trying to evacuate. The focus is on the stairwells and lobbies of the towers and the Marriott Hotel. The talk among the firefighters is that they expect to find hundreds of victims in these places. However, they are aware that only God knows what they will find. So far, nothing has turned out the way they have hoped. No survivors were waiting in stairwells or voids. Not even one.

We are still having the same safety problems every day. The attitudes of some of these construction workers, firefighters, and police officers are plain unbelievable. They do not want to wear hard hats, talk to us, or do anything they do not feel like doing. It is so frustrating to be able to help them and they ignore you. Sometimes I feel they do not want us here at all. Even some of the contractor safety personnel give us flippant answers to our suggestions. One told me today, "this is New York, and we don't wear safety glasses". Others attribute what we are experiencing as the 'New York attitude'. I do not know if that is why or if these guys are just bone tired, stressed out, or in shock. Whatever the reasons, some of these people have been extremely rude, nasty, and antagonistic. In my experience so far, the worst are some of the firefighters.

One of the construction workers in the area next to mine, where Tully is the contractor, was injured and hauled off in an ambulance today. From what information my coworkers could pry out of the company officials, this guy ignored instructions not to do something in an unsafe manner, and he ended up causing himself an injury and a trip to the hospital. It seems that the famous New York attitude did not do him any favors today.

It is like pulling teeth to obtain any information about injuries or who is responsible for work we witness performed unsafely. The contractors either deny knowledge or only provide minimal information. Personnel working in the first aid stations cannot tell us very much information other than that an injury occurred. Privacy laws prevent them from providing anyone other than their employer any personal details, including even their name. I tried getting info on a simple first aid case from a medic and could not even get him to tell me the person's type of injury, a cut, bruises, or what the problem was. Information such as that could be very important in preventing others from being in danger if, for example, if exposure to fumes from a chemical or gas was the individuals problem. By the time the information goes up through the chain of command and finds its way onto a daily briefing report, many needless exposures could have occurred. I believe in keeping people's personal information out of the hands of those that do not need to know in everyday circumstances. In cases where there may be an immediate danger to others, in a situation like this, I believe your privacy becomes secondary to the safety of others. However, no one has asked my opinion on the matter and I am too far down the food chain to be involved in those types of decisions.

I saw some celebrities for the first time today. New York Governor Pataki made a tour down West Street and later, two San Francisco Forty Niners were standing on West Street near WTC Building Six. One of them was Steve Young, the former quarterback, the other guy I did not recognize. In fact, I walked right past Steve Young and began to talk to a coworker and he said he was waiting to get an autograph. I asked from whom and he said, "Steve Young, you are standing right next to him". I am going to start paying closer attention to the people around me. Steve and the other man were posing for pictures with people and talking to others so I did not stick around to try to get an autograph. There have been many celebrities here and some of these workers have ten or more autographs on their hard hats.

I have heard some folks grumbling about celebrities showing up and slowing the work pace down. I think it is great they come here because these people need something to take their minds off what they are doing for a while. The sadness and stress of watching recovery of bodies takes a heavy toll on your psyche every day. Imagine the toll it is sucking out of the people doing the actual recoveries. I believe that it helps to improve morale. These people have lost friends, family, or have been looking for five thousand bodies day after day since September 11. If seeing, talking with, or shaking hands with a celebrity helps some of them to cope with it, I hope they keep on coming.

My legs seemed to be in better shape today, maybe I am getting used to it. I have been rubbing them down with Ben-Gay every night just in case. They are stiff and sore in the morning but once I get moving around I loosen up. I hope it is passing and I do not begin experiencing the nightly muscle cramps as I have at other times that I have spent so many hours on my feet. If I cannot walk and climb normally, I will be useless for the work I need to do on the site.

One of the things that I see almost everyplace imaginable is our American flag. It is on hats, shirts, and machines, hanging on buildings, street signs, and makeshift flagpoles. Many hang from the windows of damaged buildings surrounding the site. One flag that I see everyday has been hanging on the side of a pedestrian walkway that spans over Liberty Street, between the WFC Buildings One and Two. Debris from the collapsing WTC Tower Two heavily damaged this walkway. It is structurally safe, however about everything else is in very bad condition.

This afternoon I noticed that a work crew was inside the walkway and were beginning to clean it up and board the windows. I did not know whether they were working for Bovis or the owners, so I went up to check on the safety situation. By the time, I went through WFC Building Two and made it to the walkway, they had left this area and into WFC Building One. I eventually found them there and it turned out that they work for the building owner and are out of my area of responsibility. While walking back through the walkway, I noticed the edge of a flag sticking out of a pile of insulation, water, and other debris on the floor. It is a wonder I even noticed it as only about a square foot of it was exposed. The flag is the one that had been hanging outside from the windows. I do not know if the ceiling had collapsed on it or the workers pulled it down in preparation to board up the windows. Either way, I think a debris truck was its intended destination so I pulled it out of the mess. It was soaking wet so I folded it and put it into my raincoat bag so it would not get my knapsack soaked. I thought I could put it up somewhere else later. I forgot about it being in there and carried it around the rest of the day. When I returned to my room tonight, I pulled it out and let the water drain off in the sink and have spread it out on the chairs to dry. It is much bigger than I first thought, five by eight feet. I will decide tomorrow what I should do with it.

7

Never Trust a 'Congressman'

October 2

My coworker Matt Carney received a message on his cell phone for me from our mutual friend Cheryl Kulk. The message was garbled somewhat, but we made out that it had something to do with Paul Weatherford, my and Cheryl's friend and coworker. Paul, Cheryl, and I worked together at the Anniston Army Depot in Alabama for a few years. Paul has been ill for a few months with lung and brain cancer. I called Paul's home and his wife Kathy told me that he had passed away this afternoon in Oak Ridge. God, it seems it came so fast. I thought that he had more time. According to Kathy, he had developed an abscess in his stomach and that hastened his death. It is a shame. Paul was a smart, hilarious, and caring friend. I hope he may rest in peace. I will miss him.

It has been the same problems at the site today. The firefighters and workers just do not want to wear respirators or follow the other recommendations for being on the pile. Smoking and eating, prohibited within 25 feet of the debris field, continues unabated. We have asked the volunteers to not bring the food and drinks right out to the crews, to keep back on the outside of the 25 foot buffer area, but they continue. It is common to see someone sitting in the swirling smoke and dust eating a candy bar or sandwich. There is no telling what chemical or biological contaminants could be on their hands after hours of digging. At the Red Cross, Salvation Army, and other eating areas there are hand-washing stations. There is none of those near the recovery area. We know the volunteers are just trying to help and believe me, their generosity and kindness has caused me to cry in appreciation. However, in this case it is better for these workers health if they do not try to help so much.

Attempting to stop the smoking is futile when the FDNY Battalion Chief and his safety officer are smoking right along with them. I smoke, but go well outside of the area when I want to and there is no reason they cannot as well. I can only recommend they follow the rules, it is their decision not to. I feel that I am making some progress anyway, in spite of being ignored a lot of the time. Some of the people listen to me so my presence here is not a total loss. I will save those I can.

I spent a good hour trying to stop, or at least alter a dangerous operation in World Financial Center Two. A crew of workers put up a flimsy barricade of caution ribbon around a large section of the corner of West and Liberty Streets. They put it there so that their crews in the building, at about the thirtieth floor and up could knock out the remaining window glass. Bad idea. What made them think that no one would ignore their ribbon and walk into the danger zone, considering that people were ignoring danger and climbing over fences and wooden rails with 'DO NOT ENTER' signs on them, is beyond me. As I was walking over to check out this activity, I heard glass breaking and as I looked up, I could see a large piece falling and sailing along with the wind. I watched as it twisted and turned all the way down until it crashed and shattered in the middle of the intersection of Liberty and West Streets, 25 feet outside of the flimsy barricade and near where dozens of firefighters and other rescue personnel were gathered. It is pure luck or divine intervention that someone was not injured or killed. Other than myself, and a guy that turned out to be the supervisor of the operation, no one else was looking up and knew this glass was coming down. The group of rescuers began shouting some well-chosen words in the direction of the supervisor as I walked close enough to call him out of the area without placing myself in the line of fire. Unbelievably, this guy was standing inside the landing zone he had put up for the glass. I asked him to stop the operation and come up with another method. He said that there was not another way and he had to get this glass out of there for safety reasons! When I pointed out that glass shards exploding in every direction near a group of people did not seem safe to me, he said that he was down there to warn people about it and they could move if they did not like it! This is an example of the mindset we are dealing with everyday.

After several minutes of discussion with me, and some timely input from a pissed off firefighter, I talked him into some corrective actions. He agreed to expand the barricaded area by 100 feet, beef up the barricades, use more warning personnel, and wait until it was not so windy to knock out any glass. He also agreed to stay out of the landing area and stop the operation completely if any glass fell close to the barricade limits. My preference is for them to pull the glass into the building and carry it down, but he would not agree to that and this is an improvement. Little did this supervisor know, but as he works for the building owner, he could have ignored me and kept on working. If he had, there was not a damned thing I could do but plead with the Department of Design and Construction to stop him. It may not be a touchdown, but I gained some yards and I will have to accept it for now. Once I can get some help from the authorities, it may be another story. Fortunately, because of the gusty winds throughout the day, they dropped very little glass and without further incident.

Stew announced this morning that an OSHA compliance officer would now accompany us each day. From 7:00 AM until 3:00 PM, I will have a man named Wally from Texas as my partner. After his shift is completed, a lady named Sharon from Florida teams up with me until my shift is over at 7:00 PM. Following me around all day just wore Wally out. He complained that his feet were killing him and we stopped several times to let him rest. More than likely the several trips up the stairs in 90 West got him. I am covering a lot of ground during my shift. Sharon had no problem keeping up with me and asked many good questions. She has over twenty years experience with OSHA, adapted quickly today, and has been quite helpful.

Members of the US Congress arrived for a site tour today. As we have had continuing problems with visitors not wearing hard hats in the work zone, Stew has had hard hats made with U.S. Congress printed on them. It was a great idea because they will not be reluctant to wear them and can keep them as a memento of their trip to the site. They will issue everyone participating in the entourage one of these hard hats. Instructed to stay close to the vicinity of the proposed route and stay visible unless urgent safety matters arose, I stationed myself at the corner of West and Liberty streets, next to the largest crane on the site. This corner is the spot almost every visitor comes to view the destruction, as this is where WTC Tower Two once stood.

Stew and a few others stayed with the congressional group as they looked around. I guess they wanted to make sure they had safety representatives watching out for them as well as the military and Secret Service. I did not recognize anyone in the group. I only would have recognized Hillary Clinton, Ted Kennedy, or Gary Condit if I had seen one of them and they are Senators, not Congressmen. That is sad really, out of four hundred and thirty five Congressmen and one hundred Senators, I can only think of a few I would even recognize.

My supervisor, Jeff Vincoli, was one of our team members assigned to stay with the tour of congressional representatives to make sure they did not get into any unsafe situations. Jeff told us that while they were standing in one area looking over the damage, one of the 'congressmen' began talking to him about the recovery efforts and the day-to-day activities. As they were discussing some of the questions the 'congressman' was posing, a few other 'congressmen' behind them were also paying close attention to the conversation. After several questions, the man asked Jeff his name and introduced himself as a reporter! Jeff ended the conversation at that point.

As we were not supposed to talk to reporters, Jeff informed the bosses of what happened and hopes that they were just making conversation instead of writing a story.

This afternoon, our coworker Tony called over the radio and started repeating that he was standing next to the Super Bowl MVP and he could not believe it. As the OSHA compliance officers and I were so close to his location, we decided to walk the 1/2 block to see for ourselves. Sure enough, there were two Baltimore Ravens football players along with a small entourage. Tony was standing in the middle of them, grinning from ear to ear.

We met Super Bowl MVP, Ray Lewis, and Tony Serigusa. They were passing out hats and shirts to anyone in the area and I received one of each. Ray and Tony both autographed the shirt for me. I am going to give the autographed shirt to my son Jeremy. He will flip, as he is a big football fan.

Before the entourage began to walk through the site, we asked them if they would wear safety glasses and hard hats. We sent someone off to find hard hats while one of the OSHA inspectors handed out glasses. She gave Ray Lewis a pair that was still in the box and then walked a short distance away to watch what was going to happen. When he opened the box, he saw that she had given him a specialty pair that had the NY Jets name and logo emblazoned on them. The glasses were green and white, the Jets colors. You should have seen his face! He said "Hey! Where did that lady go? I cannot wear these! I play for the Baltimore Ravens! Where is she?" He would not wear the glasses. After a few minutes of his playful muttering about the New York Jets I got a pair of plain ones out of my backpack and said, "Mr. Lewis would you like to wear a pair of decent glasses?" He handed me the Jets ones and said, " thank you, I can't be seen in NY Jets glasses. By the way, where did that lady go whom thought she was so funny? I need to talk to her about giving me those." It was all in fun and it was hilarious. They were very gracious, posed for photos, and signed dozens of autographs. It was a nice morale booster for the troops.

There were many other visitors and celebrities at the site today. One we saw was Jesse 'The Body' Ventura, Governor of Minnesota, and his wife. I stood next to them briefly, but I did not talk to him or ask for an autograph. My OSHA sidekick, Sharon, had the opportunity to speak with him for a while. Jesse had so many people gathered around him that I thought it best to just exit the crowd and wait until she finished. I used to take the kids to see Jesse wrestle with the World Wrestling Federation (WWF). He was always one of their favorites with his pink feather boa and sunglasses. Who would have thought he would be a state governor someday?

Several Arab leaders from the Middle Eastern country of Oman also visited the site. They were wearing the traditional clothing for that part of the world, long robes and the head covering, all colored white. Their presence caused quite a stir and visibly upset a few people. No one said or did anything to them, just complained about their lack of sensitivity by showing up here. I guess some of these people cannot separate the terrorists from all Arabs yet. It is still too fresh in their minds. I have to admit that my first thought was that they had a lot of gall coming down here dressed like that. However, after thinking about it, courage and conviction is a more fitting description. They came to see what a few Arabic madmen did to their friends, just like so many other world leaders. They must have known this visit would be controversial, but they were brave enough to stay true to their beliefs and pay their respects here.

I think that the suspicion and anger will die down as some time goes by. I hope it does. I have heard some reports of Arab-Americans being attacked or yelled at because of their ethnicity and that is a black eye for our country for a few to behave that way.

I also saw NY Governor George Pataki and NY City Mayor Rudy Guiliani walking through my area with a large group of official looking people in tow. They did not stop in any one place for very long, so I only caught a few glimpses of them as they went past.

Late in the afternoon, I saw Henry Kissinger, the former US Secretary of State, standing on the corner of West and Liberty streets. I was walking out of the debris field when I saw him talking to someone. Before I could get close, they turned and began walking down Liberty Street towards Battery Park. He stopped briefly and posed with a fireman for a photo, but not long enough for me to catch up to them. I wish I could have shook hands with him or gotten his autograph. He has been instrumental in making important decisions that have affected the modern world. Henry is a legend.

When I got back to the room tonight, the first thing I saw was the flag. Now completely dried with the gray concrete dust imbedded into the fabric, it is a moving sight. I cannot help but wonder how many innocent souls, carried by September winds, passed through this beautiful flag on the journey home. Looking at this symbol of our freedom and knowing where it has proudly been hanging, I know that I cannot take it back to the site. I am taking it home to keep as a symbol of American strength, spirit, and resolve.

I am not keeping it as a souvenir. Although many of the people do take items such as pieces of the building, I feel it is inappropriate to keep anything like that as a souvenir. I personally feel a sense of reverence toward the area and respect it as a gravesite. I can take many things like signs, banners, or pieces of debris if I want souvenirs. I just do not feel it is right.

We have heard several times of people arrested for selling pieces of the buildings downtown. They can sell the commemorative T-shirts, flag ribbons, photos, and the like. In fact, displays of those for sale are just about everywhere you go in Manhattan and I am sure all over the city. Selling pieces of the building seems comparable to chipping off pieces of someone's gravestone and making money from it. However, the law of supply and demand is at work. If someone wants to buy it, somebody else will sell it.

I went on my short walk tonight and had an interesting experience. I walked to the small convenience store near the hotel. It is typical of the stores in the area as it has a deli and a hot food counter in addition to the normal items you find in neighborhood markets. While I was waiting in line to pay for my food and a quart of beer, an argument broke out between a customer and the guy working at the register. The customer said he gave the guy a five and a one-dollar bill. However, the store worker claimed that he put the money on the counter and placed a newspaper over it before nonchalantly sliding the five back into his pocket. The customer denied that scenario, so the counter man demonstrated to him exactly how he did it. He told the customer he had been working behind that counter for over 20 years and he knew all the con artist's tricks. It began to be a loud argument; nevertheless, the man behind the counter started waiting on the rest of us in line while telling the alleged con artist to leave. The customer was arguing that the store was ripping him off and would not leave. When I got to the counter, I paid for my stuff and went outside. Well, I just stepped out there when the customer came flying out the door with the bag of items he had tried to buy and a store worker was right on his heels. I looked back into the store and the counter guy appeared to be OK, but someone said the thief had pushed him and then snatched the bag and took off. I should have stayed in the store and maybe I could have helped. The worker chasing the guy came back empty handed after a few minutes, so I guess the thief out ran him and got away.

Notes

Paul Weatherford and I had worked together for over two years on my last job. He went up to Ohio and I went to Tennessee after we completed the chemical weapons incinerator on the Anniston Army Depot in Alabama. Paul had been in poor health for a few months before he sought out medical treatment. When he finally did in May 2001, the diagnosis was lung cancer. The cancer had advanced quite far already and they did not give him much hope, but I still did not think he would go so quickly. Paul had a great sense of humor that he kept right up until he went into the hospital for the last time. You could always count on Paul to find humor in any situation and he was quick with a joke. After diagnosis, Paul had taken a medical leave and had returned to his hometown of Oak Ridge, Tennessee for treatment. One day a few weeks later, he called me up and said, "Well, I'm moving to California". I asked him why California, are you going to a cancer center? Paul replied, "No I bought a house about six blocks down the street on California Avenue". Classic Paul. He was a nice man and he died too young. Paul left his wife Kathy and four children.

The flag I recovered means more to me than just about anything I own. It is not just a flag or a possession. I do not know if I can express the feeling you get when you see the flag. Just knowing where it flew and what it stands for provokes emotions of pride, sadness, and patriotism. It has a spirit all of its own

I searched high and low for a picture of this flag hanging on that pedestrian walkway where I found it. I wanted to document where it had been. It took me over three months of Internet surfing to find the picture I wanted to include with the flag. It is a close picture of NY Governor George Pataki, NYC Mayor Rudy Giuliani, US Ambassador James Cunningham, and Secretary General of the United Nations, Kofi Annan, standing in front of the flag while it hangs on the walkway on September 18, 2001. Since finding that one, I have located several others that have members of the U.S. Congress, the Governor of Puerto Rico, and Hillary Clinton in front of it. The earliest dated picture I have shows the flag hanging from the pedestrian walkway on September 14, 2001. I have not determined when or how the flag came to be there yet.

The flag now hangs prominently in a place of honor in our home. When I am on my deathbed, it shall pass on to our children and hopefully afterwards to our grandchildren, and so on. It is still dirty with the dust from the World Trade Center and it will remain that way for as long as I have a voice in it.

8

All's Fair in Love and War

October 3

It is my eighth day here, however it seems like I have been here for a month at the least. I cannot explain how weird time here seems. Our scheduled assignment here is for 90 days, and I do not know if trips home or time off are included. I think that will change to keep us from burning out. The stress is intense. We are going to need a break eventually. I do not like to be away from Janice for so long. I cannot imagine not seeing her for ninety days. I know that I am going to go home at some point or she will have to come here for a visit.

I was busy as hell today. I had climbed up twenty-six flights of stairs in the 90 West Building before 9:00 AM. My OSHA sidekick Wally kept up the pace with me for fourteen flights before becoming too exhausted to continue. That was the end of his stair climbing for the day.

It was one thing after another all day with so many problems needing to my attention. Some of the contractors are breaking every safety rule in the book and just do not seem to care one way or another for their workers. In 90 West there were workers hanging out of the windows and off scaffolding. On the ground, we had people riding up and down the street in the buckets of the machines and the never ending 'tours' of citizens into the danger zone.

My assignment here is a tough task, no doubt about it. I like to think that is why they brought me here. However, some of the safety representatives I am dealing with here are definitely not of the caliber I would expect for this situation. A few of them seem to be new to the business or just filling a required spot in a contractor's organizational chart. I work for the construction industry leader in the safety and health field, so my expectations are much higher than most. However, some of these people's behavior borders on apathy if not out and out criminal. I was told a few times that there was nothing wrong with employees being several stories up without fall protection. Their responses range from 'what are they going to tie off to? To 'that is an accepted practice here in New York'. I do not know of anywhere in the world, least of all in the United States, that falling ten stories to the street below is an 'accepted practice'. However, we did not pick these people and we have to deal with them to have any hope of getting some safe practices in use. Most of the time, finding the bad ones on site is nearly impossible anyway. They are laid up in an office somewhere or hanging out in a respite center watching TV. If you do not care about your people's safety, I guess you can do that. I have never been able to let my charges run amok, I take the responsibility for their lives seriously. We usually go straight to the supervisors or the workers and try to get things corrected. I think that probably works better anyway. As far as we go, Stew has assembled a well-balanced and experienced team. Our guys are very good at what they do.

Jeff Vincoli told us that two local newspapers ran stories this morning quoting him from yesterdays 'interview'. It turns out that two other reporters were standing behind him during the Congressional visit as well as the one he was talking with. He says the main office was not happy when they found out about it, however after he pointed out that the articles had misspelled his name terribly and gave him the mistaken title of 'supervisor with security', they realized what really happened. How was he supposed to know they were not congressional representatives? Up to this point, I have talked to clergymen, army, NYPD, and many others that I believe are part of the work crews or volunteers. We all could have something like this happen. Our instructions are not to give interviews to the news media without getting permission from our legal department first. That is common policy with most companies because you are speaking for them even if you are only providing your personal opinions on a topic. After this incident, I plan on being very tight lipped with anyone I am not sure is actually who they appear to be. Better safe than fired.

The OSHA representatives helped me get a very dangerous situation corrected today. We thought up a scheme to get the contractor to comply with safe practices. Any method that works is all right by me. After getting nowhere in my discussions on the safety of this particular supervisor's work, I went to the OSHA compliance officers and related that I was out of arguments and needed some ideas. We talked it over and thought we would go with an approach to plant a seed of legal repercussions into his mind. The plan was to go over all the reasoning again with this supervisor while my OSHA counterpart, Sharon stood quietly by my side as an implied threat of authority, muscle so to speak. It was implied because they did not have authority to 'bite' either. After futilely rehashing the problems with him, I finally said, "Let me see if I understand this correctly. You are telling me in front of this Federal Officer that you are not going to perform this job safely?" I added, "Are there any other crimes you would like to confess to while you are at it?" I played the 'cop card' and our little scheme worked. He thought it over for a second or two and decided he was now ready to do the job safely. Chalk one up for the good guys and Sharon never had to say a word.

In all fairness, most of the folks we deal with about safety issues are taking those shortcuts because they believe every second they can save somewhere is a second used searching for survivors. Therefore, they do not take the time to fix the back-up alarm on the semi truck, pick up the trash and trip hazards in their area, get the proper ladder for the task, and a multitude of other items. To be honest, I would have done many things the same way, except for putting other lives at risk. The difference now is that the chances of finding a survivor after three weeks are practically zero. They have not given up hope yet, but the time is here to stop taking these chances with fate. The situations we are trying to correct are life threatening to them and those around them. Fall protection for workers several stories up, barricading holes 20 feet deep in the ground, proper handling of the highly explosive gas bottles, and crane safety are some of the big risk items we are attempting to get under control. Any means to save a life is acceptable. Saving lives is why we are here.

As I was walking down West Street this afternoon, I ran into Bob, our NY Department of Design and Construction boss. We spoke a few minutes and he mentioned he was playing escort today. He said he would rather not have to do it but could not get out of it. When I asked whom was he escorting, he said, "Larry King of CNN is standing right in front of you". If he would have been any closer, we would have been wearing the same shirt and I was oblivious. He was wearing a hard hat that barely fit his head and he looks very frail. He had someone at his elbow guiding him when he walked. He interviewed an FDNY battalion chief and afterwards Bob took them to the other side of the site. I thought that I might end up on his TV show tonight but I did not see myself in any of the footage. I have noticed frequent filming in my work area. I am certain that I have appeared on some show at some time or another.

I had another interesting experience when I went back to the Command Center to give my notes to the night shift tonight. A guy came into the center and said there were some baseball players outside. I went out and saw two elderly men sitting on the back of an ATV signing autographs. I had no idea who they were, but I went over to meet them. One was Bobby Thompson, famous for hitting a dramatic home run in game seven of the 1951 World Series to give the New York Giants the world title. The other gentleman was Frank Branca of the Brooklyn Dodgers, the pitcher who threw that pitch to Thompson. That homerun became renown to baseball fans as 'the shot heard round the world'. I found out that today was the 50th anniversary of that home run. Instead of attending a celebration in their honor, these men came to Ground Zero bringing a few moments of relief and distraction to workers who definitely needed it. These men are exemplary all the way. I ended up getting an autographed picture and they each signed my journal as well. I am meeting people that I never imagined in my lifetime; governors, senators, leaders of countries, sport stars, and big wigs.

Our days are so busy and I have very little time at night to do anything it seems. After returning to the room, showering, changing clothes and getting my things ready for the next day, I walk about a block down Broadway Street to the corner store. I pick up any items I may have forgotten to bring or now need, something to drink, and usually something else to eat. I take a different route on the return trip so that I can look around in new areas. After that, it is back to the room to eat, make telephone calls, and watch a little television before bed. I have not yet bought or read the daily newspaper, one of my favorite activities.

I do not want Janice, the kids, or my Mom to worry about me, so I am trying to call each of them to assure them that I am doing all right. I know they are worrying anyway, but if I talk to them often enough they might begin to relax a little.

Tomorrow is my first day off.

Notes

Our daily interactions with the contractors were sometimes very frustrating because it was common knowledge to most of them that we had 'bark' but not allowed to' bite'. I guess it is easy to speed past the police car when you know the officer cannot give you a ticket. In addressing our concerns with the safety of an operation a particular contractor was involved in, some of the time we were either ignored, given excuses, told to see someone higher up, or occasionally verbally abused. To combat these we had to get creative in our attempts to convince them to correct the situations. I am going to give away a few 'Safety Trade Secrets' here but they are part of the story. If the argument that it simply is not the safe way of doing the task is not enough, we have to approach from another angle. There are several 'angles of attack', such as:

- *Legal Obligation or 'Did you know that if you knowingly ignore the safety aspects of this task and someone gets injured or killed, you can be held liable both civilly and criminally?'*

- *Moral Obligation or 'Do you really want to have to tell his or her family that they were killed because you did not want to bother with their safety?'*

- *Compromise or 'If you will change the way you are doing this dangerous task and make it safe, we will work with you on these other items.' This approach should only be used in an emergency like the World Trade Center disaster and never compromise worker safety.*

- *Personal or 'Would you let your kids do this task like that?' Or 'Have you thought about what your family is going to go through if you are seriously injured or killed?' 'Is this worth that?'*

- *Financial or 'Does your supervisor condone this? Maybe we should call him over here and see what he says.' I personally use this one as a last resort as I do not like to put anyone's employment in jeopardy. Unfortunately, this is the only one of the approaches that matters to some people, their own personal finances.*

There are a few other arguments or tricks that we use from time to time. If it sounds a little unscrupulous, keep in mind that our only reason to implement these tactics is that we are trying to save their life.

I actually did show up on the Larry King show. I watched it again on the weekend show and I notice myself walking down the road and later standing next to the guy who was escorting Mr. King. I was in the background and you would have had to know it was I - no close-ups.

9

The Funeral

October 4

It was my first day off and I was expecting to put the events and images of this past week aside for the day and relax. It was not to be as the World Trade Center disaster is still painfully evident wherever you go. While walking to the Harley Davidson store on Lexington Avenue to buy my brother-in-law, G.C. Hammac, AKA the 'G-man', some T-shirts, I happened to come upon hundreds, if not thousands of people lining the street. When I approached the back edge of the crowd at the corner of 51ST and Fifth Avenues, I was able to see what had captured everyone's attention. Looking in the direction everyone else was, I saw that a FDNY funeral procession was coming down the street towards us. The fire engines in the procession were now too close for me to cross the street, so I decided to stay with the huge crowd and watch.

What a magnificent funeral procession it was! First came two fire engines that were as clean and waxed as they could possibly ever be. As they slowly passed by us, you could see the crowd's reflection dancing along the paint and chrome. On the top of each engine, where the hoses usually lay, sat one flag draped casket. Standing on the back of each engine, holding onto the handrails with white-gloved hands, were two firefighters. These firefighters were dressed in their finest uniforms and every polished badge, buckle, and button was gleaming in the morning sun. Leather boots and belts were spit-polished to a mirror finish. They were immaculate, somber, and professional.

Next in line, were the FDNY bagpipers, dozens of them in formation and dressed in their band uniforms that include the Scottish kilts and tams. As they passed by the corner where I stood, they were playing some beautiful, but mournful song. Listening to the unique, sad sound of those bagpipes started a tear rolling down my cheek. Neither I, nor the hundreds of others could help it.

Marching slowly and eerily silent behind the bagpipers were hundreds of firefighters, also wearing their dress uniforms. It was an overwhelming sight, a very somber and touching event. I cannot think of a more noble funeral procession that I have ever seen. It seemed that everyone that was walking along the streets stopped as it passed by. Some saluted, some cried, and others stood silently watching. This solemn ritual deeply affected everyone present in some way.

The procession continued for two blocks to the church where the service was to take place. I overheard someone tell another that it was St. Patrick's Cathedral. This was such an important event that I decided that I had all day to do other things and stayed to pay my respects.

I walked along with hundreds of others the few blocks to the cathedral. Erected across the street from the cathedral, was a platform for the media. There were several on and around the platform with both movie and still photo cameras. The street in front of the church was crowded with the firefighters, police officers, bagpipers, and officials. They all stood silently and rigidly at attention until snapping into salutes as they lowered the caskets down from the trucks and prepared to carry them into the church. The family appeared out of the crowd and followed as the eight men carried the casket of their respective loved one into the cathedrals massive front doors. There were several small children in the family groups ushered along by attentive adult hands on their shoulders. The scene was a vivid reminder that these firefighters were parents senselessly taken away from their children. All of us present, and the entire City of New York wept. It was as sad of a sight as I have ever witnessed.

As they slowly carried the flag draped caskets up the sidewalk toward the cathedral, I wondered if it was possible that I have witnessed the first part of these firefighters journey to this place. Had I watched their removal from the rubble at Ground Zero? Are they two of the many people I have silently watched carried past me encased in a plastic bag, distinguished from the others as firefighters and heroes only by our flag as a cover? If they are, it is fitting that I am able to see the end of their journey. As sad as this was to see, I am strangely thankful that coincidence brought me here at exactly the right moment. Maybe it was not coincidence.

They buried two of FDNY's heroes today. There are over 350 more firefighter funerals yet to begin. They are still missing and their families held in a cruel limbo of uncertainty and delayed finality. Whether to wait until they are found or hold memorial services and proceed with their lives is an unfair choice. There are thousands more funerals that this city, this country, and the world have yet to attend.

I do not know if you can tell from the news stories just how badly hurt and stunned New Yorkers really are. From what I have observed in my time here, the wounds are to their very core. Shaken, their grief is open, raw, and consuming. It is easy to see; their eyes give it away. I notice it when we walk into the hotel at the end of our shift, our hard hats and clothes tell them where we have just came from. The people watching the news on TV's in storefront windows or scanning through the many flag or WTC shirts the street vendors are offering, all have that sadness in their eyes. It seems I can just sense it most of the time, as it is that profound. It is going to be a long, long time before they can begin to heal the wounds because the recovery is going to take months, causing the emotional scabs to be torn over and over again.

After the funeral procession, I continued on to the Harley shop and bought the 'G-Man' his shirts and some Harley pins. I also stumbled across a place called the Harley Café and I bought some shirts there as well. I found some good ones for him that have the Statue of Liberty and World Trade Center on them.

On the way back to the hotel, I found the famous Rockefeller Center. It is a nice place, very ornate. I saw the famous ice-skating rink and where they have the outdoor concerts and interviews that you see on the Today Show. I went into the NBC Studio's store there and bought my Mom a few coffee cups for her collection. She is going to love the Jay Leno, Tonight Show cup, as she is a big fan. On the way back towards the hotel, I shopped at a few other stores and bought our grandsons Ethan and Johnathan FDNY T-shirts.

The rest of the day, I just walked around and saw the sights. I did not realize that I have seen so many of these places at one time or another on TV. I recognized many places, the Trump Tower, the Garment District, David Letterman Studios, and Radio City Music Hall. New York City is really an incredible place, so different from anywhere I have been. Every block has every available amount of space occupied by a store, restaurant, laundry, deli, and anything you could possibly want or need. In front of these places are street vendors that may have a table or cart to sell from or some just walk around carrying their items for sale. Watches, flowers, T-shirts, souvenirs, show tickets, bus tours, photographs, original art work, food stands, newspaper and magazine booths, and on and on. If you cannot find what you want, someone here knows where you can get your hands on it.

There are even street entertainers performing for donations. I saw several mimes, dance groups, people playing plastic buckets as drums (they are good, too), and people that you are not sure what they are doing but they draw crowds anyway. They all are making some money like the 'Naked Cowboy' Randy and I saw on our first day here.

There are many other sad spots and constant reminders of the tragedy around the hotel and Broadway area. One firehouse has a large memorial with photos, flowers, candles, posters, flags, and letters that stretches the entire length of the block and around a corner. This firehouse lost fifteen firefighters on September 11. Today, a large crowd of people, as well as a film crew was there. I looked at several posters and letters, got a few photos, but left because the film crew was setting up on the sidewalk and I did not want to be in the way. It is close to the hotel so I will come back and take more pictures. It is a wonderful tribute to their fallen comrades.

A few blocks from the firehouse is a trailer with a bronze statue of a firefighter. The firefighter is on his hands and knees and has a look of exhaustion. There are also two large plaques on the front of the trailer, one depicting firefighters rescuing a child and other heroic deeds. The second plaque was on the street side and traffic was too heavy to go out and look. It is a very moving tribute to the heroism of firefighters. I thought this statue was a gift sent here because of this tragedy, but I found out today that it actually was on its way to Kansas City. Shortly after the attack, the truck hauling it apparently had broken down and the driver decided to leave the statue where it is now sitting. It is almost as if God intervened and decided that it belonged here. I do not know if it eventually makes it to its intended city, but I am sure that it will not be without a fight as it is a very popular spot. Visitors were leaving flowers, cards, and candles all around it and people took many photographs while I was there. I took three or four myself.

The rest of the day was uneventful. Exhaustion set in and other than going out for a long walk around Time Square later in the evening, I spent the rest of the day napping, watching television, and taking it easy.

10

The Gates of Hell Begin Here

October 5

I am back at it again today and am not starting it off in the best of moods. Randy and I had to hand in our cell phones this morning. Losing the use of the phone means I will have to walk all over the more than 16 acres of hills, valleys, and obstacles of the destruction to find the contractor safety representatives every time that I need them. As I need to talk to them several times a day, this will cause me a lot of extra walking and climbing to hunt them down. That telephone saves me a lot of time and keeps me connected to home in case I need it. I am sure that Randy needs it as bad as I do.

I was very busy again this morning as the Polish crew is giving me fits inside of the 90 West Building. It is an everyday battle with them. Some of these people just came here in the last month or so to work, according to what their supervisor tells me. The 'Land of Opportunity'. I hope that being killed pursuing that better life here is not the result. If they do, it is going to be despite my efforts; I do not give up easily. I am going in there in the morning to find what floors they are working on and talk to their supervisor about the days activities and what personal protective equipment (PPE) they need to perform the work safely. The crew is putting in shoring to help hold up the floors on the north side of the building, the most heavily damaged. The PPE is most often fall protection because of the holes in the floors and missing building face that you can walk right out. We reach a consensus on the requirements and I go back down the six, twelve, or sixteen flights of stairs to the rest of my work area. Sometimes it is within fifteen minutes, later in the day or several times a day, I see one or more of these people hanging out of a window several stories up without any fall protection on. I climb back up those stairs to get them in a safe position and explain the requirements again with their boss. I am going to get fall protection on these people or handrails put up around the holes and windows one way or another.

Most of the day, the firefighters and law enforcement groups were searching intently for bodies and sensitive information or evidence. In several areas, work stopped for very long periods while they focused on whatever item of importance they believed was there. As a result, the site became much quieter around mid-morning and it seemed everything had slipped into slow motion. With Wally in the morning and Sharon in the afternoon, we walked around most of the entire area so they could see the extent of this atrocity. The OSHA folks, other than the ones that live and work in New York or New Jersey, are only here eight hours a day for one week. Their first day is in orientation, so they do not have much of an opportunity to see all of it.

Although I had very few pressing safety problems to deal with for a change, other than the Polish crew, this day may haunt me for the rest of my life.

Sharon and I were discussing a few safety problems with a Grace company supervisor this afternoon and ended up finding ourselves in the middle of a body recovery from the WTC Tower Two debris. Although we were standing back some distance, maybe 30 to 40 feet, it was not far enough away. I saw more than I should have. Sharon briefly watched through her binoculars, but I think that was too much for her to take. I did not want see anything more than I already could.

We stood silently watching as two firefighters uncovered and then struggled to place into a body bag, the top half of a corpse. The body, covered with dust and appearing severely burned was mostly unrecognizable as a person other than the outline. One firefighter held the bag open while his partner struggled hard for what felt like several minutes to get it completely inside. I am sure it was not that long in real time, but in mental time, it seemed an eternity. After finally getting this innocent victim of madmen into the bag and onto a stretcher, the firefighters and all of us in the area bowed our heads in prayer. They must have assumed this victim was a civilian as no flag covered the stretcher. After the prayer, the body was loaded onto an ATV for the trip to the temporary morgue. As the ATV drove slowly past us on the way, those emotions of sorrow, anger, and shock churned inside again for the umpteenth time. On the outside I managed to keep it to red, wet eyes. Sharon had a pained, shocked, look on her face. If she cried, I did not notice it. I think we are both going to regret watching such a horrible sight.

I think I should have walked away as I have several other times. It would be so much easier mentally later on to have not witnessed things like this. I am eventually going to pay a price for this need or duty to see all of this horror so I will never forget and can tell others of it. I know that this sight is going to stay with me forever no matter how hard I try to erase it. It has played repeatedly in my mind the rest of the day without any conscious, self-prompting.

It was a life gone in a heartbeat, the blink of an eye, but not without having to feel pure terror while trying to escape. Innocent people should not have to die in such a terrible way. Death like this belongs to those that can conceive, plan, and carry out an atrocity like this. Those that deserve it are void of compassion, feeling, or a soul. It is important for the people of the world to know what has occurred here, just how terrible it is. The death of thousands of innocent people, the awful smell, the painfully raw emotions, hardened, grown men crying openly and frequently, the suffering of the survivors, and the hell the rescuers wade into day after day must never be forgotten. Never.

The search for important items missing in the debris at the World Trade Center is usually very low key and I do not notice anything in particular happening. You probably have not heard on the news about the many things lost in this debris. Some are dangerous to us, some are of National Security importance, some are important to major legal cases, and some are worth a lot of money. The Federal Bureau of Investigation (FBI), US Customs, Secret Service, and from what we were told, the Central Intelligence Agency (CIA) and the ultra-secret National Security Agency (NSA) are always watching with binoculars for signs of important items. The US Customs is looking for vaults filled with cocaine, heroin, ecstasy, and other illegal drugs that are to be used as evidence in smuggling trials. Other vaults contain explosives used to train bomb-sniffing dogs. The Secret Service, CIA, & NSA are looking for top-secret information that is in the presidential bunker somewhere in the basement of the World Trade Center. Rumors are that explosives are armed and ready to destroy the bunker if its security is threatened. We have not heard anything different about the bunker so I assume it is true.

There is about $110,000 000.00 worth of gold bars and $120,000,000.00 of silver bars stored in vaults under WTC Building Four and everyone is looking for that. The firefighters have been grumbling, saying that all the officials care about is the gold, not the victims. I have not seen that as it appears an all out recovery effort is taking place. Supposedly, there is other money in large quantities inside a few banks in the basement. There are criminal case files all over the buildings, especially in World Trade Center Building Six as it had the US Customs, FBI, ATF, IRS, and OSHA offices in there to name a few. We have heard that some defense attorneys are already trying to get their clients' cases thrown out of court and dismissed before some trials are to start because they have not found the evidence yet.

The FBI is looking for evidence of the terrorist plot, pieces of the plane, and I cannot imagine how many other important items. All of this missing material is important to someone. Work stops whenever there is any sign of these items or if they get near an area, where they may be. Work does not continue until they find it all or they become convinced it is not there.

In addition to searching through the site for anything and everything that may be important, everything is searched at least twice more on its trip off the site and at the landfill. After the debris is loaded into trucks, it travels to an inspection, washing, and tarping station a few blocks away. At these stations, FBI and Secret Service agents climb into the trailer portion of the trucks and look for anything that may be of interest. When they are finished, the work crew begins washing down the debris with hoses and cover it with a tarp to keep any remaining dust from blowing all over the city on the trip to the landfill. The trucks make their way to the pier and dump their loads. At the pier, it is loaded onto barges for the trip up the river to the landfill. The landfill is on Staten Island and called Fishkill. I heard that it closed several years ago, however has been re-opened just for the WTC debris because it was close and large enough for the magnitude of this effort. At the landfill, they dump and spread it out to thoroughly search it again. This last search is a detailed effort. They spread out the debris with rakes and use sifters to look for evidence, personal effects, body parts, and anything that seems important. Nothing leaves the World Trade Center site, nor placed into the landfill unless thoroughly inspected.

They do a good job of trying to keep the trucks from carrying dust off the site in other ways besides the washing operation. They also have set up several boot and hand washing stations to use when leaving the work zones. The Red Cross and Salvation Army food centers have them, too, and you do not get in their facilities until you use them. The volunteers here clean your boots off thoroughly with a garden hose and then point you in the direction of the sinks to wash your hands. There are volunteers here also that make sure you wash them, too. The majority of the volunteers at the sink area are women and we frequently respond to their gentle reminders to wash our hands with an affectionate, 'yes Mom'. They take care of us as well as our own mothers would and we love them for it. They all are genuinely concerned for every aspect of our welfare and treat us wonderfully. They are such nice people.

The staff at the perimeter boot and hand washing stations, although paid employees, has a very hard job to do. Working twelve-hour shifts, six or seven days a week as the rest of us, and most of it spent bent over our boots. They actually soap up our boots, brush, rinse, and apply a disinfectant to them before we can leave. I usually go to the same station on my way out at night and have gotten to know the crew there. The crew consists of three women, who are always visibly tired, however never seem to lose their smiles. Every night I come to the station, I make it a point to say 'hi ladies, how are you today?' I always do that because not many other people seem to acknowledge them or their efforts. They work just as hard as everyone else does here and I let them know I at least appreciate it. We have some short but cordial conversations each night and have shared pictures of each other's children and grandchildren and talked about what we normally do in our lives. They are all New Yorkers who had come down to help and hired on for this job.

The only problem with these perimeter wash stations is that people can exit the site without passing through them. So many people do not use them, just skirt by them, and walk on down the street with boots covered in crap. It is supposed to be mandatory, workers received flyers, and information posters are all around the site. It would be difficult to plug all the exits and funnel everyone through them because of all the trucks coming in and out. There are just too many ways to walk past them. Even though they attempt to stop some of them and talk them into cleaning up, the crew cannot catch or convince them all.

I saw a new sign today that the firefighters and guards have erected at one of the South checkpoints on West Street. Made out of wood with an American flag on the top, it reminds me of the sign that was so famous on the M.A.S.H television series. I think it defines the situation. This is part of what it says:

Kabul	**6,750 miles**
L.A.	**2,824 miles**
Tokyo	**6,759 miles**
Hell	**0 miles**

While I was eating lunch today at the Red Cross Respite Center that is set-up at the college, I picked up and read a few of the letters and cards that are spread out on the tables. People from all over the world write these thousands of letters, notes, and cards and the majority of them seem to be from children. Somehow, they end up in the Red Cross centers, Salvation Army tents, and even the in fire department stations. I guess they address them to New York City and the U.S. Post Office just knows they belong here. I happened to pick up and read one that is from a seventh grade boy by the name of Ronnie Syrcle, who lives in Quincy, Illinois. He wrote that he hoped the rescuers were all right, how we were examples for others, and how sad he was about all of the people that died. It was a nice letter and it had something most do not, a return address.

I am going to write and thank him and his classmates for writing to us. I think they would like to know the rescuers appreciate their caring gestures.

Notes

The notes and letters from all over the world, especially the ones from children meant so much to the rescue/recovery workers. The letters, notes, and banners were on the tables and walls at the Red Cross Centers, Salvation

Army Centers, on walls around the site, just about everywhere by the thousands. I picked up the one from Ronnie Syrcle that day.

I wrote Ronnie a letter from New York thanking him for thinking about us and included an NYPD arm patch and FDNY sticker as souvenirs of my appreciation. When I returned to Tennessee I wrote him again to let him know I was home and OK, tell him a little bit about what it was like there, and included some pictures of Ground Zero for him to keep. I am so glad that I wrote to him. I received a Christmas card from one of his teachers, Mrs. Stephenson and later on a package from Quincy Jr. High School that had another Christmas card, letters from Ronnie, his teachers and the whole class, and a picture of them all.

I corresponded with Ronnie and the class and have since learned that Ronnie shared the letters and pictures with his class at school and they frequently discussed the World Trade Center. I now feel I have the whole class as my friends. They are in Mrs. Brueggeman and Mrs. Stephenson's seventh grade class and are: Ronnie, Amanda Stepp, Melinda Pritchard, Justin Childress, Tony Young, Kevin Leindecker, Norman Pearson, Ryan Clair, Matt Albert, and Derrick Wilson. What a great bunch of friends! I have sent them a first draft copy of this story and they read it in class.

I think that our young Americans need to know and should never forget the events on September 11, 2001 and the aftermath that followed. I hope I have helped my friends in Quincy, Illinois to understand it and see the whole picture.

My friends in Quincy and the hundreds of thousands of other students and teachers that wrote letters of encouragement and love to us in New York will always have a special place in my heart. Thank you for showing me that patriotism, love, honor, and the spirit of America are alive and well in our children. You are our only hope for the future of freedom and America. Your unselfish acts of kindness have shown me that America's future is in safe hands.

My friends from Quincy are continuing to write those special letters to our troops overseas who put their lives on the line everyday searching for the fanatics that perpetrated this atrocity so it can never happen again. They know something that most of America seems to have forgotten at times, that the freedom we all enjoy and take for granted was not just handed to us by some benevolent leader. Bought and paid for with the lives and blood of our citizens throughout our history is where our freedom came from. Mrs. Brueggeman and Mrs. Stephenson are teaching the basics, reading, writing, and arithmetic as well as showing them how to be caring, compassionate, involved human beings, and Americans. Every classroom in America should have teachers like these two.

11

Arnold and Asbestos

October 6

This was a miserable day for the most part, the worst for bad weather we have had so far. A nasty cold has stuffed my head and nose and it was very windy, cold, and rained off and on most of the day. I had worn my raincoat, but definitely did not have enough clothes on underneath for this weather and I was partially wet and freezing all morning. Keeping out of the wind was the best thing I could do, but there is not any cover in the debris pile. It was either get into a building or tent to cut the wind or freeze.

After a few hours, I went to the Red Cross Center and picked up one of the donated long-sleeved T-shirts and that helped some. They told me they were out of sweatshirts already today because they had a run on them. I was not the only one who did not dress appropriately this morning I guess. I am not going to make that mistake again. The wake up call at the hotel tells you the weather forecast for the day if you listen to it long enough. I discovered that yesterday when I almost went back to sleep with the telephone to my ear. I hung up before reaching that portion this morning though.

It was extremely busy again today and it is safe to say that it will probably be that way from here on out. There is just so much work going on and problems to deal with that I rarely have time to actually relax. Sitting down for lunch or a short break at the respite centers is the only time the pressure is off it seems.

One of the crews that I have been working with closely while they replace windows in the overhead walkway that spans from the World Financial Center towards the World Trade Center corralled me first thing this morning, waving a newspaper at me. The headline said that asbestos levels were above safe limits at the site. They wanted to know if it was true. They were upset and concerned that they were going to get sick because of it and had many questions.

They gave me the paper to read the article for myself. It was a report about how OSHA and the EPA were not performing the correct asbestos tests or accurately reporting the results of the tests they were taking. The article said an independent company had performed their own tests and that the airborne asbestos was over the acceptable federal limits, not under, as was being reported. It is no wonder the crew was upset as this article prompted many questions in my mind as well.

As I knew nothing more about the article than they did, I assured them I would find out the real story and get back to them. I also eased their fears a little when I told them that with the wind blowing away from the walkway area, the protection its walls provided, and the steady rain keeping any dust down, they should not have to worry much about it today. However, as a precaution, I instructed them to go to the OSHA respirator station a block down and get some respirators for the dust and particulates like asbestos. They agreed and went off to get the respirators.

I informed our bosses about the article and they had the agencies running the site begin researching it. This afternoon they told me what they had found out. It turns out that no one could find any information verifying that the 'independent' company mentioned in the article even existed, let alone had performed any testing on the site. Their information indicates that the story is a fabrication and suspect that the group involved is attempting to stir up trouble and future legal work in lawsuits. Despicable bastards trying to profit from a national tragedy and scare the workers in the process. I informed the walkway crew of that information and gave them a copy of the OSHA asbestos report passed out in a morning meeting. I explained what the test numbers meant and assured them that if I heard anything else contrary to that information I would pass it along to them. I reminded them that I was out there with them everyday and if there was an asbestos problem for them, it was my problem too. The crew was happy with my explanation and they now know I will get them answers to their questions and tell them the truth. They now seem to trust me.

This afternoon I was standing on the corner of West and Vesey Streets watching as one of the contractors demolished a part of WTC Building Six, when a small group of five or six people walked up on my left. I glanced over at them briefly and went back to watching the work. After a few seconds, it began to register in my old brain that one of them, the guy in the firefighter's coat, seemed familiar. I looked back over to where he was standing, five or six feet away and saw one of the most recognizable Hollywood faces in America. I could not believe that I was standing this close to Arnold Swarzanegger, the Terminator! He was with some officials and the firefighter coat he wore was either an attempt at a disguise or protection. Just at that moment, a man walked up to Arnold and got him to autograph his hard hat. That broke my celebrity trance and I rummaged around in my backpack until I could pull out my journal and approach his group to ask for one too. Two other guys came up at the same time and one of the people with Arnold said he could not sign any more autographs. The group left and began walking over to the Verizon Building, which is directly North of WTC Building Six. Arnold and gang looked around outside a little while before entering the building. I continued to watch the demolition for a while before moving back into my area to address other matters.

About 45 minutes later, I saw Arnold and his entourage walking down West Street. They stopped and Arnold climbed onto the huge crane in front of the WTC Tower Two debris pile and posed for photos with the operator and friends. He signed autographs for them, however when he resumed his walk, his escorts waved anyone that approached with pen and paper in hand away. He missed a great opportunity to make some fans for life and to provide a few good memories and needed distraction for some people that really needed it. I saw him a few more times in the afternoon, but did not attempt to get an autograph again. However, it was a highlight of the day.

There is not much more I can say about Arnold other than I was surprised that he was not nearly as tall as he appears in the movies. I am six foot two inches and I had the impression that I was at least four inches taller him. He did look every bit as muscular though, even under that firefighter's coat.

Our rides back to the hotel at night are another a high point of my day. Rain or shine, night or day, there are always people standing on at least one corner along the route reserved for rescue/recovery workers. They wave flags, hold up signs of support, thanks, and patriotism, as well as cheer as we drive past them. It always makes me feel good and appreciated. Oddly, they always bring a smile to my face and a few tears of joy at the same time. I do not think my coworkers have seen how affected I am as we pass them. We always make it a point to blow the horn and recognize them as well. I am sure they feel appreciated when we do because they always cheer louder. They may not be able to work on site for one reason or another but they are coming out on their own time and doing something to support the efforts.

Arriving at the hotel at night there also is a reaction from the other people that are staying there, too. Although hundreds of rescue team members are staying here, there are many other patrons here on other business or pleasure. We are very easy to notice because we are wearing fluorescent green vests, red hard hats and carrying backpacks. Some nights the people heading out to Broadway shows or exclusive restaurants wearing their suits, evening gowns, and furs just stop and stand in silence when we walk in. Almost every night someone thanks us for being here as we walk past or ask us how our day had been. Tonight they got me a little emotional when some of them broke into spontaneous applause as we headed for the elevators.

They always let us know in some way that they appreciate the job we are doing.

I am always a little embarrassed when we walk into the hotel and especially when riding the elevators. The elevators are usually very crowded and because we smell like smoke, dust, and all the other nasty odors that waft around the site (I would compare it to the aroma of an over smoked ham) it makes me self-conscious. It is the same with the others in our crew; we always apologize for how we look and smell when the doors close. No one ever complains or make us feel out of place. They laugh off our apologies and tell us they understand, give us a pat on the arm, talk to us about how it is at the disaster site, and thank us for coming. Almost everyone gives us their support and go out of their way to make us feel good about the job we are doing.

I have never experienced anything like the support and unity that I am feeling and witnessing everyday here. It is a shame it took an atrocity to bring us together like this. I hope this part of it never goes back to the way it once was. It would be a better world all the way around if we would treat each other in this manner all of the time.

I do not quite understand how my usual stoic outside demeanor has crumbled so quickly after so many years of practice. I am no longer able to keep my emotions bottled up inside and away from outside detection. I expected my reactions to seeing the hundreds of family members in the throes of unbearable grief and the horrors of the body recoveries. A person would have to be dead inside not to hurt deeply by sights like those. It seems it is the smallest acts of kindness that affect me the most and I become choked up at the drop of a hat. I never would have expected this reaction and for the moment, I seem to be powerless to put the calm, expressionless mask back in place.

12

Paybacks, Prayers, and 'Tootie'

October 7

My cold is worse today and my head feels like someone stuffed it with a bale of cotton. I was dressed appropriately for cold and damp weather today though. After our morning turnover session and breakfast, quite a few of us attended the daily morning meeting in a classroom on the third floor of the Command Center. Based on the little desks and chairs and the crayon artwork on the walls all around the room, I would guess this is a classroom for kindergartners or first graders. It is a little humorous when you see all of these people sitting around in little bitty chairs engaged in serious conversation. The representatives from most of the twenty-six government agencies that comprise the team running the show here also attend these meetings. There was some good information passed along to us, but I became seriously irritated at the absurdity of some of these people's positions on how the work should be done, whose agency was more powerful, and who was in charge. Jockeying for position in the food chain seems to be the priority for some of these people. Others believe that their particular function or opinion is the most important and could care less about everyone else's.

After sitting and listening for forty-five minutes to mostly political and occasionally self-serving drivel, I cannot help but conclude that there are some idiots, egotists, and assholes in abundance in powerful positions of our government. One environmental agency representative spent ten minutes or longer educating us on how wonderful his group was and why everyone else is incapable of knowing his or her ass from a hole in the ground. Thankfully, most of us do not have to attend these meetings on a daily basis, only the supervisors. I do not need any additional frustrations in my daily routine, as death, destruction, and all the terrible things that go with them are enough. Besides, it would only be a matter of time before I shot off my mouth and gave someone my thoughts on their asinine position or problem. Probably best if I avoid doing that.

Based on my few observations up to this point and what I have been told, I believe a lot of the problems that we and other groups are having are primarily caused by the fact that there are twenty-six agencies ruling as a committee. They are the representatives from the Department of Design and Construction (DDC), Office of Emergency Management (OEM), FDNY, Federal Emergency Management Agency (FEMA), Environmental Protection Agency (EPA,) NYPD, and twenty others. They all have an equal vote on decisions and it is not majority rule.

It usually is a lengthy, frustrating ordeal to get any official decision or process put through this system. If one agency wants changes made, the proposed changes have to go back to every agency again for their concurrence or comments. Therein lies the problem I think. Try sitting any group of twenty-six agencies with different concerns and agendas down in a room and see how long it takes them to reach an agreement on what to serve for lunch let alone something significant. My experiences in government work leads me to conclude just five to ten of them deciding anything will make you pull your hair out before the day is over.

It seems to me that there should be an ultimate decision-maker, someone with the 'buck stops here' authority or that can at least narrow down the list of who has show stopping rights. I will say that in spite of the committee system problems, they do keep at it full guns until they reach the point of agreement. I know that some of our bosses are working late into the night trying to get procedures approved by the committee. The system may slow them down frequently, but it has not stopped them yet, that I am aware of anyway. They really seem to do a remarkable job under the circumstances, however it would not hurt to incorporate some 'lessons learned' into the system in case, God forbid, there is a next time.

The city held an official prayer service this morning in front of the WFC Building One, at the newly erected viewing stand. Built to provide the families and dignitaries a place to see the devastation, this viewing platform keeps them from having to walk out into the work area and harm's way. The prayer ceremony had several priests, rabbis, and other clergymen of various faiths, along with Mayor Guiliani and the FDNY bagpiper troupe in attendance. The entire job stopped and almost everyone gathered at the viewing stand for the services. It turned out to be a very nice, emotional, and comforting service.

One of the ministers spoke first and others after him, but unfortunately I am unsure of exactly who they were. One related a story about a biographer of Winston Churchill. This biographer asked one of Churchill's friends his opinion on what made Churchill such a great man. The friends reply was that he was 50% of this, 50% of that, and 50% of something else. When the biographer pointed out that those added up to 150%, not 100%, the man replied that what the biographer did not understand was that Churchill was not one man, he was beyond the definition of one human.

He went on to say that like Churchill, measuring us against normal men and women was impossible. He said that we had risen above the definition of ordinary mankind by putting our lives on the line to respond to New York City's cries for help and to perform these terrible tasks. The speaker said that by our actions at Ground Zero, all of us no matter where we lived, whether we were firefighters, police officers, rescuers, or food servers, we were now brothers and sisters in a way that will bond us together forever and our unselfish actions spoken about and remembered with reverence for untold generations to come. It was such a beautiful and emotional speech. It made me, and I am sure most everyone present, feel good about our decisions to come here. I wish I had a copy of that speech. I am sure I would choke up all over again every time I read it.

Mayor Guiliani said some very nice things about all of us as well in his speech. All that this man has been through in the last few weeks and he can still give such an eloquent, thought provoking speech seemingly without effort. Today and the other times I have seen him walk by, I feel as if I am in the presence of extraordinary greatness. I just want to walk up to him, shake his hand, and tell him what a great leader he has been during this tragic time.

Several more clergymen spoke and led the crowd in prayer. Between each speaker, the bagpipers played songs I never knew a person could play on those things. Songs like America the Beautiful, When the Caissons go Marching, Marine Corps song, and all kinds of other patriotic music. They played some sad songs as well and those always seem to get to me because there is that eerie and mournful sound that only bagpipes can make. As I was standing there listening to those mournful ballads, my mind drifted to golfer Payne Stewart's memorial service. That beautiful, but sad music seemingly played from somewhere in the heavens, until slowly materializing out of the thick rolling fog, came the ghostly image of a lone bagpiper.

This memorial service was one of the many that have taken place at the site. Every Tuesday at 8:45 AM, the time that the first plane hit World Trade Center Tower One, the job completely stops, and we have a moment of silence for the victims. Other religious services of different faiths take place throughout the week although the job continues for those, but you can attend if you like. There are clergy walking around the site all the time offering comfort and prayer to anyone who wishes it. I personally have spoken to Catholic priests, Jewish rabbis, and an Anglican priest in the past few days.

Right after the service completed the entire entourage of clergy, officials, and bagpipers marched down Liberty Street and right up onto the top of the smoldering pile in the Tully area, just across the street from Firehouse No. 10. Not one of them were wearing a respirator, let alone hard hats or safety glasses. If that was not bad enough, they held another prayer ceremony while the acrid, hazardous smoke swirled around them. Dozens of the bagpipers, their knees bared under their kilts, kneeled in the debris. The debris is hot, has shards of glass and metal laced throughout, unknown chemicals burning, biological concerns from decomposing flesh, and only God knows what else. We could not believe it, let alone do anything to stop them. All of the progress we have made to this point getting workers to listen to us about the dangers of working on the pile without the proper protective equipment just took a major setback.

Later this morning we heard that America began bombing in Afghanistan. One of the construction workers who direct the trucks in and out was broadcasting the latest info every few minutes with a megaphone. It seemed to brighten the mood on the site a little. Finally, we are going after the bastards that created this smoldering graveyard of innocent people, which according to their twisted way of thinking, God sanctioned. All because we are not all Muslims and think like them. I hope they are running for their lives, scared shitless, and screaming like babies right about now. If they thought, that by bringing down these towers, Americans were going to be scared and not come after them, they seriously under estimated the American people. I would have liked to have seen the face of the first terrorist that saw one of our Stealth bombers, that American eagle, come screaming towards him from seemingly nowhere and leaving nothing but an inferno in its wake. I am sure the first and last words out of his mouth were 'Holy shit'.

Most of the rest of the day I checked on the crews in the perimeter buildings. I am taking my life into my own hands every time I go into some of these places. There are so many dangerous places and buildings. There is not a sure way to know how safe they really are because buried and hidden by debris are dangerous spots.

In many places, it is like negotiating a morbid maze to get where you are going. At any given moment, there are 40 ways to Sunday to die.

In addition to the buildings, holes, machinery, and hazards, it is always on everyone's mind that another attack is not out of the question. What better way to add insult to injury than coming back and killing the rescue workers? They have begun to allow the commercial jets to fly over the site again and the first few that came over sure caused some anxious moments. They were on a low approach to the airport and you could see almost everyone look up toward the jet engine noise, watch the plane approach, and then slightly duck their heads as it came over. All of us wondering if it was another suicide attack. I am not used to them coming over like that yet. I always have to watch them until they are safely out of range.

The helicopters that hover and circle overhead of the site every day make me nervous too. The US Coast Guard and Army have helicopters up there almost everyday, even on the extremely windy days. I do not think terrorists can get to one to hijack it, but I worry that one will crash. I have watched as they circle on those windy days and buffet back and forth. They sometimes seem to barely make any forward progress. It appears they might stop in midair and fall in the middle of us during the next wind gust.

Late this afternoon, I went to the Red Cross Respite Center to write down my notes for our turnover to the night shift. I had some coffee and enjoyed the 20 minutes or so off my feet while I sorted out my scribbled bits of notes and made out my list of observations and safety concerns. After I had finished, I began to walk down the hall towards the elevator. As I entered the elevator foyer, the doors opened and a familiar looking woman walked out. She was a very good-looking African-American woman with long braided hair dyed blond. As I watched her walk past, I got the feeling that I had seen her before and she was someone famous, however I could not put my finger on who she was or where I might have seen her before. She walked a short distance to the food serving area and went directly behind the counter. I delayed getting on the elevator and watched as she took off her coat, said hello to the other people behind the counter, and unceremoniously began scooping out food to the workers in line. Seeing her serve food, I figured that I must be mistaken and began to head back towards the elevator. However, I could not shake the thought that I should know her so I walked back near the food line and looked at her again. That second look was all it took as her name popped into my head. It was Kim Fields, AKA 'Tootie' from the Facts of Life television show. Our kids, especially Jennifer A. and Julie used to watch that show, as well as the reruns everyday after school. As I was digging into my pack for my journal to get an autograph, one of the workers yelled "Tootie' and they high-fived each other. When the line of people getting something to eat trickled to a stop, I approached and talked with her for a minute, thanked her for coming down to help, and she gave me an autograph.

Ms. Fields took time out of her busy schedule (she is currently starring in a play on Broadway) to come down here and help feed the rescue workers. About two hours later, I saw her walking through my area on her way out of Ground Zero after she had finished serving food at the Respite Center. She sure has earned my respect and made the top of my list.

Notes

As with any major catastrophe such as plane crashes, floods, tornadoes, and these attacks, an emergency management system is activated to do what it is created for, managing the emergency. These systems tie together all the information and respective agencies so they are working together and have all the information they may need at hand to make quick and efficient decisions to protect the public. They have information such as maps for escape routes, shelters, utilities, special rescue, and emergency operations groups all at their fingertips. New York had a brand new, state of the art emergency management facility for just these kinds of emergencies. The only problem was that it was located in the World Trade Center.

The City of New York pulled off a Herculean task of rebuilding an Emergency Management Command Center. They assembled it in a warehouse at one of the piers in Manhattan. This effort included installing computers and tying them into the appropriate agency systems and each other, setting the place up to accommodate the hundreds of people to staff it and making it all run smoothly and quickly. I feel New York did a commendable job handling a catastrophe bigger than any that had happened to any American city before. The obstacles they had to surmount when looked at singularly are formidable:

1. *One of the world's largest buildings destroyed and the surrounding buildings with their stability questionable.*

2. *Thousands of dead and missing people.*

3. *Fire, rescue, and police departments sustaining heavy casualties and loss of equipment.*

4. *Thousands of citizens in need of evacuation and shelter.*

5. *Unknown enemies that may not be through attacking and you need protection from them.*

6. *Fires, disrupted utilities, and contaminants.*

7. *The need to coordinate rescue efforts and support the thousands of rescuers.*

8. *Keep the public from panicking and maintain civil order.*

I am sure there are many concerns and problems that I have not even thought of yet. Add all those other things that arose as this unfolded and you can see there was an outstanding response by New York to begin to manage it all.

13

How Dare You Keep Me Safe

October 8

What a lousy day this ended up to be. My cold seems to be worse, it was very windy at the site, which caused a lot of falling glass, and it seemed that it was one problem after another all day long. The normal daily problems seemed to be getting worse today too. On top of all that, an ironworker verbally abused me for no apparent reason and it almost turned into a major incident. Being in the middle of this death and destruction over eighty hours per week is extremely stressful during the best of days without having days like this one. I am stressed out, exhausted, and can definitely say I have earned my pay today.

The glass is a major concern and danger on these windy days. There are literally thousands of broken windowpanes all around the site. A piece of sharp, jagged glass falling from heights anywhere from one to forty or more stories could go right through a person on the ground. On days like today, you can easily see the larger pieces of glass being blown out of the windows and falling. Some drop straight to the ground and others seem to float on the air currents and you have no idea where they are going to land. The small, fine pieces are a different story. Unless the sunlight is behind the particular area and reflecting off them, you cannot see this rain of fine glass. More than once I have noticed a dusting of glass on my backpack and shoulders. My biggest concern is getting some into my eyes. It could shred them before you even knew it was there. I keep my safety glasses on all the time and wash my face anytime I can get to a bathroom with running water. Not much else you can do about it.

Crews have been working to put protective netting around several of the buildings over the last few days. Other crews working for the building owners are removing broken windows and replacing them with plywood. However, both these efforts are slow processes and many buildings have no protection in place at all. Other areas have been fenced or barricaded off, and in a few others, scaffolding erected to provide some overhead protection. The glass does not always cooperate and stay in these protected areas. We keep the workers away from these areas as best we can and to my knowledge, no one has suffered an injury due to falling glass. We are performing glass damage reports every few days to mark the progress of getting the area into a safe condition. You might think that the broken windows are just on the sides facing the World Trade Center and most are, but actually, there are windows broken on all sides of the buildings up to three to four blocks away.

The wind is our enemy in other ways besides the falling and flying glass. The concrete dust that is all around the area, for blocks in every direction, is very hard to keep out of your eyes on calm days, let alone when it is blowing around. The dust cloud that everyone witnessed on TV rolling down the streets on September 11 was from the concrete used to build the World Trade Center Towers. When they collapsed, the concrete just pulverized to practically nothing but dust because of the height it was falling and from all the weight of the steel and more concrete that piled on top of it. I have not seen a piece of concrete larger than I can wrap my arms around. Most of the pieces I see are no larger than softballs.

The wind is wild here because of what they call the Skyscraper Effect. The huge buildings that are so close together cause the wind to funnel through the streets and alleyways, rendering it faster and stronger by concentration. Some places seem calm until you pass in front of an alley and suddenly the wind becomes so strong that it is difficult to keep on your feet. These gusts frequently knock over barricades, tables, and even collapsed one of the tents the Salvation Army had erected. I dodge blowing debris almost daily.

The incident with the ironworker abusing me today is the worst incident I have had so far, but others in our group have related some nasty encounters with other workers. Mine today started innocently enough. My coworker Charlie and I were walking between the perimeter of the WTC Tower Two debris and the 90 West Building when we spotted a full oxygen gas bottle lying on the ground, a bad practice as well as an OSHA violation. It was lying on its side in a spot where one of the machines or trucks may run over it, which could cause all kinds of problems. These bottles are under a great amount of pressure and should the nozzle be broken off, it becomes a missile. In that case, it can easily kill and cause a lot of damage until it finally exhausts the gas inside. These types of bottles can 'launch' for hundreds of yards and travel through concrete block walls, and most anything else in the path. It could also explode, throwing shrapnel in every direction. The release of pure oxygen could combine with a hot exhaust system and start a vicious fire. Charlie and I stood the bottle upright and began looking for a spot we could place it and tie it off so it would not fall over.

Well, the ironworker was watching us and apparently did not like the fact that we had stood his oxygen gas bottle up as it was supposed to be. He seized the opportunity to call me over and ask me what we thought we were doing. I explained about the dangerous position it had been in and the OSHA regulation in a polite manner. He proceeded to explain to me how stupid OSHA rules were and how I was even dumber for not agreeing with him on the subject. I tried to explain that I was only doing my job, which was to assist in preventing workers like him from suffering injuries during the rescue/recovery operation. He responded by calling me a few choice names and telling me to "get the fuck away from him". I took that in stride, as this was not the first time I experienced verbal abuse by a worker in my career and probably will not be the last either. I told him I was not going anywhere until we took care of the bottle. He became irate and repeatedly told me to get the fuck away from him. About this time, one of his coworkers showed up and he instructed him to lay the bottle back onto the ground. I said, "OK, do what you want, we were only trying to prevent an accident". "However, with your attitude, I can guarantee that whether it is today, tomorrow or ten years from now, your careless attitude is going to catch up with you".

At the time, I did not know my supervisor had walked up behind me and had heard most of the conversation. After I had walked away from situation and the idiot before things became worse, he came over and told me that I had handled it well. He called his supervisor and reported the incident. As the incident information went up the chain of command, someone decided that this guy needed arrested and removed from site. I was to 'hold' them until the officers from the Department of Environmental Compliance arrived. Someone with the ironworker's company heard that broadcast over the radio and hustled him and his coworker out of our sight. The DEC police never showed and since the ironworkers had disappeared their supervisor received stern instructions that abuse of our team was intolerable and another instance could get them thrown off the site. Nothing much else left to do. I did not feel that the abuse of me warranted arresting him, but combined with all the other similar incidents we and others have been experiencing, I guess they wanted to send a message.

I am not the only one of our crew to have a run-in with unruly workers. The other evening, Randy Bailey witnessed an incident and became involved in an ugly episode of verbal abuse. Randy saw a crane operator in the AMEC area who was playing around with a crane. He was moving the boom in a manner to cause the hook to swing back and forth, low enough to the ground to hit someone. It quickly became evident that the worker had a particular purpose for his actions; he was trying to knock over a welding cart with acetylene and oxygen gas bottles in it. I have already mentioned all the potential consequences of that dangerous scenario. The guy succeeded in his game, hitting the cart and knocking it over onto the ground, much to the delight of his coworkers. They began to applaud, hoot, and whistle congratulations at his success at damned near killing them all.

After checking to make sure that there was no danger of the bottles going off, Randy went over to the operator and his boss to request he shut the operation down and to see the operator's credentials. Before Randy could finish his question, the boss started verbally abusing him. "Get fucked and get out of my fucking area". "Where were you thirty days ago when we got here"? "Do you even know a fucking thing about cranes?" "Do you think this is unsafe"? The abuse went on and on for quite a while. It got ugly enough that Randy had concerns of assault, so he contacted the Captain of the Department of Environmental Compliance who was in charge on night shift. The captain arrived with three officers in tow and requested to talk to the offending boss and the crane operator. The contractor ignored him as well and did not produce either employee as requested. After hearing Randy's side of the events, the captain told them in no uncertain terms that our safety department worked for him, the city, and state of New York. If there were any other incidents like this, he would personally handle them and someone was going to jail. He was particularly upset over the "where were you thirty days ago" question. He asked them "where were you when I was running for my life and escaping a collapsing tower on September 11?"

Despite the controlling police supervisor being involved and a subsequent letter to the city requesting action, nothing came of it. We troops in the trenches can only conclude that they can do or say, just about anything, they want to us and we are powerless to do anything about it. I know that I am just going to walk away and contact a supervisor from now on. There is no point in me arguing with anyone and risking a fight. Help the ones that want it and leave the others for someone else with more stroke than we have.

There have been many other near-miss incidents where it was just luck that someone was not killed. Another in particular that happened on the night shift had our crew pretty worried for a while. A driver of large dump truck parked on uneven ground had raised the bed to dump the load when it became top heavy and rolled over onto its side. Randy and Denny Blackwell were near it and said the ground shook violently when it went over. They at first thought the slurry wall was collapsing and the ground was shifting and were debating whether to run north as was the only instructions they knew. Upon seeing people running, they followed and saw the truck. They went over to make sure that no one was hurt. They thought everything was OK until Denny pointed out a communications radio lying on the ground next to the bed of the truck. Until they verified that no one was in fact under the truck, they were worried that the radio had flown out of someone's hand as the falling truck bed was crushing them. They never found out how that radio ended up where it was.

For the remainder of the day it seemed like I could not get ahead of all the problems or catch my breath. One problem after another, chasing down supervisors and listening to many of them give excuses why they could not do it safely. Some of the supervisors are just great people and will do anything they can to protect their crews. Others it seems could care less if their worker could fall eight stories or not. I heard some poor explanations for putting people at risk. "That is the way we do it in New York, it is called area practice". " This is an emergency, we do not have to follow all those stupid rules here because it wastes time". "What, he is hanging on up there, what else is he supposed to do?" Some of the pitiful excuses would be funny if someone's life was not on the line. It was all I could do to feel comfortable enough that no one was going to die in the next hour so I could take time for lunch and write my notes this afternoon.

I have thought a lot about going home today. Frustration and homesickness are starting to set in and creep into my thoughts every time I have a spare moment. I have made a commitment to do this job and I plan to keep it. My problems are miniscule compared to what the families of all these dead people are going through. What is that old saying? I used to cry because I had no shoes, until I met a man with no feet. I need to think of that every time I feel like packing it in. Besides that, my parents taught me that a person's word is his bond. I gave my word I will stay here and I will even if it kills me. I wish that I knew how my Mom and Dad instilled these values and ethics in me. I really do not remember a specific conversation or event when these values came up and I retained them. I find myself puzzled at times wondering how I know something or how I came about some of the core values that make up what I call my personal code of life. I can only hope that I have passed these values onto my children and someday they will wonder how I did it.

14

The Bathtub Springs a Leak

October 9

This was another very busy day. The OSHA inspectors that accompanied me last week have left for home so I have a new guy with me today. His name is Richard and he is from Columbus, Ohio. We went just about everywhere on the site today. These tours are getting to be the standard events on the first day of a new OSHA inspector. It gives them their first opportunity to see the large scale of this mess and become familiar with the locations of the important services like first aid, bathrooms, and Red Cross Respite Centers. I remember how I was totally disoriented my first day so I try to get them comfortable with where they are and where they should not be. In addition, it would not go over well if I 'lost' my OSHA counterpart somewhere. I am afraid that I pretty much wore him out though. We went to the Red Cross Center to get him some cushioned shoe inserts before 11:00 AM. He hung with me all day though without a complaint. He did have the normal reaction to all the safety violations going on all around the site. Things that we would never allow in normal circumstances are not high on the priority list here as there are bigger fish to fry. It will take him awhile to get over the initial shock of the open defiance of safety rules, not to mention of the devastation.

There is not that much new here today other than some concerns involving the damaged slurry wall that surrounds the World Trade Center. It has become the focus of a whole lot of attention. Based on what I have been able to grasp of the situation, the wall holds back the Hudson River and if it fails, things will get very ugly. Depending on which 'expert' you talk to, the result of the slurry wall failure could be minimal problems or could result in the ground turning to mush and the surrounding buildings would begin to collapse. They have nicknamed this wall system 'the bathtub' although its design is to keep water out, not in.

An Army Corps of Engineers employee told me that the area was once a trash dump filled in to build the World trade Center as well as other buildings. It was filled in and the slurry wall built to make more land space on Manhattan Island. The wall, building foundations, and soil depend on each other for stability. In other words, the wall keeps the river water out and the soil and underground structure keeps the wall from collapsing. What the engineers are concerned about is that as the removal of debris and structure progresses, the slurry wall is beginning to shift towards the created void. The southern tip of Manhattan depends on that slurry wall staying intact. If it fails, a very large area is in jeopardy of ruin.

In my area, between the 90 West Building and WTC Tower Two, there are cracks appearing in the soil along the slurry wall. I checked out these cracks today and they range anywhere from six to twelve inches deep, six to eight inches wide, and one to eight feet long. An engineer told me that there is also a large crack in the wall itself near WTC Tower One. They continually survey this wall to detect any movement and dozens of engineers are inspecting as they try to determine a solution to alleviate the problem. They have decided to pour sand into the voids of the basement to replace the removed debris. Workers will set up conveyors and have them running around the clock pouring the sand in the void. The wall will have holes drilled into it and tieback anchors installed. Installation of de-watering wells around the wall to remove water from the surrounding soil is the plan. I hope this plan works. The only instructions I have heard in case the slurry wall collapses is to run north. Does not seem like much of a plan, but I intend to run like Hell if they give the word. I just hope I am not inside the 90 West or World Financial Center Buildings if it does go belly up. If I am, a fresh batch of rescuers will be digging for my remains.

I wonder if the lunatics that planned and carried this out ever imagined that all of this damage would result from their insane act. If they knew all of these engineering issues would happen when they slammed those planes into the buildings, they are a whole lot smarter than anyone has ever given them the credit for being. It is a shame that people with that intelligence would waste it killing people halfway around the world that did not do a damned thing to them. Think of the things they could do to actually help their own people instead. People living in caves, tents, squalor, and barely getting enough to eat let alone an education or having hope for a future. This attack was not about making things better for the Arab people. It was about power and ego.

Richard and I saw them bring out a body this afternoon. It was his first time to experience this ritual. He was quiet and pensive, more than likely processing the same thoughts I had the first time a week or so ago. I do not think you really get used to it, but learn to deal with it so it does not affect you as badly as the first few times. The search for bodies is always a disturbing part of my day. Sometimes it is slow but other days it seems they are bringing out quite a few. They locate areas where they are usually with the help of the search dogs. It is a common sight to see the dogs going back and forth over an area and sometimes even going into a void or hole in the debris to search. There are many, many search and rescue teams here from all over the country. New teams are showing up all the time to relieve the other crews. Most all the teams have dogs and they work sometimes until they cannot go on. The dogs are happy when they can find something, that is their job and they want to please. Those dogs do a lot of work at Ground Zero. Unfortunately, everyone they find is already beyond rescue.

The fires burning under the rubble pile are a continual problem for the rescue/recovery crews. The smoke is always hanging in a haze around the site unless it is a real windy day, which does not help that much, because it fans the exposed hot spots. They also never know when they are going to open a very hot spot while pulling out pieces of debris. When that happens, a mixture of smoke and steam envelops the operators of the machines as the firefighters begin pouring on the water. The operators and ground personnel will usually back off and wait until the firefighters can get it cooled down enough to allow them to move back in.

These fires are strange phenomena because they are almost entirely under the pile and rarely do you see any actual flames even when they do open the pile up to expose it. At those times, you usually only see a deep, cherry red glow. That a fire of this intensity is even burning under all that concrete dust and steel piled on top is amazing. A firefighter told me that the fire is getting most of its oxygen from the tunnels and open areas underneath and that the pile on top is acting like insulation and helping it to keep it's heat. He compared it to a mine fire and said the temperatures underneath the piles are running around 1,000 to 1,800 degrees. He said that they believe the fire fuel is a combination of the mountain of paper that was in the offices, aviation fuel from the planes, and maybe some wood from office furniture. From what I understood of his explanation, the fire will consume the fuel much slower than an open fire because of the compaction.

In some areas, the workers can only stand in any one place for short time periods because their shoes will melt! That problem is improving now due to the firefighters continually pouring water on the piles to cool them. It also helps to keep down the choking dust kicked up from the machines. It has also rained a few times but none of that is slowing the fire raging down below. Water cannot travel down to the fire in sufficient quantity to make a difference due to the densely packed debris. At one point, to no avail, they attempted to inject foam fire retardant down into the piles to cut off the oxygen supply by smothering it.

The US Coast Guard takes overhead infrared photos from their helicopter circling the site every day. They post that information on large maps at the FDNY Command Center several blocks from here. I have only attended one of their morning meetings and it was very informative. I wish I could go more often but I was just filling in for the regularly assigned person that day. A US Army Corps of Engineer employee has told me that the photographs over the past few weeks have shown that the fire is actually growing outward and getting hotter. They do not think they can put it out quickly, just a little bit at a time as they uncover it.

The acrid, biting smoke is my worst problem and is definitely an inconvenience most of the time. It stings my eyes and at times when it blows to the outer reaches of the site where respirators are not required, it causes me to struggle to breathe. I wear my respirator everywhere in the exclusion zone and most of the surrounding areas when it is bad. I try to keep upwind of the smoke as much as possible. That is about all I can do.

At the end of my shift, I made my way back to the Command Center at the school for the turnover to the night shift. We spend about half an hour or so at the Command Center twice a day at these shifts turnovers. In addition, we attend some of the morning and afternoon meetings, but that is not that often for me, the bosses usually attend those. It has a Salvation Army food kitchen, a supply area (I was given a new pair of work boots there) and has various services like first aid, massages for about the first week we were there, and other amenities. They did a good job of setting it up in a hurry. Well guarded, I feel very safe there.

The Command Center is in a very nice neighborhood with a great view of Manhattan and the river. There are stores, delis, and apartment buildings all around the immediate area. Tonight we found out that it is a very exclusive neighborhood to say the least. Some of our crewmembers were standing outside talking to an NYPD officer who is guarding the area while they waited for the rest of us to leave. They saw a woman exit a deli, cross the street to enter one of the apartment buildings, and commented to the officer that she must be a model because she was so beautiful and well dressed. The officer told them that they were probably right, that many models lived there as well as some other high-income people. He said that the starting rent at that building was $15,000 a month! In less than eight months of payments at that amount, I would have my house paid for. I cannot imagine earning enough to afford rent like that or even paying that if I did.

My cold is still hanging on, but it seems a little better today. I finally was able to talk to Sara today, but Jeremy was not at home. I finally caught up to her by a borrowed cell telephone from the site. Typical teenager, she is either on the Internet or the telephone or in her case, both at the same time. I have a very difficult time getting in touch with her and Jeremy with my limited window of calling time at night. It means a lot to me to talk to everyone and let them know I am OK and not to worry. Talking with them reminds me of the important things in life and keeps me from taking too many chances. However, I have not told them that I take a chance every time I walk onto the site.

I am exhausted tonight and can barely keep my eyes open any longer. In hindsight, I should have thought to bring a tape recorder so I could record my thoughts and the events as they were happening. It would be so much easier to be able to write it down accurately on my days off than each night like this before I forget it or fall asleep.

15

The Saddest Place in America

October 10

What an emotional day. I made a very big mental mistake today and I think this one is going to haunt me for a while. I do not know what I was thinking. My OSHA counterpart Richard and I were not as busy as usual and he mentioned that he wanted to look around the surrounding areas and see some of Manhattan. We wandered around a few of the surrounding blocks that had minimal damage and I decided to take him down to the waterfront to see the Statue of Liberty. That was the beginning of my mistake.

On the trip, which was only a few short blocks to Battery Park and the waterfront, we had to pass directly by the spot where, after their visit to the site, the relatives and friends of the victims leave flowers, Teddy Bears, cards, and notes. The area appears to be a small park. It has a short stonewall that starts at the few entrance stairs and continues part way around it in both directions. It is known here as the 'Teddy Bear Wall'.

Directly across the sidewalk from the Teddy Bear Wall is a makeshift memorial for the members of the New York Police Department, Port Authority Police Department, and Fire Department (FDNY) killed in the attack. This memorial is set up on the courtyard of a permanent memorial that honors the members of the NYPD that have fallen throughout New York's history. Here there are pictures of many of the victims, letters, newspaper articles, fire helmets, flowers, and the notes from relatives and friends. A priest is on duty at this memorial to provide information and comfort to those that are overwhelmed by their visit.

Richard wanted to stop and look at the memorials. He and I went into the Police and Firefighter area and looked over all of the photos and items left there. Fire helmets with the victim's pictures attached and signed by their families and friends were tough to look at for very long. Packed into this small area are so many touching tributes to these fallen heroes. I read a few of the notes and poems posted on easels and boards erected here for that purpose. One note in particular made the tears begin to well up. It was from a son describing how his father was a hero and always would be in his and the world's eyes for his courage on September 11. Young sons and daughters should not have to be in this position of having to write tributes to their parents taken from them so early in their lives. Such a sad place, but it was going to get worse.

Walking across the road to the Teddy Bear Wall, Richard and I silently began to look at the flowers, Teddy bears, and letters placed here so lovingly by the surviving relatives and friends. The bears and flowers are intermixed and packed tightly together. Notes and cards, written by those buried in grief, left here for stolen loved ones that will never now read them. Randomly placed among the notes, flowers, and bears, are trinkets of a personal significance that I can only speculate. Richard and I were standing side by side, but not a word passed between us, both of us lost in personal thoughts and emotions.

Had we just continued our trip to the Statue of Liberty at this point I would have been all right. However, we did not and I was about to realize that I had made a painful mistake. I began to read some of the personal notes, the first one sad, but emotionally manageable. The second one, a letter from a wife to her husband who had perished in the attack was my downfall. The hand written letter began by telling him how they had been together for such a very short time and that those 34 years of marriage now seemed as if only a few short weeks had passed to her now. The time since their wedding day until now was not enough. I could not read any farther had I wanted to. Feeling as if punched in the throat, chest, and stomach all at the same time, I could not seem to breathe. My throat hurt so bad that I could not swallow. I had to look away from the wall, the sight of the Teddy bears was now more than I could handle. All I could think of was how painful that letter was for her to write and how she did not deserve having to. Then my thoughts turned to my wife and children and how I hoped they never had to write something like this. My God, the profound grief that has filled in the void left in these survivor's souls is unimaginable. I feel like I cannot seem to escape the sadness that has taken up residence in this place.

I could not leave there quickly enough so I wandered around in the general area trying to get my composure back until Richard was ready to move on. Afterwards, Richard and I continued on to the waterfront and sat for quite a while on a bench, silently gazing out across the river at the Statue of Liberty and Ellis Island. My emotions were still at the surface, however they began to change for the better while viewing our symbols of freedom. We left the bench and walked along the riverfront walkway, talking and trying to relax. At the mouth of the harbor sat a U.S. Coast Guard ship, quietly keeping vigil on our safety. The ship was blocking the harbor entrance from any unknown enemies who might foolishly try to slip in and strike New York City again.

When we went back into the site, Richard began watching the firefighters as they worked at uncovering a body in our area. I took care of other matters in the surrounding area because I really have no desire to see any more of that awful process. Richard just wants to see and experience everything while he is here for his weeklong tour. I really cannot blame him for that. I started out wanting to make sure I burned these experiences into my memory as well. There are some though that I may want to erase later and will be unable to. I am trying to avoid the obvious ones and I have already reached my limit today with my mistake at the Teddy Bear Wall.

Told on the first day that the firefighters do not like people to watch them during body recovery and I have always tried to respect that. All kinds of people are always right there in the middle of it watching every day and I have never noticed anyone seeming to mind. You cannot help but see it all as it goes on all around you, especially in my area. This is where they died. It is a painful thing to see. Knowing that the person they were removing had hopes, dreams, families, and life just like you and that it was gone in an instant. It also is a very difficult task for the rescuers, mostly firefighters. I have seen one firefighter so overcome with grief that a coworker had to lead him away. The last that I saw him, he was trembling and sobbing uncontrollably. Apparently, he had recognized the badge number of the firefighter found. It could have been his son, brother, or a friend.

The other day, one of the counselors at the Red Cross center told me about a firefighter who had just recovered one body too many for him to deal with and he broke down during lunch and she helped him. Everyone has his or her breaking point and it was good that his came when it did so that he could get help from a professional. I wonder how many others have reached their breaking point and disintegrate at home after work and deal with it on their own. I think that the psychological damage suffered here is going to be a significant problem in the years to come. Whatever it is, Post-Traumatic Stress Syndrome or PTS, battle fatigue, or just painful memories, eventually they may be too much to handle. Some people are going to be waking up screaming in the middle of the night for a long, long, time. I really do not know if I will be one of them.

My mistakes today just keep coming. Reliving this as I write it down in my journal has not been easy. I am right back in the emotional state I was in earlier. Janice and my Mom called tonight and I tried to talk about it with each of them. I could not get the words to come, but the tears I could not stop. I tried silently crying so they would not know how upset I was. It did not work and although they did not say anything, they knew. I do not think anyone up to this point in my life, knows how badly some things like this bother me because I try hard not to show it. I let out my emotions slowly and try to keep them buried and private. My wife Janice, who knows me better than anyone, probably sees those emotions churning under my mask. However, she never mentions it.

Notes

I wrote this chapter on January 19, 2002, a little over three months after I first wrote in my journal about that day, October 10. I had read the rest of the journal several times, but could not bring myself to read the entry about the wall and letter until then. This was the one memory that I had not been able to mentally revisit. I would not have tried then had I not been writing this book. I cried all over again as I thought would happen. That letter affected and hurt me worse than anything else I saw at Ground Zero, and I saw some terrible things.

Passing the Teddy Bear Wall was a frequent part of the daily routine at Ground Zero. After October 10, I could walk past it, look at it, and I even stop and take a picture of it. I could handle it just as long as I did not think about that letter or read anymore. The 'Teddy bear Wall' is the saddest and most emotionally upsetting place that I have ever stood. If there is a worse place than this, I never want to see it. That day's experience has left a painful and permanent scar on my soul.

You learn very quickly, what you can handle and to avoid the things that you cannot. It only took a few times of inadvertently finding me in the midst of the victim's families during their visits to the site for me to go somewhere else. As long as I could not see them, I was all right. Not all of the family visits that I saw were disturbing but a few times family members collapsed and had to be taken to the Disaster Medical Assistance Team (DMAT) first aid station or helped away by the grief counselors. I could not always avoid them easily. My area is where they came, actually right up to the debris pile until they built the viewing stand, but that was in my area, too. So at times, it was just unavoidable.

I do not know if it was a conscious or unconscious decision in my case to put up an internal protective wall around difficult experiences. The letter and seeing body removals will continue to haunt you if you do not. With something like the World Trade Center disaster, the devastation, and the loss of life, you have to have the ability to cope. To do what you have to do, you must protect yourself from your breaking point by adapting the way you deal with a situation. In my case, it was looking or walking away and occupying my mind with other matters so that I did not cross that fine line of composure versus emotional breakdown. I only had to do this for a month. How did people that were at war for years do it? It is remarkable how your mind can protect you from potentially damaging experiences. Unfortunately, as with the firefighter I mentioned above, it does not work for everyone.

16

Sightseeing

October 11

My day off and I need it. I got up at my usual 5:00 AM and met Randy after his shift and we had breakfast at the Howard Johnson's across the street from the Marriott Marquis. It costs about twice as much here as it has at any other HoJo's I have eaten at around the country. However, it was quiet inside and we were able to have a great conversation. We filled each other in on our experiences on our shifts this week. It is always an interesting hour or so listening to the trials and tribulations of the night shift. Surprisingly, they have as many problems as we do on the day shift. In our normal work, the night shift is usually slow and relatively quiet and relaxed.

After breakfast Randy went off to get some much needed sleep, while I walked down to Rockefeller Center again, this time to get Janice a Today Show coffee mug at the NBC store. While I was in there, I thought about taking the tour of the NBC studios they offer, but decided to wait until I can bring Janice here some day and we can do it together.

I wandered around the area awhile before heading for the train station so I could get over to Newark, New Jersey to buy my brother-in-law, G. C., some more Harley Davidson shirts. I have not been in a train station since I was in the eighth grade and then the tour guide took us wherever we needed to go. Seemed a simple enough endeavor though. All that I needed was ticket to get onto a train going to Newark. People coming and going packed the station in intermittent waves it seemed. One mob would replace another as trains arrived and departed. I kept looking over the schedules they have posted all over the place and could not figure out which train I should take. I gave up, swallowed my male pride, (we never ask directions!) and just went up to a ticket counter and told the lady where and when I wanted to go. Without any mention of my inability to find my way out of a train station, she sold me a ticket and pointed me in the direction of the loading platform where my train would stop in about 20 minutes. When the train showed up I found out you have to be quick. People surge toward the doors and pile on in no time. I do not know why though as the train was not even half full and did not leave for a few minutes. I guess it is habit from when it is crowded. The trip over was uneventful, not much to look at outside other than buildings and fields. Inside the train, there were a few strange characters, either talking to themselves, or wearing some weird outfits. No one bothered anyone else and I made it safely to Newark. It was a wasted trip as I found out there is not a Harley Davidson shop in Newark. I looked through the phone book for something else of interest in the area and there was not anything else I wanted to see or do. I found my way back to the train station without assistance and rode back to Manhattan.

The trip I took down to the post office was fun though. I went past the bus station on the way there and it has a statue of Ralph Kramden of the 'Honeymooners' show out front in honor of his being a bus driver on the show. There also is an underground K-mart in the bus terminal, which came in handy for me. I bought some mailing supplies and a few other miscellaneous items. I have not seen any shopping centers or malls here yet, only specialty shops and the K-mart. The post office is right across the street from Madison Square Garden, the site of so many sporting and entertainment events. The 'Gaahden' as they call it here, is where Paul McCartney will put the big benefit concert on October 20 for the victim's families. I had hoped to buy a ticket, however the news last night announced it is a sellout already. The tickets cost hundreds of dollars anyway, which is way over my budget. I continued to roam in whatever direction seemed interesting for a few hours until the inevitable exhaustion caught up with me and I went back to the Marriott and slept.

17

Anthrax

October 12

Well, this was a stressful day for me in particular. Early this morning, someone announced over our job radios that the news media was reporting that anthrax was in Rockefeller Center at the NBC Studios. The report did not say what part of the building in particular it was, only that Rockefeller Center was closed and under quarantine. My heart leapt into my throat as I was in parts of that building yesterday on my day off. Information was sketchy and slow in coming most of the day. I watched a few minutes of television news at the Red Cross Center after lunch, however did not hear anything specific.

Anthrax. I would never have imagined my ever being concerned about anthrax. Of course, before September 11, no one was concerned about many of the things that we are now. I was worried all day about my possible exposure because we were getting so little information on where it was found, if the public was exposed, or what to do if you thought you had been. Hell, I did not even know a single symptom of anthrax exposure that I should be worried about if I were to get one. I also thought a lot about our children and grandchildren's future and safety in the new, uncharted society we now live in. The irony of my exposure to death or serious injury on a minute-by-minute basis here at the site and the possibility I may now be in worse danger because I had a day off did not escape me either.

When I went back to the Command Center at 6:30 PM tonight for shift turnover, the small television they have there was on the CNN station. As the night shift was not there yet to begin going over my notes, I stood and watched until the news topic turned to the anthrax at NBC studios. They began the story by showing film of the sign that is at the entrance to the NBC Rainbow Room. The cameraman must have stood in the exact spot as I did yesterday when I took a photograph of the same sign. Since seeing that sign, I became very concerned that I actually might have been in an area where my chance of exposure was possible. I had wandered all over the first floor of the NBC Store and the surrounding outside areas. After about five minutes into the report, they finally said that the anthrax was isolated to one office and the public normally would not visit there. What a relief, I could finally relax a little. Just in case this report was inaccurate, I informed my supervisor that I had been at Rockefeller Center the day before and what buildings I was in. I sure am glad I decided not to go on the NBC Studios tour yesterday.

Now I have to wonder what is waiting for me everyplace I go from now on. Is it safe to go to the post office, the Laundromat, or a restaurant? I have all of this paranoia because apparently the world has gone completely nuts. I am naturally cautious when I go anywhere new, but now I will try to be keenly aware of my surroundings. Thoughts as 'could this place be a target?' or 'are there any suspicious vehicles or people in the immediate area?' will now be considerations when going to public places. The sad part about this is that anywhere is a target to these maniacs as long as it kills Americans. The worst part is they will use any means possible, no matter how unimaginable by sane people. Who would ever have thought that 19 people would commit suicide to kill Americans in the belief that they would go to heaven to receive a reward of 72 virgins and as martyrs to God, no less?

I am afraid for the future of our children, grandchildren, and the untold generations to come. How do you stop this madness? Suicidal lunatics flying planes into buildings and now someone is attempting to poison us. We may have to completely change the way we live, lose some of that freedom that we enjoy so much. These people involved in the World Trade Center attack have proven they hate us so much that they are willing to kill anyone of us and in any manner. America, the greatest country that the world has ever known, with the greatest military defenses, and brilliant minds, and here we are ducking when planes go overhead, suspicious of the mail, and not knowing what the hell may be coming next. What a way to have to live your life, suspicious of everything. I think we have taken too much for granted and it was easy to do. Our greatness, freedom and might, have caused us to become complacent, comfortable and negligent. A valuable lesson taught to us in a most terrible way. I hope and pray that we have learned our lesson well and can get our safety back for our future generations.

Another busy day for the recovery teams as they uncovered and retrieved a few more firefighters today. I do not know how these people can emotionally handle unburying their friends, coworkers, and relatives day after day. They spend hours of effort in performing tedious and exhausting work knowing that the result is going to be additional grief and pain. It takes immeasurable courage, humanity, and dedication to expend so much of their energy and soul knowing their only reward is recovery of the dead. This tragic activity never takes time off; it goes on everyday, twenty-four hours a day.

Our crewmembers have all had some problems with individual firefighters from time to time. Some have behaved in an extremely rude and pompous manner for absolutely no reason known to us. Some have just ignored our advice and continued placing themselves and others in dangerous positions. However, the majority of the firefighters have treated us with respect and appreciated our efforts to assist them. I believe some of the negative behavior relates to the fact that they have suffered such a great loss of friends and relatives and are now suffering through the grim task of finding their remains. I cannot think of anything more difficult or stressful than that. Nothing that I have experienced with a few individuals so far has changed the feelings of respect I have for most of these people.

As misfortune would have it, it seems that my prediction for the ironworker that verbally abused me the other day came true. Richard of OSHA and my coworkers told me that yesterday he was in a man basket (a crane suspended work platform that workers ride and work from in high, difficult areas) when the lift line caught on another crane. They said when the line slipped free, the basket swung violently two or three times into the WTC Tower Two façade. The ironworker suffered arm injuries caused by, ironically, a gas bottle that broke free in the basket after the collision with the wall and fell onto him. Everyone that witnessed it is of the opinion that he was one lucky individual to survive it. I have not seen him here today, he may be off work, or they put him somewhere else. It is too bad; I hate to see anyone get hurt. However, when you ignore basic safety practices or have the attitude this man has, you will suffer for it eventually. It just caught up to him quicker than most.

As I was standing in front of the large crane in my area with another man watching the removal of beams from the Marriott hotel and WTC Tower Two area, he pulled out a disposable camera and took a few photographs of the work. I mentioned to him that photo taking was off limits to my group based on the NYC edict, but I wished I could take some. He said that he had been told the same thing, but had been watching the firefighters, police, and every visitor that came onto the site taking photos and videos for two weeks without repercussions and decided he was going to get some too. I feel the same way. Supposedly forbidden for anyone to take photos, it seems that selective enforcement is the rule. The only people ever stopped from doing it are the construction workers. I think I will pick up a disposable camera tonight for myself. I could bring my good 35 MM camera down here if I thought they would not confiscate it if they caught me. The army guards sporadically search our backpacks when we come arrive in the morning. I can afford losing a $10 camera, but the $250 one is a little steep for a few photos.

Yesterday, October 11 was the one-month anniversary of the World Trade Center attack. The guys told me they had a very nice ceremony again at the site. One month gone by already and the recovery of victims, let alone the clean up of this mess has barely scratched the surface yet. This must be what a reoccurring nightmare is like. Only here it starts when you wake up.

18

Beyond Courage

October 13

I saw at least two, maybe three firefighter remains recovered today. I do not know if there was others found in other locations. It seems that they only find a small number of bodies each day. I would guess that there are probably more than I actually see each day because there are several areas that crews are searching in. However, I am usually too busy taking care of other matters to notice those activities. In addition, the civilian recoveries are more low-key than the solemn, ceremonial atmosphere that occurs when it is a police officer or firefighter body. You do not seem to notice the plain black body bags as they are driven off the pile during the frenzied pace of the normal daily activities. On the other hand, it is difficult not to notice six or eight firefighters carrying a flag draped casket out of the pile and up the middle of West Street on their way to the morgue.

Nearly everyday there is a rumor or discussion that they are nearing a location in the debris that it is thought a hundred or more firefighters or victims are thought to be located. Up to this point, none of that speculation has panned out and they find only a few of the thousands of victims. I hope that for the sake of the families and recovery workers, the pace and number of the recoveries will increase soon. Perhaps some of the survivors can begin to heal and rebuild their lives once they finally find their loved ones. Waiting for weeks or months like this must be very difficult.

I was busy as usual most of the day, but at least the weather has been sunny and warm. It was in the eighties today. The problems were relatively minor in nature today and most easily corrected. I am getting a lot of cooperation from Ray, the safety manager at Bovis. Ray is a very intelligent guy that is trying his damnedest to correct the safety problems in his area. It is going to take a lot of time and effort, but he is willing to go the extra mile to get it done. We could use several more safety guys like Ray here.

Richard, my OSHA counterpart left for his Ohio home today. I asked him where in Columbus he lived and it is right near my wife's son John Bellestri and his wife Brandee in Pickerington, just outside of Columbus - what a small world it is. Richard has turned out to be the best OSHA representative that I have worked with so far. He overcame his initial panic at all the safety violations going on and settled down quickly. That first day with him, he was grabbing me every few minutes and saying things like "Look at that! That guy is not wearing safety glasses." Well, no the person was not wearing safety glasses but neither were 99% of the other people on site. I was happy if they were wearing a hard hat, work shoes, and not doing anything completely crazy. Richard soon realized the enormity of the problems and adapted very quickly. I enjoyed our entire week together. We had some great conversations, solved some difficult problems and actually accomplished a great deal. We did a lot of walking around and investigating things, just taking it all in. I wish he could have stayed and worked with me for the rest of my time here. I think we could accomplish a lot more together.

As far as finding safety violations goes, it is like shooting fish in a barrel, there are 147 of them in every direction at any given time. What Richard was able to do, that some of the other OSHA folks and others as well have had trouble with, is to prioritize the problems. There are so many very dangerous situations occurring all the time that you cannot take the time to sweat the small stuff.

Richard and I went up on the roof of the World Financial Center again so he could look over the entire site once more. We chatted about the site and the many problems facing we safety people here. The future of America was another topic. I took some photos with the disposable camera I bought at the souvenir shop by the hotel last night. I covered the automatic flash with duct tape so it would not draw the attention of anyone. It is ironic that I worry about getting in trouble with the police for taking photos and they are taking as many as anyone else is. Rumor has it that the police are making the people they catch with cameras rewind the film so it is not ruined and they can get it developed to keep as their own. I do not know if there is any substance to that rumor or not. During our wanderings, we talked to some of the people Richard had met. Richard and I then said our goodbyes and he headed for the airport.

As the weeks go on, I am beginning to recognize and become familiar with a few of the firefighters and police that are usually in my area. The firefighter sector and battalion chiefs are whom we normally talk over safety concerns with, but some in their crews are becoming more talkative and friendly. As I have mentioned before, a few firefighters seem to have a chip on their shoulder and act as if it is beneath them to show us some civility.

One particular firefighter seems to be different from any I have encountered yet. I have noticed him here frequently. Thinking about it, I may have seen him almost everyday that I have been here. He is probably in his fifties, it is hard to tell age because almost every one is exhausted, dirty, and looks haggard and older. His presence has stood out to me because he is very quiet and polite. He usually says only a few words when someone speaks to him. He spends hour after hour on the debris pile. Many other firefighters spend a lot of time there as well, however he appears to be always one of those digging in the middle of the recovery activities. Today I have found out why.

As I was standing in front of the firefighter's tent, which is my area's FDNY satellite command center, talking to another firefighter, this man walked past us on his way back to the pile. I said hello and he only nodded politely without speaking as he usually has when I have greeted him. I casually mentioned to the firefighter I was conversing with that this man seemed to work many hours. He replied that the man had been here working 12, 16, and more hours every day since September 11. He then added that he would keep coming here every day until they find him. I asked what he meant and he told me that the man's son, a firefighter like his father, was one of those killed in the collapse and he remains buried in the debris pile. Until the day that they find his son so he can take him home and give him a proper burial, he will be here. My God, the pain and grief he must be suffering every second he is here must be excruciating. Yet, he quietly spends countless hours here continuing a search that if successful can only have one horrific conclusion, he will find his dead son.

Only a parent that has lost a child can understand what pain this man is going through. As a parent that lost a child at birth, albeit no comparison to losing them in adulthood, I think I know a little of the 'what if' battle he is fighting over and over in his mind. Why was it not he lost instead of his boy? He no doubt is cursing the day he became a firefighter and laid down the footsteps that his son eventually followed. He is blaming himself for the loss of his son, not the people that did this. Grief, guilt, and what ifs are terrible combinations to carry around at one time.

If you think that the worst that could happen would be to lose your life in something like this disaster, you are mistaken. There is a fate worse than your own death. Sometimes surviving is a curse and this firefighter tragically is experiencing it. However, he is not alone. Many more have survived the loss of their sons, daughters, brothers, spouses, and other family and friends in this horrendous tragedy. There are others looking for family as well.

The strength, courage, honor, and sense of duty displayed by this man will forever remind me of what my father's examples taught me so long ago, what it means to be a man and a father. Hundreds of heroes perished on September 11, but not all of them, I met one of them today.

19

Where Are You Now?

October 14

A few of our crew were standing around talking when Mark, one of our other crewmembers joined us. Mark told us that he was walking in my area this morning and happened to look down, and discovered someone's amputated hand partially buried in the dust. The hand still had what Mark thought appeared to be a wedding ring on a finger. He waved for a firefighter to come over to recover it as told to do our first day here. Participating in recovering bodies or body parts is not our role here, not that any of us want to anyway. Mark pointed out the general area where he found it to us and I realized that I had just spent an hour walking all over in that area. Thankfully, I am not the one that found it. I do not know how I would have handled it. I never imagined my being a part of anything like this. I would give my life to keep our children and their children from ever having to live through something like this.

It is a wonder that I have not stumbled onto something I do not want to see in my daily walks all over the site. I am continually scanning the debris to watch where I step because of all the sharp objects, holes, etc. This terrain is comprised of beams, wire, concrete, piping, and other building materials thrown together into mountains, mazes, valleys, and just about any configuration imaginable. The fire also rages underneath the pile and it is not always evident on the surface. What dangers lay just beneath the surface is a mystery. One misstep could lead to a serious injury, a fall into a hidden abyss, or death.

In addition, I am always on the lookout for signs of the 'Black Boxes' that were on the planes. On our first day on site and while going through the badge process, we received a color flyer with pictures of the boxes and the flight recorders. Everyone gets one when arriving on site for the first time. The officials mention frequently in the meetings the importance of finding them. Posted all around the site to remind everyone what to look for, the posters are unavoidable. Black Boxes have a wealth of information on them that will help the National Transportation Safety Board and the Federal Bureau of Investigation in their investigation of this attack. I would be surprised if they survived the fire and collapse of the towers, but I continually look for any hint of the fluorescent orange color of them. Strange how they are not black at all, but called 'Black Boxes'.

I also see grim reminders of the lives of the people that had worked in these buildings. I am sure that many of these items belonged to some of those buried here as well as the survivors. Shoes, I see shoes all of the time and there are lots of them. They are everywhere it seems. Scattered in the debris, the streets, and some of the surviving buildings are tennis shoes, high heels, loafers, and just about every kind imaginable. I get a real bad feeling in the pit of my stomach every time I see one in the debris pile, wondering if there is a body attached, or perhaps someone's amputated foot is still in them. Thankfully, there has not been anything but the remaining shoe. I suppose that most of the shoes were extra pairs that people had kept in their offices. Either way, it is unnerving to happen upon one in my travels during the day.

Other items that I run across always give me pause to think about how this could happen to any of us. Computer parts like a broken mouse, keyboards, broken picture frames, and other office items. Occasionally there is a shirt or other clothing, but firefighters usually pick those items up right away. Papers by the millions are everywhere for blocks in every direction. In some areas, the paper is knee deep. I found a visitor's ID card the other day. I believe it was from the Morgan Stanley-Dean Witter Company. I picked it up and as I looked it over, I wondered if someone had been wearing it on September 11 and whether he or she had made it out. I set the badge down on a curb instead of tossing it back into the debris. Someone else must have picked it up because it was gone an hour later when I passed back through. I also saw a bowl that appeared to be an expensive one, very ornate and intact in the Marriott Hotel, or World Trade Center Three. I left it where it was, as I feel this stuff is sacred and should not be kept as souvenirs. All of these buried articles are reminders that before 8:46 AM on Tuesday, September 11, 2001 life in the United States was unfolding as it normally did.

Walking on the debris pile is necessary to do the work. It is always in the back of my mind that I am walking on a graveyard with thousands of missing people below my feet. My parents taught me to be respectful when in a graveyard and I always am. Unfortunately, not all people share that view and today I was involved in my third incident of disrespect in a week. Today, I saw a truck driver get out of his truck and urinate on the ground next to it. The Port-A-Johns were no more than 100 feet from where he was. I caught up to him before he could get back into his truck and asked him what in the hell he thought he was doing. I told him that some of the firefighters and police officers within sight of him had lost friends and family here. To them and just about everyone else here, this was sacred ground. If they saw him doing that, they may kill him. He could not apologize enough and felt terrible that he had been so thoughtless. He explained that he was new to the site and did not know where the facilities were. I showed him and he apologized several more times. I think that this guy will regret that lapse in judgment the rest of his life.

In the other two incidents, the same thoughtless, self-centered person committed them both. He was a machine operator and I watched him climb out of his machine and urinate on the debris pile. As this upset me quite a bit, I immediately approached him and told him that I thought it was disrespectful as well as disgusting. He said that he understood and just was not thinking at the time. Two days later I saw him do it again right in front of dozens of people, including women. He does not care one iota for anyone's feelings but his own. He left the area when he saw me coming because he knew that I was angry. I informed his supervisor of the two incidents and he was mad as well. He told me he would personally take care of it. Whether he has or not, I do not know.

I thought a lot about the mysteries of life and God today. Standing here looking at this destruction and misery day after day prompts you to wonder and ask yourself some very deep questions. Why do tragedies like this have to happen? Why is this carnage, the lives lost, others changed forever, the suffering of the injured and survivors, the terror, all part of God's master plan? What did these people do to deserve this? Where is this God now and why does this creator of all allow this? It is a puzzle too complex for me to figure out, as much as I would like to know the answers.

I am not a religious person by nature, I am scientific minded, but I know that this entire amazing universe got here somehow and it could not have just happened. It must have started with a superior intelligence guiding the way. The diversity of life is just too amazing to have happened by chance. Overall, I have a great awe for this wonderful place that we live in. We are not even close to figuring out how big and complex this universe is, no matter which scientist or religious leader claims to know all of the answers. I have heard people from both sides stand up and try to tell us how it is or how it has gotten to be here. I have never heard one explanation that I believe to be totally correct.

All I know is that somewhere, somehow, sometime, it began. The Big Bang theory is a good explanation for the expansion of the universe, but how did the expanding matter get there in the first place? That is the elusive answer and I for one believe that a superior intelligence, God if you will, was involved. I cannot think of another explanation that fits. Of course, then there is the question of how God got here too, but for now I just want to know where God is and why this has to be a part of life.

Is this 'free will' as I have heard religious leaders claim? Was God's plan, to create all this, give us a book of instructions, and leave us to our own devices? It is so obvious that mankind does not understand God's message and is floundering on this planet. We are on the brink of destroying it and ourselves. One worldwide appearance proving God's existence to those billions of us that have not figured it out yet and need some kind of proof would probably change the world from this madness. Sounds like a plan to me and what does God have to lose? We need all of the help we can get, and soon.

I think it was so much easier to believe and follow God's teachings in the past because there were events that confirmed its truth. The parting of the Red Sea, Lazarus raised from the dead, water changed into wine, and God speaking to humans were some of the miracles or events that gave evidence of the Creator. We do not have those 'miracles' in our time and I think we need something similar to reinforce the message. If acts such as planes slammed into buildings to kill thousands of innocent men, women, and children in the name of God do not justify a miraculous response, what does?

The rest of the day I was very busy. I feel we are banging our heads on the wall most of the time. We have no enforcement power so they just walk all over us. I received my share of dumb looks, smart remarks, and ignoring for the day. I can try my damnedest; however, I cannot help them if they do not want to help themselves. Now that I think of it, maybe God is thinking the same way.

I was walking down to get a coffee at the Salvation Army tent on Liberty Street when I encountered a group of women on the corner. There were several of them and one of them approached me and asked if I had a pen she could borrow. I gave her one and she went back to the group and started signing autographs. After she signed a few autographs, she passed my pen around to the other women and they began signing also. I had no idea who they were. After they had finished, the lady brought my pen back and I asked her if I could get her autograph too. She gave me one and then she had another lady sign my journal as well. Turns out they were Olympians. The lady who borrowed my pen, her name is W. White, has been in five Olympics in the track and field division, starting in 1956 through 1972. The other lady is Mary Riddell, who will be competing next year, but I do not know in what event. Gathered up off to the side of the group were six or seven more female Olympians and I now noticed that some of them had on clothing with the Olympic insignia. They appeared to be very upset from looking at the devastation. They were hugging and crying and I did not want to intrude in this obviously emotional time for them. I left and continued down Liberty Street to get my coffee without bothering them for an autograph.

Everyone seems to react differently when seeing this atrocity the first time. I have seen everything from stunned silence, tears, to a total mental and physical meltdown. The family members seem to suffer the worst of it for obvious reasons, however many others take it very hard as well. No one walks away from seeing Ground Zero without some type of emotional scar unless he is one of the bastards that are responsible for it.

20

Heroes and Villains

October 15

Our crew's frustration is getting worse every day that passes. One of the guys was at the big meeting last night, the one with all the government agencies involved in the recovery effort here. He said that they asked why we are not doing more to stop the NYPD, FDNY, and visiting big wigs from wandering around the site without hard hats, respirators, and other personal protective equipment (PPE). What a bunch of crap that question is. Apparently, they are not looking at our daily reports because noted on every one of them is our summation that it is out of control and we are being ignored. Every one of us has repeatedly told them that they should be wearing PPE and to follow the rules that have been set-up, but we are powerless to do anything if they refuse. The reason we have no authority is that the same people that are asking that stupid question will not give it to us. They have fixed it so that OSHA cannot even do anything about it, so what the hell do they think we are supposed to do.

When an FBI agent escorts a government official wearing a skirt and high heels into the middle of a smoking, hot pile of mangled debris, we talk to them and advise that they get her the proper PPE or stand on the sidelines. When he whips out his FBI badge and sticks it into our face, are we supposed to argue with him, wrestle him to the ground, or what? I am not going to piss off the FBI, Secret Service, NYPD, or God knows what other official agency only to find myself swinging in the wind. I gave up on going to the government higher ups because they do not make them follow the rules either. It seems to me that someone is trying to shift the blame in case one of these people gets hurt. Politics, in my opinion is the root of the cause.

All I know is that it is no way to run a safety program. It is the same crap, just a different day, however it is slowly getting worse.

It is a classic 'Catch 22', damned if you do and damned if you do not situation. The FDNY is in charge of the site as long as rescue/recovery is continuing so the firefighters can and do anything that they want. Some become downright rude and put themselves in danger despite of anything we suggest. On a few occasions, I had felt that they went into dangerous places just because we had told them that they should not.

Some of the NYPD and other government hotshots are just as bad, some worse. Probably all of us in our group are given the 'do you know who I am?' Or the 'I am a New York City police officer, or city official, blah, blah,' routine. I am weary of it and I finally told a firefighter how I felt about it. He had just defied my advice and walked into an area that we had barricaded because Bovis was dropping a beam from twenty stories up. I was standing at the barricade to assist Bovis in warning people away because no one was positive this beam was not going to bounce out of the planned landing area. I told him to go ahead and kill himself despite my professional advice. He turned around and glared at me with a look as if I had no right to suggest anything to him because he was an FDNY firefighter, after all. Well, excuse me for trying to do my job and save your life.

We also have many problems with visitors sauntering all over the place without wearing any appropriate protection and clueless to the danger of the situation. We have other women besides the FBI agent I mentioned, in skirts and high heels walking around in the debris pile. I cringe seeing the older people that can barely walk as they are trying to navigate between moving machinery. The worst of the lot are the ones that bring their small children out there.

I just cannot understand why anyone would want to bring a young child to see what has happened and what is going on here. Body removals take place only a few yards in front of these kids. The smell alone is a bad experience and they are in danger just by being here, as we all are. My God, I cannot imagine what in the hell these parents thinking. I do not believe in hiding or lying to kids about bad things. I think it is better to be honest and try to explain it in a way that they can understand. It is my opinion that they are just asking for problems dealing with this tragedy somewhere down the line. One of my most vivid memories as a small child (I think I was four or five) is accidentally seeing a man who had drowned. I remember it clearly like it happened yesterday and at the time, I know it bothered me a lot. The fact that I remember it so well is evidence that it left a lasting impression on me. Why would anyone deliberately expose small children to something like this, a disaster that describing as terrible merely scratches the surface? It is incomprehensible to me. I just do not understand their reasoning.

The reason we have these visitors all over the place is the FDNY, NYPD, and other government agency are bringing in their friends, relatives, girlfriends, neighbors, and who knows who else to see Ground Zero. Some of them are actually escorting what looks to be tour groups through and we cannot do a thing about it. I report these types of incidents every day.

I think I now have the best incident of someone walking around the site that should not have been where they were. I looked out into the debris pile today and there was this guy walking around the moving machinery, no hard hat or safety glasses, wearing loafers, and a kilt. Yes, a genuine Scottish kilt. I called my supervisor on the radio and told him what I had out there and I had to repeat it three times before he would believe it. I have no idea who the guy was, but firefighters seemed to know him and were getting their photos taken with him. He could be part of their bagpiper band.

A few people let in by a friend somewhere make the mistake of not having an escort and end up tossed out of the area. One incident the other day that I was involved in was a classic. I was walking down West Street toward the Bovis office when I noticed a guy climbing up onto a stack of plywood in front of World Financial Center Building One. Once up there, he set up an easel, got his paints out, and began painting. I stopped to watch him, as in a way it was quite humorous. He was holding up his thumbs to line up what he wanted to paint, had a paint pallet in one hand, and was wearing one of those French berets, almost as you would see in a cartoon. I watched him begin his painting and was fascinated at how he quickly had framed the outline of the standing façade onto the canvas. He made it look effortless and though I do not know much about art, it was looking like a good start to me. As I stood watching him, two NYPD police officers walked up to me and asked who he was and who let him in. I told them I did not know so they went over to question him. Well, the guy began explaining that he had a friend of a friend and he was not quite sure what his friend's name actually was, but he swore that he had permission to be there. He knew his friends name of course, however he was not giving them up to the police. These officers were not buying his story and after a few more minutes of listening to him, they told him that he had to leave. The guy became very animated and started arguing back and forth with them about it and insisting he had permission to be there. This went on for a minute or so until a gust of wind came up and blew his painting over, wet paint side down into the dust. Well that was too much for him. He threw his hands up in the air in despair, looked like he was going to start crying, and then finally took on a look of utter defeat. Then to add insult to injury, the police officers threw him off the site. It just was not that guy's day.

The recovery teams are not finding any bodies in my area for now. They still believe that groups of firemen may have congregated in several areas during the evacuation and the firefighters are itching to get into those areas to find out. However, piles of debris are blocking the routes into them and it is not safe for the time being.

The construction crews are steadily working on getting these areas cleared, but it takes time to untangle this mess of twisted iron and mold it into a size and condition to load into trucks for transport. Most of the time, these firefighters will wiggle into places that would scare the hell out of most people. I think that most of these teams have realized that the odds of finding anyone alive now are a billion to one and unnecessary chances are no longer worth it. Not all of them believe this though. We still have people foolishly risking their life on a daily basis to recover a body and taking exception to anyone calling the operation a 'recovery' instead of a 'rescue'.

I had quite a bit of activity at the 90 West Building today with lots of work and problems taking place. One case took up a good deal of my time and boosted my heart rate and blood pressure a few times. This is a perfect example of the types of things that prematurely ages us safety folks. One of my darkest fears is watching someone die before I can intervene to fix the situation, whether it is their behavior or something else. Someone falling to his or her death would be the worst for me as I have a fear of that myself. This is how it happened.

Falling debris from the tower collapse has damaged the scaffolding around the 90 West Building. In several places, portions of the scaffold structure are bent, twisted, or missing pieces. This scaffolding rises all the way up to the roof and covers three of the building sides. The stability of it was one of the first questions I had asked my second day on site. The subcontractor told me that engineers had inspected it and classified it as stable and usable. I had my doubts, but deferred to the experts and they confirmed they considered it sound. The inspecting engineers were from the scaffolding company that originally had built it, so they definitely had an interest in its stability. The size of the scaffold mandated that a professional engineer must design it. That is an OSHA regulation.

The subcontractor tasked to repair this scaffolding and secure the protective netting on the outside face of it is not the same company that originally built it. Bovis said that the original builders were too busy working on other buildings to get to this one right away, so they hired this group. The netting is to keep the broken window glass from falling onto workers below. The use of the scaffold creates several fall protection issues that I need to address and these concerns are more difficult due to the attitude of the scaffold subcontractor. They just do not think it is important to keep their workers tied off at any height and continually allow them to be at serious risk.

I have spoken to their supervisor on a few occasions, a Scottish gentleman that gives me a litany of excuses in a rapid speech style made all the more difficult to understand because of his thick Scottish accent. The guy that they identify as their safety representative echoes his boss in the excuse department, however he speaks slowly and in an Irish brogue. Their part of the conversations sound something like this: Aye man, ye can't mean ta be a saying ye wan ta lad ta be tethered onta da building there whilst he moves about now, can ye? I have to say; at least they are speaking English or a form of it anyway. I can usually understand most of it, unlike the Polish crew. I cannot understand a single word they say to me. I may not be making much headway in the safety arena here, however I am getting a cultural lesson. Feel like I am touring Europe some of the time.

This morning I observed six employees climbing the framework of the scaffolding up to the level of the eleventh floor. Not only were they not supposed to climb up on anything other than a ladder, they did not tie off at any point on the way up or when they reached their destination. They wrapped their legs around some of the scaffolding, hung on for dear life, and began pulling up materials by rope. They were at least 110 feet up without anything but their own strength and luck keeping them from falling to the street.

I tried everything to get them to get to tie off or move to a safe area. I yelled up to them, used hand signals and spoke to their supervisor. All to no avail as they all ignored me. I hunted down their safety representative, explained the situation and my concern to him. In the Irish brogue, he said it was customary practice for this kind of work and they did not have anywhere to tie off to anyway. Then he walked off into the building without showing the least bit of concern. I could not believe it. I immediately went to the oversight contractor's office and attempted to get them to correct the situation. The safety representative, Ray, who would have immediately got the situation under control, was off site. All the supervisors in the office did was to pass off responsibility to someone else in their organization, most which just happened not to be there either. After several minutes of talking and pleading with four different supervisors without any progress, I went across the street to the OSHA tent.

I explained the situation to two OSHA compliance officers and they accompanied me to the work area. We located the same safety supervisor I had spoken to earlier and they got the same result, ignored. In normal circumstances, these compliance officers could bring an immediate halt to the work and start issuing citations. They do not have that authority here and can only act in an advisory role. They have no more authority than I do. We went back to the OSHA tent and talked over our next step. One of the officers came up with the idea to act as if they actually have the authority to stop work. In other words, he was going to try to bluff them into compliance. They decided they needed permission from an OSHA supervisor before jumping into this plan with both feet. We found the OSHA Regional Manager and laid out his idea. After weighing the pros and cons, she said the situation is so dangerous to go ahead and give it a shot, but to back off if we encountered resistance.

We went back down the street to the scaffold and the OSHA officers yelled up to the crew and told them to tie off or get off the scaffolding. These guys looked down at him as if he was merely a minor inconvenience and then continued working. Well, this pissed him off and he whipped out his OSHA ID badge and yelled "I am a federal OSHA officer and you had better come down now!" It worked like magic. Those people could not scramble off that scaffold and through a window onto the eleventh floor fast enough. After several minutes, the supervisor whom had ignored us rushed over and said he would do whatever it took to make it safe so they could go back to work.

We informed the Regional Manager of our success and began discussing how we should try this in other situations. She began to chuckle and said she knew that once we won one, we would not want to stop at just one victory. She reminded us that OSHA was under strict direction from Washington, DC not to stop the work unless it was immediate danger like this one. Actions like this one today were going to be the exception, not the rule. Damn it would be nice to have that in our safety tool kit here. Nevertheless, at least she let the good guys win one important battle today.

All the valuable items left in the 90 West Building has caused quite a bit of commotion on the night shift. My friend, Randy, the night shift supervisor, spotted a guy coming out of the building acting suspicious the other night. Randy and a co-worker followed him and some others accompanying him as they tried to leave the area on an ATV. They kept driving around to different checkpoints as if they were looking for an easy one to pass through. Randy informed an NYPD officer nearby of what was unfolding and the chase was on. Randy said it looked as if 400 police officers were running after them. They finally caught up to them and the one guy had some CD's, liquor, and a wad of dust-covered money in his pocket. They released the others in the ATV for not being involved or aware he had stolen these items. The NYPD officers were angry to say the least. Looters are the scum of the earth at Ground Zero in most of our eyes. After the looting incident, the NYPD placed guards in the 90 West Building.

That incident is not the only suspicious activity that took place in 90 West. I heard about this incident today from a reliable source that claims his supervisor was involved. This incident has potentially worse implications than the case of the guy with the stolen liquor and cash. However, it could have been innocent enough. I will let you be the judge.

A couple of construction crew supervisors in the 90 West Building happened to run into woman who was acting suspicious on one of the upper floors. She appeared nervous and unfamiliar with the building. They began questioning her about her business inside the building and she was very evasive in her answers, but said she was with an NYPD officer. She told the supervisors that she was in there with the officer to retrieve her belongings that she had left on September 11. There was not an NYPD officer in sight and she did not know where he was in the building. The supervisors decided that something was wrong with the whole story because the woman did not have any belongings with her nor was she looking for anything when they initially saw her. Deciding to further investigate and verify her story, they went looking for the officer. After several minutes of searching, they found him standing in an office area on the other side of the building and on another floor. As they were walking up to talk to him, a small safe came over an office partition and landed on the floor near the officer. An accomplice or companion of the officer obviously threw the safe and it became clear to the work supervisors that the woman lied about her purpose there. Now facing an uncomfortable and awkward scenario, they were unsure what to do. The officer was not clear on his purpose for being there either, nor did he offer an explanation regarding the safe. The supervisors recorded the officer's name and badge number and they reported the story to the NYPD supervisors. As far as I know, they have not received an explanation. According to the man that told me this story, the supervisors were very nervous to think they may have witnessed a robbery situation involving a police officer as an accomplice.

Investigations into other alleged criminal activity are ongoing as well. The NYPD and FBI are investigating the 'diversion' of truckloads of the steel columns and beams to warehouses supposedly run by organized crime. The news reports said that some of the truck drivers were bypassing the drop off points and unloading at their loads at warehouses. The alleged purpose of this was to later use the steel in the making of souvenirs to sell. There have been several raids on some of these warehouses and the questioning of suspects occurring over the last week or so.

Greed motivates people to do some disgusting things. Looting a national disaster site and stealing from victims is about as low as you can get. There are many stories of other looting incidents. There are rumors of what became of the looters after taken into police custody too. One story that I have heard several times involved a man stealing watches from the dead at the temporary morgue. Rumor says that he did not survive to make it to jail. I do not know if it ever happened or not.

The company I work for, especially a few employees who initially led the way to this effort here deserve a lot of credit. One of our employees was working in New Jersey on the day of the attack and came over to help in any way he could. He ended up invited to some meetings where many questions about safety came up and he answered as best he could. He also informed them of the safety expertise and resources our company could provide. By the time, the meetings were over, he had more things to do than he could possibly accomplish on his own, so he called our Corporate Manager of Safety, Stew Burkhammer, for assistance. Stew immediately assembled a small team of safety professionals and support personnel and headed to New York, arriving the next day. The company had some discussions with the high-level government officials in charge and pledged our assistance, and so that began our involvement.

My company has provided so much towards this effort to help New York City get the necessary safety items in place. They have written the site safety and health plan and used their contacts to help get massive amounts of safety equipment on the way. They assembled teams of engineers and safety professionals to help assess the situation and provide expertise and assistance for wherever needed. The company stepped up to the plate and began assisting without hesitation or request. They have done a tremendous amount of work to get this effort rolling but for those of us that work for them, it is no surprise. That is how they operate and why most of their employees will tell you that we work for the best company in the world.

Nothing mush else out of the ordinary happened today. Well, at least ordinary for here. The terrible day-to-day sights, sounds, and sorrow never take the day off. I did hear that Dennis Quaid was here on the site somewhere, but I did not see him.

21

Flirting with Disaster

October 16

Well the contractor flirted with disaster today and in the process scared the hell out of me as well as a bunch of other people. However, everything came out all right other than they received an extreme ass chewing by the city. Fortunately, the contractor had put safety measures in place and they worked. It sure did stir up the site for a while though.

The contractor was torch cutting on the façade of WTC Tower Two. The façade is the skeleton like walls of the towers shown repeatedly on television. They had been cutting on this section with torches for several days, attempting to get it to the point that they could pull it over. These façade portions need to come down now because they are holding back huge amounts of debris and their stability is in question due to the forces pushing on them. They are made of steel beams that are five inches thick in places and covered with aluminum sheeting for decoration. The superintendent of the company doing the work had told me they were the toughest pieces of steel they had ever tried to take down because they had to cut them about 90% of the way through. He said that normally they would cut no more than 45% of regular steel to be able to bend it over, however they had tried that and could not budge these. I had watched when they tried it that time and all the wall did was rock back and forth until they finally broke the cables and went back to the drawing board.

This is how it works. They begin by putting ironworkers into a man basket attached to the crane hook. The crane lifts them up to the places that they need to cut. The basket is about the only way to get up there as scaffolding or ladders would be too dangerous. The ironworkers begin cutting the façade steel on each column to a point where the wall should still stand on its own. This process takes several days, as the steel is so thick and the sections span a hundred feet or so. The next step is to cut holes through the façade in various places, mostly near the top, so they can place one end of the steel cables through them, and tie it to the façade. The cables are approximately 150 to 200 feet long and the other ends wrapped around 10 foot pieces of beams on the ground. The purpose of the beams is a means for the grapplers (big machines with tracks and huge vise-like jaws on them) to grab onto them and pull the wall over to the ground. Once the cables are in place, the ironworkers resume cutting on the façade until it is approximately 90% cut through. Once those cuts are completed, the grapplers will begin their dance. In unison, they move back and forth, rocking the façade until it comes down, the cables break, or it stands fast. That was the plan on this piece too.

These operations are a big safety concern for several reasons. One is that the landing zone, and a very large area beyond, has to be clear of people. Obviously, you do not want anyone under the façade as it falls. In addition the cables are approximately two hundred feet long and if they break at a point near the façade, they can whip back two hundred feet or farther behind the machines. Because they will stretch, you have to have at least a four hundred and fifty-foot area cleared. A whipping cable will cut a person in half. Even with those dangerous conditions, I have had problems keeping people out of the exclusion zones during these operations. In one case, an engineer argued with me about letting him and other people do their work. He said we safety people were always bothering someone. Even my pointing out that he was directly in the line of fire of a potential breaking cable fell on his deaf ears. I guess that the engineering school he attended skipped over the laws of physics and decapitation.

The contractor had planned to drop this wall yesterday, however they had to reschedule it for today due to it required more cutting than they had anticipated. They announced in today's

morning meeting that they would be ready to do it at 1:00 PM. They
had completed the set up of the exclusion zone in the morning,
connected the cables to the façade and beams, and were performing
the final cuts at around 11:30 AM. I was standing just outside of the
exclusion zone watching and talking with a few workers while a fire
truck was backing into place to hose the area down for dust control.
The grapplers were in position for their portion, however their
massive jaws were still empty of the beams, and their engines were
idle. The operators were milling around waiting for word to proceed,
which they anticipated to be over an hour from then. The firefighters
had just parked the fire truck next to me and had not even started to
set up their hoses yet when suddenly there was the sound of a loud
crack, then another. I quickly wheeled around to look towards the
façade and I saw the last 25 feet or so of its premature fall. It hit the
ground with a force that rocked and shook the ground. Instantly, a
thick cloud of concrete dust and debris shot into the air in every
direction. It was so dense that I could not see anything inside of the
huge exclusion zone. The cloud quickly overtook the dozens of us on
the fringes of the zone and I pulled my respirator to my face and just
held it in place as I pulled my radio out of my pocket and tried to
notify my supervisor what had happened. I told him the wall had
fallen over prematurely and I did not know if there were injuries yet.
He could not understand me through my respirator on so I took it
away from my face and yelled that the wall had fallen. That was
about all the words I could get out before the dust overwhelmed me
and I began to cough and struggle to breathe. I quickly put my
respirator back on and tightened down the straps. The dust on
September 11 must have been a thousand times worse. I do not know
how they got enough air to escape it.

I was sure that someone was dead and I was not the only one
who was concerned. Several firefighters and other people began
disappearing from my view, probing deeper into the expanding dust
cloud, searching for anyone who may have gotten back in there. This
was a possibility because unfortunately our experience so far has
shown us that there are a few firefighters and rescue teams that will

not listen to anything when looking for a body. With my eyes so full of the biting dust that they were heavily watering, I began looking for the man basket with the men that had been behind the wall performing the cuts. I could see nothing but dust where they had been just moments ago. I looked up until I spotted the tip of the crane boom and began following the cable down into the dust cloud. I could hear the crane motor whining as it was reeling the cable in as fast as possible. Several seconds passed before the basket broke through the top of the dust cloud and into view. Thankfully, the ironworkers were giving the 'thumbs up' sign, letting everyone know they were safe.

As the dust began to settle and confirmation came that no one had been injured or killed inside of the exclusion zone, emotions bubbled over and heated questions started flying. Let me tell you, a representative of the Port Authority Police Department (PAPD) was about as mad as you can get and he called an immediate meeting with the contractor and a whole slew of other officials. I reported all of the information on the unfolding events back to my supervisor. He told me to get into that meeting somehow. I spoke to Ray, the Bovis safety manager and he took me into the meeting.

The meeting was with all the parties involved, the FDNY, PAPD, DDC, and other officials. Quite a few of their tempers were flaring during the discussions of the incident. The PAPD representative was so upset because he had people performing work underground almost all of the time. Any unusual activities that could influence the safety of the work underground had to be carefully coordinated to protect those workers inside these secluded and dangerous areas. Anything causing a collapse of those tunnels, parking garages and stores would be a catastrophe. It would be difficult and dangerous to get rescue teams down there to help them.

Fortunately, there was not any crews underground in that location at the time, however as the PAPD representative heatedly pointed out, that was purely by chance, not because of the required well-coordinated effort. The Bovis lead superintendent, Charlie Vitchers, began explaining to the group about all of the precautions that his company had taken before proceeding with this task. Charlie told them that although the wall did come down earlier than expected, it was within the time communicated to the proper officials. There was much debate over exactly what officials these were and whether they should have passed the information to the other groups or Bovis should have. Charlie also explained the unknown factors involved with removal of the façade and some of the other large debris. As I was listening to Charlie go over the details, it was evident to me that he is very knowledgeable about every aspect of this type of work. Charlie has been around the demolition block once or twice and I could see why Bovis placed him in charge of this effort. By the time, he finished explaining the ins, outs, and unknowns lurking within this unprecedented clean-up effort, the charged atmosphere in the trailer had begun to cool off. Afterwards, the PAPD and other officials made it clear that improvements in communication were going to be in place and strictly followed before they would allow any more work of this kind to proceed. No one disagreed that better communication was necessary to keep the thousands of people here safe. This is a wake up call for all of us here; we are very lucky this has turned out the way it has.

This afternoon, at the corner of West and Liberty Streets, I walked up get a Coke® at the Salvation Army tent and noticed a small crowd of people were gathered in front of it talking to someone sitting in an ATV. As I got closer, I saw that he was Senator Bob Dole. He was signing autographs, posing for photos, and shaking hands with the workers gathered there. Unfortunately, he was trying to leave when I got close enough to get an autograph or shake his hand so I missed out. Bob Dole is a great American, a World War II veteran as well as a public servant and it was an honor just to see him. I have to say that he should quit dying his hair though; it was obvious that he colors it. However, to each his own, I will just keep letting mine turn whatever colors it wants as long as it does not turn loose as the saying goes.

Tonight after work I walked a few blocks past Times Square to
see what was around there. I went into a convenience store that had a
deli and picked up some Chinese food and a drink. I had just walked
out of the store and was starting back towards the hotel, when all hell
seemed to break loose. I was near a subway station entrance, the
stairs leading below the street level to the boarding area when police
cars, as well as police on horseback and on foot converged out of
nowhere all at once. Officers jumping out of cars, running towards
me, and cops on horses galloping up the street to join the rest of them
were all around me. I did not know what in the hell was happening,
but initially I thought they were going to grab me. Fortunately, they
ran past me and down the stairs into the subway station. After what
seemed like dozens of officers had passed, curiosity got the best of me
and I followed to see what was going on. A crowd of police officers
and a few civilians were standing around a handcuffed guy laying
face down on the platform. It appeared that he must have put up a
struggle as his eye was swollen and his face appeared to have been hit
a few times. His clothes were also torn. A lady was animatedly
describing the encounter to two other officers and from what I could
hear of it, this guy apparently tried to rob her and several of her lady
friends while they were waiting on the platform for the subway train.
After a few minutes, the police pulled the alleged crook to his feet and
led him out and into the back of a police car for his ride to jail. The
rest of the walk to the hotel was uneventful.

22

Lead, Follow, or Get the Hell Out of the Way

October 17

Stew informed us at this morning's shift turnover meeting that the contract for us to manage the World Trade Center safety for the duration of clean up and a recovery activity is not going through as planned. He said that unless something changes in the coming week or so, we would be going home. He gave us a preliminary schedule for departures and my day to leave is to be on October 27. This information was somewhat unexpected as I thought the negotiations were going well and as we were already here, it was just a formality. I have to say that it will not break my heart to go home, but as shit changes so quickly in this business, I am not going to get my hopes up or tell Janice yet. I do not want to let her down either. I will see how it goes for a few days before I mention it to her. I miss home badly and we are not able to do what we came here for so I am ready to go if that is what happens.

Word travels fast on the site and before I even mentioned it to some of my contacts here, people were coming up and telling me how sorry they will be to see us leave. They said that they think we have done a good job considering that we have tried to fight a battle of biblical proportions with our hands tied.

Most of our crewmembers feel that we are not making enough progress out here to make the needed difference. One of our team coworkers, Rob Jones, (who works for a different company than I do) is so frustrated that he sent a letter to his boss saying he wants no part in this anymore because his demolition advice and the legal requirements are being ignored by the contractor responsible for demolishing WTC Building Six. Rob fears that someone is going to die on his watch. Rob is very knowledgeable and good at his job and he is right. We are all concerned that it is going to happen eventually. Rob has had a lot of difficulty with the contractors and their lack of demolition plans. They are not supposed to start demolishing any standing buildings until they have an approved plan in place. The fact is that they do not have one and it does not seem to faze them in the least. They are trying to tear something down every time Rob turns around.

I had some OSHA folks today that just got in my way and raised my frustration level because they could not differentiate from their normal inspection mentality and what is necessary here. In other words, they could not think on their feet. This following scenario played out this morning when two OSHA inspectors met up with me during their first hour at Ground Zero. The first thing they did was to look at some gas welding bottles secured to a fence while I was watching the work activities in my area. The OSHA regulation says that the oxygen and acetylene bottles have a separation of twenty-five feet when stored. Well, these guys measured the distance between them and it was only twenty-one feet. A minor issue but these guys wanted me to immediately walk two blocks to try to find the Bovis safety manager, Ray, to have these few bottles moved four feet. I told them I would be seeing Ray at some point later in the day and would pass along the information then and note it on my daily report as well. These two guys just were not going to accept that I was not going to immediately get this minor item fixed and began to insist I had to do something now.

They were so insistent that I finally had to put it into my perspective for them. I told them that I " had over a dozen firefighters next to the hotel that were about to get killed because they were going to go into an area that was too unstable and dangerous. In addition to them, over at the 90 West Building, I had someone hanging out of the sixteenth floor window without fall protection on, and by the way you two are about to get run over by that truck backing up behind you." I did not have time to worry about moving the bottles; I had many much bigger problems to deal with. I told them to take a walk around the entire site to get familiar with what they were dealing with here. I added that when they finished their walk to come back and hook up with me in my area, which would be easy because I am usually there except for meal times. I have not seen these two guys since.

I am by no means saying that they are no good at their jobs because not everyone has the experiences or the ability to do what they call in the medical profession, triage. Triage means categorizing according to condition. The most severely injured, ranked a number one priority for treatment, mid range injuries ranked a two, and so on. You take care of the Number ones first, than turn your efforts to the number twos, etc. Same concept applies here; you do not let a person fall to his death from the fourteenth floor window while you are busy getting safety glasses on someone else.

Affecting our judgment is the magnitude of the devastation, the death, and terrible things that we see every day. This is outside of most everyone's experience. It is difficult to focus at all some of the time, and it takes a while to get over the shock of it all. After you are acclimated, the only way that you can be effective in any way is to prioritize where you are needed the most.

The problem today was relatively minor, more of an irritation than anything else was. Actually, it was probably just my impatience caused by the stress of this week. It is my day off tomorrow and maybe some rest will help me become a little mellow for a few days anyway. I do not realize most of the time how much the stress takes its toll on me. Even though I try to put the bad images and feelings in a mental box somewhere, to deal with later, they must still be working on me subconsciously. I am going to have to start taking a deep breath and mentally count to ten when I feel the irritation and impatience bubbling to the surface.

Overall, we have had some great OSHA representatives to assist us. I genuinely like almost all of them and we are comrades trying to keep people safe the best way that we know how. Unfortunately, they do not have any authority to stop the work either, but those federal government badges sure carry some weight and cause a few of the contractors to back off when we are desperate to get some cooperation. Most of them do the best that they can as we do. The others at least stay out of the way most of the time.

I had an ambulance shoot past me today and it went over near the 90 West Building. I still had a crew in there so I went right over to see what had happened. One of the building owner's workers had become very ill while working and had went to the Red Cross Center next door for help and they determined that he needed to get to a hospital. When I arrived, the man's supervisor was talking to the Red Cross nurse and complaining loudly that this was the second member of his crew who had become very ill while working in the building this week. He was attracting quite a crowd of people who were working there as well and they were listening very intently. The bystanders began to talk among themselves about what the problem could be and some mentioned they had not felt well for a few days too. I questioned the supervisor about the man's symptoms, what he observed and thought it could be. I then reported the findings to my supervisors. A request that some additional air monitoring and an investigation be started to see if there was fumes, vapors, or any other hazards in the building that would be of concern went up the chain of command.

This is an office building, thoroughly inspected to identify any hazards, and work ongoing there since day one and no chemicals or other contaminants identified that are out of the ordinary. Dozens of people are working or entering the building every day now for weeks, including the NYPD and myself without becoming ill. I am at a loss for a job related explanation of his illness.

In situations like this, it does not take that much to get rumors started. They get worse as they pass along the line and then the anxiety level begins to get other people ill as well. This happens all the time in schools and offices where someone smells something unusual and feels ill and before you know it, you have a multitude of people ill and the situation spins out of control. The commonly known name of it is Sick Building Syndrome. Panic and the power of suggestion are usually the drivers for the other people's complaints. Most of the time, investigators find no cause for the illness. However, the illnesses are very real to those people; just not caused by a contaminant but by fear. In cases like these, it is very difficult to ease their fears because of several factors. They were actually ill. It is naturally difficult to get them to believe that it was psychosomatic in nature and their natural suspicion that 'they are hiding the truth from us' because of the knowledge that some authorities have created distrust in the past.

I just missed getting to meet Robin Williams today. My coworker Matt Carney called me over the radio and I went right over to where Matt was but Robin had already left. Matt was able to meet him and get his autograph. Matt's eye is patched because he got debris into it yesterday in his work area, despite having his safety glasses on, so used that as his introduction. He walked up to Robin Williams and said that he could not see very well, but someone had told him he was Robin Williams and if he was, could he have an autograph? Mr. Williams laughed and signed one for him. I heard that he also was talking on the phone to some of the workers wives. I wish I had caught up to him, as Janice would have loved a phone call from Robin Williams.

Notes

There were thousands of documented injuries and illnesses during the rescue recovery operations at the site. My experience in this business led me to conclude that many minor injuries remained unreported for one reason or another. Many people, myself included, do not report the scratches, minor

153

*cuts, banged elbows, etc unless they are serious. In a case of this magnitude
and the early sense of urgency to attempt to save victims, the rescue teams
would feel that reporting an injury would only slow them down.*

*Reflected in the story related to me by a nurse at the site is an
example of this mentality and courage. She said that in the first few days
after September 11 several rescue workers had come into the first aid stations
with serious injuries. She told me about one firefighter who reported he had
injured his finger and when he removed his glove, his severed finger stayed
in it. He asked the first aid personnel to 'tape it up so I can get back out there
to search'.*

*Gathering the statistics must have been a difficult task in itself
because there were so many locations that you could go to get treatment. The
Red Cross, Salvation Army, D-MAT group, etc all provided first aid services
in many different locations around the site. It was also hard to get a clear
picture of on the job relationship for some of the illnesses because they did not
have the time to get a detailed history each time and many of the reports were
vague. Recorded on the first aid summary reports given to us every few days
are headaches, colds, flu, and even unknowns. If you asked for a sinus tablet
or an aspirin, it went on the books too.*

*Below I have listed the statistics provided to us for the first month,
September 11 to October 11, 2001:*

Abrasions:	132
Blisters:	410
Burns:	134
Chest pains:	43
Concussions:	10
Contusions:	66

Crush injuries:	16
Dehydration/heat exhaustion:	22
Eye injuries:	802
Nausea/vomiting/fever/diarrhea:	132
Fractures:	30
Headaches:	664
Lacerations:	342
Lung injuries:	611
Other:	2, 160
Psychological stress:	103
Skin irritation/rashes:	280
Sprains/strains:	373
Unknown:	830
Total for one month:	**7,160**
Construction workers accounted for 32% of the injuries or:	2,315
Police 20% or	1,446
Firefighters 15% or:	1,080
Unknown 11% or:	773

Other 10% or: 733

Medical personnel 5% or: 357

Military personnel 5% or: 334

Red Cross personnel 2% or: 122

The most serious injury I was involved in should have never happened in the first place because the worker was not supposed to be there and was not working at the time. He had come in early to watch the activities and was standing on some stacked steel beams watching firefighters recover a body. Somehow, while he was standing there he slipped and fell onto a sharp foreign object sticking out of the steel and suffered a very bad puncture wound. That got him hauled out in an ambulance and into the hospital for a few days. You would think that ten to twelve hours a day of watching body removals would be more than anyone could take let alone coming in early to watch more. Whatever his reasons were, he ended up with a lot of pain and time off work.

We had other incidents that could have been much worse but for some luck and timing. We had people struck in the head from debris falling out of trucks, falling down in the debris piles, and a few vehicle collisions. With such great potential for injuries on the site, the fact that no critical injuries or deaths occurred is miraculous. The debris pile covered a sixteen square block area containing thousands of sharp objects, hidden holes, rough terrain, with machines and vehicles running all over it. You had to be looking intently at every place that you set your foot and the activities around and overhead of you every second. I have not heard of any serious injuries at the site since I have left. However, at the rate injuries were happening while we were there, I would expect that the total injury and illness count is very much higher now.

23

Tales of the City

October 18

It is my day off again and I got up early to have breakfast at McDonald's with Randy although I could have slept in. I enjoy talking with my friend as he is very intelligent, funny, and I trust him. We have known each other a long time and although we do not always see things in the same way, (I am more liberal to his conservative) it never has mattered because we respect each other's opinions and do not let it affect our friendship. Five or ten minutes a day to talk during turnovers is hardly enough time to cover all the things going on here. I want to know about his shift and he about mine. There are many things that we were missing being on opposite shifts.

According to Randy, the night shift is having most of the same problems that we are, but they seem to be getting better co-operation on wearing respirators. As the supervisor, Randy has to type up the shift reports and does not get as much time in the field as he would like. I would like to be on the same shift with him, but I am not that fond of working nights. My body clock has always worked well on days. It usually takes me several weeks to adjust to other shifts and the different sleep patterns. There are drawbacks to either shift here though. There is a lot more activity and people on days with all of the tours, sightseers, and family members to deal with throughout the day. I think it would be worse seeing this tragedy in the daylight and not under artificial light and softened by shadows. Then again, the night shift has to navigate in those conditions and it renders it all the more dangerous for them.

After breakfast, we walked several blocks down the street to pick up his laundry. We chatted for a while longer and then he went to get some sleep before his shift tonight. After he went off to his room, I made two trips to the post office to mail out souvenirs for the family. It cost about $40.00, but it was well worth it as I think they will like what I bought them.

I did not do much else other than walk around and look at the sights in the area of the hotel. This place is just something else. People are wandering everywhere and there is always something interesting to watch. I wandered around several blocks and took in the atmosphere of the neighborhood. It is such a different lifestyle here than I have ever experienced. Very fast paced it seems. I tired quickly and decided to go back to the hotel for a nap.

Later on this afternoon I went back out and decided to eat at a TGI Fridays located in Times Square. I ordered a $13.00 hamburger and sat in a great window seat so I could watch the activities taking place in the square. I believe I could sit and watch the comings and goings in this neighborhood for hours. I like to people watch and this place has thousands of them going by non-stop.

As I ate my burger, I watched a young couple outside of the restaurant that appeared to be homeless. They were young, maybe seventeen to twenty one years old, carrying backpacks and sleeping bags, giving the appearance they had been staying outdoors. The girl did not have enough clothes on for the weather as she was shivering and looked miserable. She also did not appear to be very happy with her situation or her companion. The man was counting money and I got the impression that he was seeing if they had enough for a room or food. He said something to the girl and they appeared to argue about it for a while. A few minutes later the man walked off down the street in a huff, leaving the girl sitting on the sidewalk alone and near tears. I could not help but wonder if she has run away from home with her boyfriend and has now found out just how hard life can really be. She sat there quite awhile looking so out of place and as if her world was collapsing all around her. After 10 or 15 minutes, the man came back, grabbed her by the hand, and roughly pulled her off down the street and out of my view.

Other people I see passing by I generally can place into a few categories by their behavior or appearance. Tourists usually give away their identity by their slow pace, cameras or maps in hand and the excited pointing when recognizing landmarks. I would fit into this group easily enough as I wander around the area with my head twisting in every direction to see the sights or trying to find out what street I am on.

The locals are different breed altogether. Most walk quickly and navigate deftly through the crowds with there eyes focused on the path in front of them, ignoring the virtual circus unfolding around them. Spotting these veterans is relatively simple I have found. It is in the way that they interact with the overwhelming traffic. At corners with traffic lights and walk/do not walk devices, the people waiting for them to change in their favor either are visitors or slowed by age or physical conditions. Healthy natives do not normally wait and they will dart through any opening in the traffic flow that provides them an opportunity to gain a few feet towards the other side. I have seen many narrow escapes mixed with blaring horns, a few choice swear words and gestures, and even a few instances of banging on someone's car hood. It is an ongoing game of chicken pitting man against machine.

The remaining players in the circus are some that make their living hawking souvenirs, food, entertainment, or in some cases themselves. Others in the mix are here for the excitement of the atmosphere, to prey on the weak, or because they are stuck here with nowhere else to go. Many are homeless and living a vicious cycle of self-abuse and an inability to rise above it and move on to better lives. It is a continuous free show of so many of life's dramas playing out here on the street everyday for anyone like me that takes the time to watch.

I am beginning to realize just how exhausted I am now and have been for the last couple of weeks. I think it must be primarily mental exhaustion from the never-ending stress because other than walking and climbing stairs each day I do not do that much physical work. I think I really have not noticed it much except on these days off because every day at the site is such an intense experience. I think that on most of the work days I run wide open on a combination of caffeine, nicotine, and adrenaline.

On these days off I have I have the whole day free and so many things to do in New York City at my feet. However, I simply do not seem to have the energy or desire to take advantage of it. Even after taking a three-hour nap, I am still exhausted and am going to bed early.

24

Volunteers of America

October 19

Overall, most of the day was uneventful. It seemed that things are getting better, but just in the safety arena. Another subcontractor told me that he would be sorry to see us leave because we have helped him a lot. That made me feel good and it is nice that some of them recognize that we are here only too help them perform this monumental task safely. We could accomplish so much more if the government people in charge would let us. However, unless something changes in the next week, we will turn over safety responsibility to some other group that the City of New York hires. I have not a clue what other companies are even in the running. All I know is that whether it is our team or someone else, it is a difficult task.

It is unusual, but not too many problems of significance or out of the ordinary for me to deal with today. The ever-present body removals and a few family visits took place, those I am trying not to dwell on too much. It does not do me any good to think about them each day because tomorrow I will have to see it all over again. Not that I am becoming immune to the pain and suffering, on the contrary, it still bothers me each time I see these things. I suppose that I am learning to deal with it on my own terms for the time being. I am afraid that is only a temporary condition and one day it will all burst through the thin wall I have built around it.

I talked with another Red Cross counselor today. These people volunteered to put their lives on hold, some their counseling or therapist businesses, to be on hand to listen to whatever it is that is bothering us. Whether it is the horrible sights, sounds, and smells here or even a problem at home, they want to help you. The counselors seem to circle around the tables in the Respite Center engaging in small talk, asking how you are and if you need anything. They frequently ask leading questions, attempting to determine if you are handling all of this all right. Occasionally, they seem to zero in on someone and give him or her personal attention. Whether I answered her questions incorrectly or she has a sixth sense about these things, I briefly became her project this afternoon. She asked if she could sit with me a while and talk. I was eating alone as usual and told her that I did not mind. She asked how I was feeling and I told her that I think that I am fine, but I have had a few bad moments here and there. I said I had tried to prepare for much worse than I have seen so far.

We continued the small talk for a few minutes and she was asking me about my work, what I did, and where I was located on the site. I then asked her what she thought of the damage and devastation. She replied that she had not seen it as they have instructions to stay at the Red Cross Center and not to go out to the site. I told her a little about what it was like and we discussed my opinion on the counselors not allowed to see what has happened here. I told her that I thought she had to observe what we were doing, seeing, and living with day after day to understand the mental and physical toll it is taking on us. I am sure there is psychological damage that all of us have suffered that we are not even aware of yet. How are they able to really zero in on what might be bothering us without seeing the horror for themselves? She agreed with me and thought that I was on to something that would help her do her job better. She said that she would bring it up to her supervisors. I offered to take her and others on a tour if the bosses agreed. They need to see it and spend some time watching the work, especially what the firefighters are doing. They need to walk in their shoes for awhile to know how badly their feet hurt, so to speak.

Lord knows that most of us will never be the same as we were before. For most of us, we will be stronger; more compassionate, and better human beings. Sadly, some are going to spiral into depression and a host of other emotional problems that may haunt them to their grave. I am afraid that nervous breakdowns, alcohol and drug abuse, and even suicide will become a problem with the rescue/recovery workers.

The Red Cross and Salvation Army volunteers are such extraordinary and nice people. They are willing to feed, clothe, medically treat, and counsel us. They will do practically anything they can to help make our life here a little more comfortable and tolerable. Some of the volunteers wear badges that have a 'no' with the circle and slash through it meaning **'no'** is not an option. If someone has a reasonable request for some kind of service, the volunteers will do everything they can to see that they get what they need. I cannot say enough nice things about the volunteers here. They have left their homes and families from across the country to come here just like us, except they do it without payment. Awesome people. The Red Cross is the largest and most involved presence at the site as far as I can tell. They have set up 'Respite Centers' where we can go to eat and get a host of other services. These centers are open around the clock and going to them is one of the best parts of our day, a welcome relief from our terrible tasks.

The food provided by the Red Cross, Salvation Army, McDonalds, and others is wonderful. I eat better and more here, than I have in a long, time. I usually eat three meals a day at the site, starting with breakfast at the Command Center. They have eggs, potatoes, sausage, pancakes, bacon, rolls, juice, coffee, and the works every morning. Lunch and dinner has the same great food and the volunteers serve you and ask you all the time if you have had enough or would you like more. I have had baked salmon at least ten times for lunch or dinner. This is just an example of the great food they are providing to us. The food is all donated or purchased with money contributions from the American public and companies and is prepared mostly at NY restaurants. A few of the Respite Centers have small kitchens for cooking some items but restaurants that donate the use of their facilities prepare the bulk. It seems that everyone is pitching in here, in one way or another. In spite of eating like a king, I still am losing weight and it is quite a bit for my frame too. Although I am snacking in-between the full course meals, and eating again when I get back to the room, I have lost at least ten pounds. I did not realize the weight loss until just recently. My pants are practically falling off and nothing else seems to fit right anymore either.

In addition to all the great cooked meals, you have your choice of practically every type of snack food and candy bar ever made. It appears every cookie maker in the country has sent products here for us to eat. I am in heaven as I love cookies and could eat half a box at a time. Cashews, raisins, fruit, even yogurt candy is there in great quantities and the volunteers are constantly offering you some. I always have granola bars, candy, nuts, and crackers in my backpack to snack on all day.

The Respite Centers are very well coordinated and operated staffed facilities. They are located in buildings evacuated because of the attacks. St. Johns University has one and the other ended up in a Marriott hotel two blocks from the site. The center in the Marriott had originally been on a boat docked at Battery Park and named the Spirit of New York.

The volunteers offer so much more than great food. They have a supply room where you can get clothing, work boots, raincoats, toothpaste, first aid supplies, over the counter medicines, gloves, and more. Americans have donated all of it (and I am sure other countries too), to provide us with all of the things that we may need. You can also sleep, watch TV, get on a computer, read books or magazines, get a massage, or just get off your feet for a while. These centers are instrumental in keeping this whole operation running and are a vital part of Ground Zero.

The Salvation Army also has food and relief centers throughout the site. These are usually mobile kitchen trailers and tents but they are every bit as important as the Red Cross centers. They are usually closer to the work site than the others are and some provide full meals, others have beverages, donuts, candy, etc on hand for you to snack on while you take a break. They have clothes and personal items that you may need as well. The Salvation Army volunteers also drive around the site in ATV's with water, soda, coffee, and other drinks to hand out to the workers if needed. The Salvation Army volunteers are just as wonderful as the Red Cross people are. They practically beg you to come in and eat or pick out the supplies that you want.

There are so many other groups offering many different services, too. The telephone companies brought in mobile phone banks that you can call anywhere in the country for five minutes free of charge. They also provide telephone cards with 15 or 30 minutes free calling time and in some places have cell phones with unlimited talk time. I am using the telephone cards every night to keep in touch with my family spread across three states. Church groups are holding services, offering counseling, and providing food, clothing and any help they can. Many of their clergy walk throughout the site offering us solace, prayers, or just conversation to let us know they are here for us if we may need them. McDonalds, Uncle Ben's Rice, and others have kitchens set up and bring food out to us in the field. I really would not need to move from my area to get what I need. In a typical day, I am offered Big Macs®, soda, water, candy bars, rolls, you name it, by groups making their rounds to see that we are taken care of. Whether you take them up on their offerings or not, they still are concerned that you are doing OK and make it a point to talk with you a few minutes.

Other people here are unselfishly doing whatever it takes to assist this effort, too. Doctors and nurses donate their time to see to our health needs, either treating wounds, personal illnesses, or renewing prescriptions that we are unable to take care of on our schedules. We can get a massage and chiropractic care, see a podiatrist, and get psychiatric counseling anytime we may need it.

This is a massive effort by charities, corporations, and volunteers from all over the world. We are almost a small city within New York City created out of a desperate necessity and the kindness and compassion of the human spirit. Their humanity is incredible and bottomless. They have all touched my heart and soul in more ways than I can count or could ever thank them for adequately enough.

I saw Governor Pataki escorting dignitaries through the site again today. He seems to be here quite often. There also was a Buddhist or similar group performing a prayer service or some type of ceremony on the viewing stand at the corner of West and Liberty Streets. I watched them for a while as they were chanting, walking around in circles, and playing tambourines or some sorts of drum like instruments. They were wearing orange robes like the Hari Krishna people that you used to see in airports all the time. I did not understand exactly what they were doing, but they seemed serious about it and had an elaborate ritual they performed. Someone mentioned that they thought it was the Dalai Lama and his entourage. I do not know what the Dalai Lama looks like, however I doubt that it was he, as I did not see any media present filming or interviewing anyone.

When we went back to the Command Center for our nightly turnover, they had a small award ceremony for Greg, one of our joint venture coworkers. Greg received his company's highest award for service, the President's Award plaque, for being instrumental in getting several firefighters out of harm's way. While Greg was observing a work operation on the night of October 8, he noticed that one of the cranes was beginning to lift a large steel beam out of the debris and directly over a hole that several firefighters were in searching for bodies. Greg stopped the crane lift and convinced the firefighters to climb out of the area and stand back a safe distance.

Thankfully, they listened to him and it probably saved their lives. As the steel beam lifted off the ground, the steel connection point separated and broke, dropping the multi-ton beam into the spot that the firefighters had been in just seconds before. A crushing death under all of that weight awaited them and Greg stepped in. He sure deserves this award for his efforts in going the extra steps to assure their safety. As I have mentioned before, sometimes dealing with certain firefighters can be a difficult, stressful, and occasionally an exercise in futility. Saving lives is something we are all hoping to do in one form or another. After all, it is what we do for a living.

Another hero has risen from the ashes of the World Trade Center, common people doing extraordinary things. Way to go Greg.

I finally told Janice tonight that I am supposed to come home in a week. I hope it does happen as planned - I miss her and she was excited. I have rambled on enough tonight. I think I have caught up on all of my notes. It is difficult to force myself to write in the journal every night. I cannot even begin to cover what I experience every day before exhaustion takes over and I fall asleep.

The guys told me that Vice President Dick Cheney and Keith Richards of the Rolling Stones were at the site yesterday, which was my day off. Now there is a pair I would like to have seen together.

Afterthoughts

I cannot ever say enough to adequately express my appreciation and thanks to the thousands of volunteers that supported us in every way during my time at Ground Zero. Thousands came from all over America and many other countries just to help us in any way they possibly could. They worked as many or more hours than we did everyday, were always trying to take care of our every need, smiled the whole day through, and they did it all for no pay or expectation of gratitude. They were the backbone of this gargantuan task and accomplishing it would never have happened without them. They not only deserve the respect and gratitude of every rescuer and worker who set foot on Ground Zero, America and the entire world owes it to them as well. In my view, you have set the example of human compassion, love, charity, and what it means to be an American and a member of the human race that at best could be equaled, but never surpassed.

I wish that the entire population of the world could have witnessed the actions of the volunteers of America as I did. What a different planet this would be if only they could have experienced it for their selves. For too brief of a time in our history, we became the people we should always have been and should strive to ever be. From one end of this country to the other, we shared the same gaping, painful hole in our hearts, a deep and pure compassion, a collective consciousness, and an identical goal. We shook off those asinine social and historical chains that have restricted our human relations for so many centuries. Unencumbered by those restrictions of differences in race, ethnic origin, religious views and practices, sexual orientation, social status, and other petty differences, we freely ran to the aid of our neighbors in this time of tragedy, pain, and grief. Suddenly it mattered to no one whether we were rich or poor, homosexual or straight, an atheist or Anglican priest, had black, white, or green skin, was a corporate executive or a garbage collector. We worked side by side, looked out for each other, and genuinely cared about our brother and sister's welfare. We shared stories of our lives and families, extended our hands and souls in friendship and assistance, and embraced each other as we cried our eyes out. We were family.

Unfortunately, in any society or civic unit as we became, there are the bad apples. Some people took advantage of the generosity of the American people by taking as many clothes and supplies as they could carry, not just what they needed. Others stole items from other workers or looted the abandoned and damaged buildings. Fortunately, those worthless bastards were only a miniscule flaw in the fabric woven of people that were truly astounding in their love and respect for their fellow man.

So many of the volunteers touched my heart and soul in one-way or another. I wish I knew all of their names and could thank them personally. Here are some people that I wish to acknowledge and thank. I hope either they or someone who knows them recognizes their description so they know how much they meant to me.

The Red Cross worker at the Respite Center in the Marriott hotel who looked like Santa Claus with his white hair and beard, who shook my hand everyday, asked me how I was and if I needed anything. I know you worked at least twelve hours a day, six days a week and never lost your smile. I looked forward to seeing you everyday. Thanks for the smile and for caring. You will never know how much it meant to me each day to see your smiling face.

The lady who walked around the site every day offering massages to the workers right in the work area. I never took you up on one, however I saw you help so many folks that needed it. I was amazed how you could give that many massages in a row without your arms seizing into knots. Thank you for wading into chaos to help my coworkers.

Michelle, a counselor and a Mormon from out west somewhere. You so skillfully steered me into a conversation about some things I did not want to talk about, but somehow knew I needed to anyway. Thanks for traveling across the country to help keep us from going off the deep end.

The DMAT counselor who stopped and talked to me every time he saw me. You spent five or ten minutes of your time just to see if I was all right or needed to talk. Thank you for caring for a perfect stranger and pulling my attention away from mayhem for a while.

Two of the wonderful ladies at the Red Cross Respite Center in the Marriott Hotel, one, a chiropractor who spent five minutes talking me into my first back adjustment, put me at ease, effortlessly twisted me around and took the pain out of my back. Not done yet, you then pushed me over to the massage table for round two with lady number two, who took the tension out of me from head to toe. I had resisted doing that for weeks because I was afraid it would feel too good. I was right; I was as limp as a wet noodle when you were done with me, but I felt great. Thank you for the weeks without back pain and curing my suspicion of chiropractors.

The three smiling ladies at the boot wash area on West Street. I admired your work ethic and wonderful attitude while performing a very hard job 70-80 hours a week. How you managed to stoop over to scrub our boots 12 hours a day yet always seemed to stand back up smiling is beyond me. I looked forward to seeing those smiles and our talk of family each evening on my way out. Thank you ladies.

So many more gave a smile, a pat on the back, offered coffee, a sandwich, a prayer, or just stopped to see if I was OK. Thank you sincerely. You will forever have a special place in my heart for your kindness and for opening my eyes again; to see what wonderful people we can be when our neighbors need us.

I cannot leave out the American people for the things that they did. Continual streams of semi tractor-trailer trucks unloading food, bottled water, soft drinks, and every other kind of supplies that were needed. So much arrived that they eventually had to request people to send money instead. All of it came from every city, town, fire department, Rotary Club, church group, charity, corporation, or citizen that wanted to help his or her fellow Americans. Whether you donated money, food, your time, sent a card, or just prayed for us, thank you. Those of us working on the site knew and appreciated what you were doing for us.

America is the greatest country on earth. They can attack us, wound, or kill some of us, but we stand tall and together. To conclude, I would like to swipe a quote from a letter sent to the editor of the Knoxville, Tennessee, News-Sentinel, shortly after the attacks. The writer informed the terrorists that attacking and killing thousands of us was futile in their objective because they did not understand about Americans. He wrote, "You see, we do not live in America, America lives in us". That may be the greatest quote I have ever heard.

25

New York's Finest in Action

October 20

The pace of the work, the body recoveries, and everything else seemed to move in slow motion today. Most everyone seemed to be working relatively safely and sensibly today. I cannot help but wonder how long this change of pace and attitude is going to last. I did not have anything other than minor problems that I can think of and that is an anomaly here. I do not know whether exhaustion caught up with everyone all at once or it is just my mind playing tricks. The change I feel in the site atmosphere could be because now that we are supposed to be leaving next week, the fire and adrenaline are beginning to subside in me. The job almost seemed routine for the first time other than an incident at one of the apartment buildings. It is amazing how even this place could become almost just like any other job, even if it is for one day.

With the lack of life threatening problems popping up every five minutes, I had plenty of opportunities to talk with many of the people I have come to know here. It is common knowledge now that we are supposed to leave at the end of next week and surprisingly, even the people I have had some confrontations with are friendly and told me they think we have done a good job overall. One supervisor that I have had an on going battle with asked me who was going to keep him in line if I left. I had once threatened to have him arrested if his employee fell out of a window because he would not make him wear fall protection gear. It is nice to know that some of the workers are sorry to see us leave and actually appreciated our help. Those kinds of comments today seem to even the score with all of my head banging in frustration these past weeks. We may not have gotten our message through to all of them. We certainly seem to have reached many more than I would have guessed.

The incident I witnessed today at one of the apartment buildings near the site was a classic. I had walked down to the Salvation Army Center tent on Liberty Street, about a block away from the site, and had just gotten a cup of coffee when I heard an argument going on very close by. Curious and not too busy for the moment, I walked towards the sound of the ruckus and found it at the entrance of an apartment building. The building has damage, mostly broken windows, and the residents evacuated on September 11 have still not returned to living there. There have been NYPD officers there for the last week or so guarding the entrance to keep any looters and thieves out, but to allow the residents and work crews to get in. Up until then the fence gate remained locked most of the time and I did not notice much activity. Now I saw that the officer was in a face-to-face argument with a young woman. She was demanding entry to the apartments and he was telling her she did not have the proper identification or an access permit. She said she lived there and wanted in and he said he had his orders and she was not.

The argument escalated and heated up as she kept maneuvering back and forth in an attempt to get by him. It was quite a show, almost like a boxing match without the punches. She would lunge to the left suddenly and he would back peddle into position to block. She would feign a move to the right; shuffle her feet and charge in another direction. The officer deftly kept her at bay by reacting to every move and quickly stepping in her intended path. All the while, he calmly and repeatedly informed her that he could not let her in until she had the proper paperwork. The argument about the rules seemed to be going nowhere with this lady and it seemed she was getting madder by the minute.

The battle seemed at a stand off until as luck would have it, one of the contractor's work vehicles pulled up to get in and the officer was momentarily distracted. She instantaneously recognized the opening in the officer's defense and made her run for it. Her luggage in tow, rolling behind her, she dashed past the officer and headed towards the apartment building.

This is about the last thing you want to do here, run through a security checkpoint at this heavily guarded site of a terrorist attack and with everyone's nerves on edge. The NYPD, Army, and others guarding the site have authorization to shoot first and ask questions later if needed. A stupid stunt that could have resulted in her shot full of holes.

Fortunately for her, this officer kept his head and just ran after her on foot, yelling for her to halt. Not any surprise, she ignored his commands and kept heading towards her target. She had made it several yards into the parking lot before he caught up to her. The officer grabbed her by the arm and tried to lead her back to the gate peacefully, but she was not going to give up her quest that easily and the struggle was on. She put up a formidable battle, swinging her arms about and digging in with her heels, however in the end was no match for the officer. He physically had to drag her to the gate and shove her out to the sidewalk. He pulled out his radio and called a supervisor for assistance. While waiting the few minutes for his back-up assistance to show up, the lady restarted the 'dance' in another attempt to get past him. Failing in her first run for it and being dragged out never phased this woman or altered her mission in the least. In fact, she was even more determined to win. Jumping back and forth, circling, and repeatedly charging in an effort to get by him, she pulled out all the tricks. She also was screaming, swearing, and waving her arms the whole time. This officer had the patience of Job and was a supreme professional throughout her renewed attacks and name-calling. He was quiet, but determined in performing his job without having to manhandle her again. He did it successfully. After a few minutes, but what must have seemed like an eternity to him, his supervisor finally drove up. While continuing to block the entrance, he related the facts of the situation to his boss. Meanwhile, the enraged, combative, foul mouthed, crazy lady stood off to the side and began raising the game to a new level. She pulled out the hole card, the one that works so well in times like this, she began to cry. She looked so helpless, distraught, and pitiful that if I had not just witnessed the previous battle I would have went over and tried to console her. This lady was good, a natural born manipulator to say the least.

The mood definitely changed now from electrically charged to a sad melodrama. The police supervisor went over and spoke to her for a few minutes. Between the sobs, sniffles, and wiping away of her tears, she was nodding her head in agreement with whatever he was saying. It appeared that she now understood why she could not go into the apartment complex. When the supervisor finished his conversation with her, he spoke to the officer for a minute or so and then left in his police car. It appeared that all was well and good. I started to walk away, assuming the show was now finished, but decided to watch for a little bit longer to see where she went. I must have had a feeling this was not quite finished.

She bent over, fiddled with her luggage, and appeared to be preparing to leave. However, she also seemed to keep an eye on the NYPD supervisor's car as it disappeared down the street. A second or two after the car was out of sight she stood up straight, grabbed the handle of her luggage, and rushed head on into the officer at the gate again. The battle now resumed and it was evident that this woman was no longer playing with a full deck of cards. Unbalanced or mad with rage, she made it obviously clear that she was not going to give up peacefully.

Between fending off the lady's multiple charges at him, called a bastard, son of a bitch, and a few other choice words, the officer managed to call again for backup. The response was very quick this time, and when she saw the additional officers, she stopped the fight and turned to flee. They easily subdued her and led her about a block away from the area before they stopped to talk to her. After a few minutes, they walked with her until they were out of my sight. I do not believe that they arrested her, but probably either escorted her out of the protected area, or took her to a hospital for evaluation. I hope that they at least took her temporary badge away so she cannot come back. The NYPD officer looked relieved that it was finally over. He showed great restraint in dealing with the situation and the confrontation ended without anyone suffering injuries.

Nothing else of note happened today. We still are not sure if we will be leaving next Friday or not. Stew said this morning that the negotiations are progressing day by day and to be prepared for anything.

I am watching Paul McCartney's concert on TV while I write this tonight. I am struggling to stay awake and do not think I will make it to the end of the show, as 5:00 AM seems to come earlier every morning.

Afterthoughts

The incident with the irrational woman could have ended up badly and not all of the people who tried to violate the security rules were as fortunate as this young woman was. Another evening when I returned to the Command Center at the end of our shift, there was a heated exchange in progress outside of the entrance door. The argument was between an Army sergeant, two NYPD officers, and a handcuffed man. I could not get into the door, which was the only allowed entrance at the time, so I stood back and watched the encounter. Apparently, the man in handcuffs became irate when denied entry to the building for one reason or another. From what I could gather out of the shouting, he had confronted the Army sergeant and a scuffle ensued. The NYPD, who use the Command Center as one of their gathering points and check badges on the street corner, responded and subdued the man. Even restrained by handcuffs and surrounded, he was still arguing about his rights as an American Citizen. His wife was standing off to the side shaking her head, obviously upset, and trying to get him to calm down. He ignored her and kept up his tirade at the sergeant. Finally, the poor sergeant pointed to his uniform and told the guy that the reason he had the authority to stop him from entering was that he was ordered to by the United States Army and he did not appreciate him assaulting him or disrespecting what that uniform stood for. After that, this guy went into a patrol car, directly to jail, did not pass go, or collect two hundred dollars. His embarrassed wife apologized to everyone involved.

This was a war zone, security had a serious job to do, and they did it well. They took a lot of unnecessary verbal abuse from people who thought they were immune to the rules and handled it professionally. The abuse was frequent enough that they finally put up signs at their posts outlining the rules and why they were just doing their jobs. Guards checked us all of the time to see if we had the proper access badge to enter the areas and there were many checkpoints. I would estimate that guards checked my badge at least 20 to 30 times a day.

Whether the guards were Army, National Guard, Marines or NYPD they were always courteous and I treated them the same way. I told a few of them when they thanked me for showing them my identification that I did not care if I had to stop and show it to someone every five feet because I knew it was for my own safety. The only way to keep a terrorist out was to verify that you were who you said you were. Too simple for some people to understand though, so justifiably, they suffered the consequences.

Well protected by land, air, and sea, the site was secure. The US Coast Guard was protecting the harbor and river around Manhattan. The USS Campbell and some other large ships were sitting at the entrances to the harbor. There were several smaller Coast Guard boats on river patrol. These small boats had machine guns mounted on the bow and the crewmembers carried M-16's. I do not know what kind of weapons the large ships had, but I am confident they were heavily armed.

Although I did not see where they were set up at, I had heard that the US Marines and Army had a camp in the area. I do know that both of those groups were on guard duty at the checkpoints everyday. I also saw military helicopters on several occasions flying to and from a site near the World Trade Center. I am sure there were many other defense systems in place we did not know about.

On one occasion, I saw a military fighter jet flying off in the distance. I had mixed emotions when I noticed it. On the one hand, I felt proud, safe, and secure. On the other hand, I felt fear and uncertainty as I wondered if they were on their way to shoot down a hijacked airliner that was now heading towards us. Before September 11, Americans would not have even dreamed these unfathomable thoughts or had this fear of mass murder on our soil by foreign enemies.

26

Oprah, Meg, Adam, & Friends

October 21

This day was not very busy, however it was very unusual and noteworthy. The rescue teams found several bodies in my area today and work was mostly at a full stop while they searched for and recovered bodies. The removal of bodies just continues on and on and they have not even scratched the surface yet. Thousands of people are still missing. They do not even know exactly how many are lost in this massive debris pile because we hear revised estimates every few days. At least the estimates are lower each time. The stress that these firefighters and rescue/recovery groups are under must be unbearable. What a terrible thing to have to do day after day. I do not think that I could handle it the way they seem to be.

They seem to be rotating the rescue/recovery groups in and out, so they are not staying on the front lines too long. I am seeing new towns and states printed on their shirts. They are from everyplace, Michigan, California, and even one from Japan. I am not sure if the firefighters are rotating their crews as well. I hope that FDNY is getting them out of here after a week or so. A person can only take so much of this terrible thing. There are so many of them here that it is hard to tell if they are new or not. I recognize a few of the chiefs as having been here continually since I arrived on September 27. To do my job, I have to talk to them quite frequently so am getting to know some of them.

There were many processions carrying bodies out today. One of those was out of the ordinary, very different than most. The rumor mill had told us that a recovery team had located a police officer's remains this morning. Based on the amount of police officials gathered around the area of the remains, he must have been someone

important. They placed the flag draped stretcher in an ambulance
that just sat there for a very long time. A firefighter related to me that
the police knew who the officer was and an NYPD Chaplain and
other police officials went to pick up his family. Once the family
members arrived, they held a prayer service. Afterwards, the family
walked in front of the slow moving ambulance, leading it down the
street towards an exit and out of our view. Every time I think I have
handled the worst of the emotional sights, another one proves me
wrong. This ceremony was very touching to witness. The victim's
wife walked proudly down the street, head held high, leading her
hero home for the last time. My God, I do not know where these
survivors keep finding the strength to carry out these things. My
heart ached at the sight of it alone; her pain must have been
unbearable.

There were many safety problems all around my area in spite
of the work stoppages. As there were so many search crews,
firefighters, and police officers on the debris pile, I spent a lot of time
out there in it trying to get most of them to wear respirators. Some
listened and some did not. I try to not become upset over it any
longer. I just keep trying to do my best to convince them to protect
themselves. Respirator use has improved somewhat lately, however I
would estimate that well below 50% are wearing them at all, let alone
all the time.

What made today so noteworthy was all of the celebrities that
visited the site. I almost felt as if I was in Hollywood at times. Most
of them had participated in Paul McCartney's benefit concert last
night at Madison Square Garden. It all started this morning with Meg
Ryan. My coworker, Rob Jones was in my area checking on some
demolition concerns, his area of expertise, when he noticed a man and
woman walking around in the work zone without hard hats. Rob
approached them and introduced himself as a safety representative
on the site. Rob requested that they walk over to the Salvation Army
tent on the corner of West and Liberty Streets and obtain a couple of
hard hats. The woman had a scarf wrapped around her neck and

covering her face, Rob assumed because of the odor of smoke and death, as it was not cold out. After Rob's request, the lady lowered the scarf, stuck out her hand to shake Rob's, and said that it was very nice to meet him. Rob replied that it was nice to meet her too, but would they please go over to get a hard hat. They replied that they were leaving anyway and started to walk off. As they took a few steps away, it hit Rob who the lady that he had been talking to was. Rob said "Meg". Meg Ryan turned around and said "yes". Rob being a big fan of hers lost most of his wits at that point, but managed to get her autograph and then start calling me over the radio.

I had just walked out of the debris pile of WTC Tower Two and was removing my respirator. I was about ten feet behind him when I heard his call on the radio. I walked up and asked him what was up. About all Rob could manage to articulate was "Meg Ryan". I did not believe him until he pointed her out to me. It was her all right, curly blond hair and wearing those John Lennon style sunglasses that I have seen her wear on TV. I saw her start to walk away so I hurried over to her and asked if I could have her autograph. She said sure and leaned against me to steady her on the uneven terrain so she could sign her name in my journal. I thanked her for the autograph and for coming down here. She said goodbye and walked out of the controlled area towards Battery Park. (Note- I tried to embellish the story a little when I got home, but neither my wife nor anyone else seemed to believe that Meg Ryan would flirt with me).

I walked back over to where Rob was standing and while we were admiring our Meg Ryan autographs, I glanced up and saw actor Mike Myers and his wife standing less than ten feet from us. He gave us his autograph, too, and we talked to them for a little. Mike and his wife were very nice to everyone who approached them for an autograph or photo. He must have signed dozens of autographs and posed for several photos. I wished I had brought that disposable camera with me today. The Army guards had searched our backpacks a few mornings ago as we came into the Command Center so I have not been carrying it in fear they catch me with it.

Now, Rob and I were standing in front of the Salvation Army tent at Liberty and West Streets admiring our two autographs. As we were talking, I noticed Mayor Giuliani was over on the visitor's stand. I mentioned it to Rob and we speculated about whom the person was standing next to him. After a few seconds of observing, I realized that it was Oprah Winfrey. As we watched them, Rob and I decided we were not going to try to get her autograph because she seemed so distraught at what she was seeing at Ground Zero. It appeared that Mayor Giuliani was actually holding her up it and she had her hands up to her face that had a look of utter shock. Oprah and Mayor Giuliani were up there on the viewing stand for several more minutes before Oprah seemed to regain some of her composure.

After they came down the steps of the viewing stand and as she walked towards her car, she began signing a few autographs for the people gathered around. Rob and I decided it must be all right and went over to ask for one, too. There were only a few people in front of us when we arrived. I was the last one to get an autograph and almost did not. She was just getting into the car as Rob got his and her bodyguard said no more, but she reached out for my extended journal anyway. I was going to have her address it to my wife because she is such a big fan and would have loved it, but my mind went blank when she asked me to whom to address it. Being that close the legendary Oprah, it is a wonder that I could manage to remember my own name. Oprah wrote a nice message for me and signed her name. After handing the journal back to the bodyguard at her door, I thanked her and she thanked me in return. Within a second, Oprah regained the distraught look on her face and seemed to sink back down into her seat as if all of her energy just evaporated. She seemed to deflate like a balloon. I immediately felt bad that we had bothered her during what was obviously a very emotional event for her. I am amazed that she could or would compose herself and put on her 'game face' for a few minutes to sign our autographs. I saw Oprah's true professionalism and public persona that most people probably only see when in her presence. However, I think that I had a brief, but rare glimpse of her that most people may never witness, the emotional facet that reminds us of what we seem to forget about celebrities, that they hurt, bleed, cry, and mourn just like the rest of the us. We should have left her alone.

A short time after leaving the company of Oprah Winfrey, Mayor Giuliani began walking around with some other unknown dignitaries. He was pointing out the damages as they walked along. The entourage stopped near Rob and I and we ended up getting the mayor's autograph as well. I have wanted to meet him since I first saw him at the site in my first few days. Standing next to him was an honor, getting his autograph was a bonus.

The celebrity onslaught took a break for a while; at least I did not see anyone else for a few hours. It was back to the work of keeping people safe. I did my usual 90 West Building tour to check on the Polish crew. They have been doing quite well lately. Without my having to tell them to, they were putting up handrails over the gaping holes in the walls and at windows before they started putting up shoring. That was a welcomed relief because I have been afraid that one of them was going to fall to their death on my watch and I do not know if I would ever get over that. It also makes my job much easier not having to climb those several stories of steps every few hours to check on them. Thankfully, they started on the lower floors and worked their way up so my legs had time to toughen up for these daily trips up to the sixteenth floor and beyond.

My trips into the smoking debris pile were not as frequent today. With the pace greatly slowed due to the locating and removal of victims, most of the heavy equipment was idle and the torch cutting activities at a minimum. There were many more firefighters, rescue/recovery personnel, and police officers out there though. Besides the continual respirator issues, they just stood around watching basically, and did not get into harm's way often. Occasionally, they would wander under the hanging steel and debris by the façade or the hotel, but they were not in those areas much today.

After another of those infrequent trips in and out of the debris this afternoon, I happened to walk up next to who I thought was just another worker. He was dressed in work-type clothes and was wearing a hard hat like the rest of us. He was talking to someone else and as I walked up within earshot, I recognized the voice that I had heard performing a skit last night on the Paul McCartney Benefit. It was none other than Adam Sandler. I asked him for an autograph and got one. I thanked him for it and he said 'no, thank you for coming here and what you are doing here'. I think that it was nice of him to come down here and spend some time with us. Word spread that he was here and more people started to show up to see him. I called Rob on the radio to let him know, however he was back at the Command Center for a meeting and could not head my way. I got back in line and Adam gave me another autograph for Rob. It was the least that I could do for the guy that introduced me to Meg Ryan a few hours ago. Mr. Sandler was in front of the Salvation Army tent for quite awhile as he signed autographs, conversed with the workers, and many pictures taken with them. He was not only very gracious, but he also seemed to be a regular guy like the rest of us, not one who made the big time and forgot where he came from.

About an hour after Adam's visit, Lou Pinella, the former New York Yankee and now manager of the Seattle Mariners, appeared almost the same way. I was standing at the corner of Liberty and West Streets drinking a Coke®, when all of a sudden he was in front of me. I pulled out my journal and he gave me an autograph and asked how I was doing. After I stepped out of the way for someone else to get one, a lady that I believe was Mrs. Pinella approached me and we talked for quite a while. She was very nice and had many questions about the work operations. We talked about the plan for removing the debris, where the trucks took it, and a little about the body recovery. Both were there a long time, Mr. Pinella signing autographs, posing for pictures, and talking with the workers about the final playoff game for the American League Championship tonight. Lou's Seattle Mariners and the New York Yankees are playing for the pennant and a berth in the World Series. *(Note* The New York Yankees won).*

   We are still in limbo about whether we are going home Saturday or not. It is possible that we some us will stay on a while longer if requested by the city. According to Randy, I will be one of those asked to stay. I have mixed emotions about that. I will definitely stay if they really need me here. Part of me would like to go home for good, however I made a commitment to stay here for ninety days. I will honor that commitment no matter how homesick I get. In our line of work, it is common to be away from home for a month or longer. It is hard to explain, but it seems like I have been here for months and months. Working the long hours can account for some of that feeling, but I think it is the sheer intensity of the situation. We handle more things in a day here than we would in two weeks on our regular jobs. I think I have experienced more in this short time than I could have in years anywhere else. I would just like to go home for at least a week to see my soul mate, take care of some business, and sleep. I miss Janice and our dog Paco, too. It is funny, when I call home Janice puts the telephone to his ear and he talks to me with little growls and woofs. He will not go near the telephone unless she says its 'Dad'. My dog misses me too.

Peace!

Meg Ryan's autograph

184

27

Even Heroes Stumble

October 22

Today is my Mother's 71st birthday. I took time out to use one of the phones at the Red Cross Center in the Marriott Hotel to call and wish her a happy birthday. She was not planning anything special for the occasion just staying home for the evening. She sounded as if she was doing well now. A few weeks ago, she was still hurting from the trip from Michigan to our house in Tennessee and back. It took a toll on both her and my sister Sue. Sue had back problems and Mom's knees suffered from riding in the van that long.

After today's events with some of the FDNY firefighter's arrogance, their aura is really starting to fade in my eyes. I am not the only one either as most of our team, contractors, and many others on the site are complaining about their behavior. At first, there seemed to be very few that acted as if they could walk on water and were better than everyone else. I chalked up most of that attitude to stress or the American public's adulation had gone to a few of their heads. Now it seems the surly attitudes, smart-ass comments, and the 'who do you think you are talking to' arrogance is becoming the rule instead of the exception.

They are not only treating us in this manner, as the NYPD appears fed up with them as well. Based on the conversations that I have overheard lately, the police officers are upset at what they perceive as total disrespect and disregard for their missing officers. They believe that the FDNY cares only about finding their own comrades and overlook the areas that may contain the remains of police officers. They complain about the 'Hero Attitudes' and their refusal to acknowledge that other departments had heroes lost during the rescue attempts on September 11 as well. It is an emotionally

charged topic and some are very pissed off about that subject. I have
heard these comments for a while now and even see it written about
on the Porta-Johns® walls. I have not noticed many differences in the
recovery efforts other than the types of ceremonies for each group.
However, I am not watching as closely or have personal interest in it
as those who have lost friends and coworkers. Talking amongst our
group, the consensus is that this rift is going to get worse and cause
problems eventually, whether here or long term resentment down the
road.

My problem with the firefighters today started when I saw
several of them in an extremely dangerous position. There were
seven or eight of them digging for bodies directly underneath tons
and tons of steel beams and other debris that is hanging over the side
of what is left of WTC Building Three, the Marriott Hotel. The debris
in this location is not packed as tightly as the debris in the tower
footprints and is more than likely unstable. No one knows what is
holding it together because it is just a hodge-podge of piled up and
twisted masses of steel beams, concrete dust, wire, and whatever else
was in the building. Adding to the danger mix is the work with the
heavy machinery that is continually going on in the areas next to it.
Evidence of the effects of the vibration created by the machines was
visible in the small streams of dust and marble sized concrete pieces
trickling out of the debris and down onto the firefighters below. The
machine vibration or even just gravity alone could have shifted and
toppled the debris at any given moment. Had this house of cards
began to come apart the firefighters had little chance of escaping its
onslaught.

I broke one of my Golden Rules by putting myself in harms
way in an attempt to get them to leave the area. I do not do that at
any other time or place for obvious reasons, however as the whole
world knows, this is not anything like other times and places. I went
down the hill of debris and into the hole under that mess of instant
death hanging above to talk to the recovery crew doing the digging.
A few bothered to listen to me while the others kept digging with

shovels or poking into the debris with the long probes they use to locate bodies underneath. After I listed all the reasons why I thought they should back off and wait until the area rendered safe, my small audience silently turned around and went back to digging. It could have been worse I guess, they could have verbally abused me as well.

Not willing to give up and leave them to their own fate, I found an FDNY captain watching the action from the sidelines. I laid out all of my concerns to him. He politely listened and then informed me that they believed some firefighter remains were in there and they intended to find them. Then he turned his back to me and walked off down the street. Strike two. It took me quite some time to find someone in authority that thought more with his or her head than emotions. He was a Deputy Chief and he agreed with my concerns and finally ordered his men to pull out of there.

I just do not understand how the FDNY leadership can allow their people to jeopardize their lives in such obvious risk to recover a body, even if it may be one of their own firefighters. I know it is an extraordinary emotional burden on them to know that buried in there is their friends and coworkers. However, they all know that no one is coming out of there alive. Hope has long passed of ever finding a survivor here, so why risk killing or maiming more. If I thought for a microsecond there might be a survivor in there I would be right in there with them digging, the risk be damned. Unfortunately, that is not going to happen.

As a safety person, I am continually aware of the hazards involved with any given task and the probability that those hazards could become a factor. This situation is no different except the severity of the consequences if it goes bad. In our business you identify the hazard and either eliminate it or develop controls to minimize the risks involved. In this case, I know the hazards and the only reasonable solution is to remove the overhanging steel or keep personnel out of the danger zone. It is a simple solution to me, but apparently not with this group. I cannot do anything except suggest, cajole, and state my case; even scream if I thought it would help. The decision is ultimately the FDNY chiefs to make and I have to accept that no matter how much I disagree.

I found another American flag laying in the debris pile today. This one is small, three by five inches and is on a stick. It looks like those that most of the grapplers and other machines have taped on them. It is filthy with the dust and I cleaned off the loose dirt and stuck it into my backpack. Any flag that has flown at Ground Zero is sacred as far as I am concerned.

Stew told us this morning that the schedule for us to leave is still the same, but to stand by because anything can happen at this point. I hate being in limbo. I always like to know what is going to happen and when. Unfortunately in this business, you rarely ever know anything with any certainty. Come on Saturday!

I have been worried about Stew for the last week. He arrived here September 12 and has been working more hours a day than we have. His schedule is unbelievable. He is at the site most of the day and afterwards attends meetings late into the evening. He is looking extremely tired, however he keeps running at that incredible pace day after day. I do not think anyone can talk him into taking a day off to relax and recharge his batteries. He is as dedicated to this job as you can be. Stew has led our company to be the safest construction company in the world.

Rob Jones and I were hoping that more celebrities would show up today. We especially looked forward to an appearance by Paul McCartney, Elton John, or Mick Jagger. I did not see anyone although I did hear that actor Steve Buschemi was on the site somewhere.

28

Déjà vu All Over Again

October 23

I saw Mayor Giuliani several times at the site today. Out here a lot lately and he mostly gives tours to the bigwigs in our government. Sometimes Governor Pataki is with him, but I did not see him around today. It seems like every fire, police, rescue department, state, city, and official from all over the country and world have been here at one time or another. After watching what they do when they come into my area, it is hard to tell if some of them are here to help, learn, or just be able to say that they were here and to get their photo taken. I have watched some just walk out to the edge of the debris pile, make sure they had the façade behind them, and smile while someone with an expensive, professional camera snapped photo after photo of them. Of course, it is not only the politicians doing that. The NYPD, FDNY, etc, escort people in and out of here all the time and many get their photos taken the same way. I even saw a group of clergy posing for photos.

Well, yesterdays firefighter problems I dealt with turned out to be just a warm-up for round two today. They were back in harms way again this morning, in the same spot as yesterday only over 15 of them at risk this time. Once again, I put my safety and common sense on hold and waded into that damned catastrophe waiting to happen. I might as well have just talked to the empty grappler sitting there for all the good it did me. All I managed to do was get ignored and disrespected. Although there were many more people under the hanging steel beams today, I had less of them bothering to listen. After I again said that I thought they should get out of there, they turned their backs to me and continued to work.

Written on one of those backs were the words Safety Chief. Here was their Safety Chief right smack in the middle of it all with them. I caught his attention and he stopped long enough to talk to me. I went through my concerns again and he conveyed the same message I had heard yesterday, they were sure there were several bodies of firefighters in there and they were going in to get them. I practically begged him to pull his men back until the machines brought down the debris hanging over them to the ground. I explained to him that I understood his crew's feelings on recovering their friends and that all I was asking was for them to search in another area until I could get an operator into the grappler that was sitting there to pull that knotted mess of steel down before it collapsed onto them. He seemed to think about it for a few seconds before he asked me if I was a structural engineer. I told him I was not, however I had a lot of experience in safety and it was my opinion that the area was too dangerous as it was. He turned around without another word and went back in to continue digging with his men.

I guess he did not think I was qualified to have a worthy opinion unless I was an engineer. Well, I know dozens of engineers and they are extremely bright and talented people. Engineers can tell you how to build a building so it will stay up and what it will do in a hurricane or earthquake. However, the unknown configuration of these piles of debris, where it is anyone's guess as to what exactly is holding it up, forget it. There is not an engineer born yet that can possibly tell you that with any certainty. You might be able to parade a herd of elephants over it and it will not even budge or you could move one piece an inch and the whole shebang would collapse. The only way to be sure it was safe was to get it on the ground.

I gave up trying to get anywhere with them and went to find a Battalion Chief. I found one across the street at their mini command post. All I can say about him is that he at least listened and was courteous. He did not do a damned thing either though. I called my supervisors, filled them in on the situation, and told them this needed the involvement of someone with authority. It took several hours and calls by Stew to people way up the New York City political ladder to finally make the decision to get these firefighters out of harm's way. During that time they had located three bodies so they marked the locations and pulled back only because of orders from up above.

I stood on the fringes as they huddled with some engineers and discussed the plan forward. The firefighters wanted to know what action they needed to take to eliminate the danger so they could continue their search. After much discussion, the engineers decided that the way to accomplish this was to get an operator into a grappler and pull that knotted mess of steel beams down before it fell on somebody. Brilliant idea, wish I had thought of it. I mulled over confronting my buddy, the Safety Chief, to ask him why he now thought that was such a good plan, but decided to let it go and accept that there was a victory, even though someone else was getting the credit. At least the Safety Chief and I know. *

(*Note. These piles of steel over their heads were much larger and complicated than I or the engineers had realized. It took crews two days of steady work with the grapplers and crane to untangle and remove all the steel from the hotel and make it safe to allow the firefighters to resume body recovery there.)

Thank God for the small victories. It is a shame that the fight has to be so damned tough at times. Nevertheless, I will take it. I like to think of it as maybe I helped save a life or two today. Despite the stress, hassles, insults, and potential for catastrophe, it all worked out without anyone being injured or worse. Not a bad day's work if I say so myself.

Although I broke the 'Safety Golden Rule' a few times again today, it is the last time that I plan to take any risks. My goal is to go home in one piece in spite of the fact that some of these people do not seem to want to themselves.

The part of these events with the FDNY today that really bothers me is that they are willing to risk a few dozen lives to recover three bodies.

This is only one example of the foolish things done during the rescue/recovery operations. Read on.

Afterthoughts

I have mentioned a few times throughout about the trouble we had getting people to wear their personal protective equipment, respirators in particular. We were constantly reminding firefighters, policemen, contractors, and visitors to put them on. We got some cooperation but not much. Firefighters in particular were not complying with the requirement to wear them within the restricted twenty-five feet of the debris zone. When we were not just plain ignored, we heard excuses like 'the damage is already done, I was here the first day,' 'I am a firefighter and I do this for a living and I know when I need a respirator,' and my all time favorite: 'where were you on the day it collapsed? I did not see you here giving me a respirator when I really need it.' These are just a few of the ridiculous excuses heard day after day.

Posted all over the site for all to see were respirator warnings. They were on the Salvation Army kitchens and tents, walls, poles, etc. Handed out in the daily meetings and to every agency and contractor was respirator zone maps. We also listed it as a significant safety problem nearly everyday on our daily reports to the NYC Department of Design and Construction (DDC) who we were reporting to at the time. We brought it up in countless meetings with the entire twenty-six agencies that were involved in the day-to-day operations at the site. Those meetings also included officials from the FDNY. The agencies accomplished nothing of significance regarding respirators other than issuing more directives that no one enforced anyway. So, it is easy to see why we were so easily ignored. They tried everything short of actually making them wear them, which was the only way to correct the situation. No one in charge appeared willing to take the problem on for some unknown reason.

We knew that it would come back to haunt them one day and it has, only a lot sooner than I personally thought it would. A few months after I left it was reported that many firefighters needed to be re-assigned to areas different than Ground Zero because they had significant lung damage and breathing problems that have arose from their time spent there. What a surprise. I believe that they are only the first of multitudes that are going to be suffering from lung damage because of not listening to us, OSHA, and everyone else that tried to get them to protect themselves.

The lawsuits that have arisen from the respirator issue are a significant number, and more cases and more defendants are added to the list almost weekly. Based on the reports I have read, the firefighters have filed a majority of those alleging that NYC did not adequately protect them from respiratory exposures by not providing them the proper equipment. The dollar amount asked in these lawsuits is several billion dollars. In addition, city workers (which firefighters are) may also file for Social Security benefits and receive three-quarters of their last year's salary tax-free for life if it is determined a line-of-duty injury forced retirement. As NYC is self-insured, the taxpayers are going to be in debt for a very long time. Billions of dollars in health care, lawsuits, and compensation, and so many of these cases were so easily avoided.

So there, you have it. It has come back to haunt us and will for a long, long, time. Psychic? No just an ordinary guy that knows his job and is a life long student of human nature. Knowing how people think, act, and react are is a very large part of the work that safety people do. If I do not understand human nature, I cannot be effective in getting people to change their behavior to work safely. We understood the problem; we just could not overcome the many roadblocks placed in our way.

I do believe that every New York City employee, injured or ill because of this tragedy, be assured if receiving proper medical treatment for as long as it is required. If unable to work, they should receive compensation commensurate with their salaries. With many of these lung problems, the injured parties caused them by their own negligence and disregard of professional advice and that needs to be taken in to account. I do not believe they should be allowed to sue the City of New York, the World Trade Center, the airlines or anyone else but Osama bin Laden and his terrorist organization. I honestly feel that the federal government should place a ban on any lawsuits such as these.

How we ever got to the point that we believe our government, companies, and others are entirely responsible for every bad thing that can happen in life is beyond me. We have gotten to the point that we expect anyone with authority in government or business to foresee every possible thing that could go wrong and protect us from it, even if the problem is our own stupidity or negligence. Yes, there are many times that an entity's negligence requires them to make it right, to take care of those injured. In those cases, those responsible should pay a fair price for it, no argument there. This is not one of those times because lest we forget, this was an act of war, a sneak attack by enemies of our nation. To hold anyone responsible other than the perpetrators is wrong.

Did the victims and survivors of Pearl Harbor sue the hell out of everyone because no one saw the attack coming? No, because during that period of our history people knew and accepted the fact that no one can protect you from everything. They also had honor. They waded into that inferno of death, destruction, and personal danger in Pearl Harbor to help their comrades and fellow human beings the same as people in New York did. The difference is that they thought of it as their duty and responsibility for their fellow man. They accepted the risks and consequences with honor. They did not want nor expect additional payment for it; they walked away with pride that they had helped their neighbors. They did not run to a lawyer the first chance they got and demand that someone pay lots of money to them because it was not their fault this happened and they have suffered because of it. No, they had honor, duty, and pride. Somehow, somewhere since we have lost that and replaced it with a belief that we are entitled to live our lives without a single rough spot in the road, or by God someone has to pay dearly for it.

I am going on record here that in the unlikelihood, something from my time at the World Trade Center kills me tomorrow; it is not the fault of my employer, New York City, the owner of the World Trade Center, federal government, or anyone else. I chose to go and help and was honored to have gone. For anyone in my family to sue over it would only taint my memory.

There was only one way of protecting the rescuers who did not have immediate access to respiratory protection (let us not forget the firefighters did have access) on September 11 and a few days afterwards. That was for Mayor Giuliani or Governor Pataki to tell them they could not try to rescue anyone and to leave until the respiratory supplies became available. The firefighters, police, and other rescuers would have killed them if they tried that. I saw the efforts to find victims two weeks later and they would have still killed you then if you tried to stop them.

I realize that my observations and opinions are not going to make me very popular with some of the people who read this, especially firefighters. Throwing stones at heroes is not a good way to endear you to anyone, but I feel it needs said because I believe it to be true. The truth always comes out somewhere in the end and I know I am not the only one who shares this opinion. Many of the people who were there with me also have the same feelings. I know because we discussed it.

However, the facts that I have presented here in no way take away from the heroic deeds of these rescuers. I have said repeatedly throughout this book that many of them are people of extraordinary courage, strength, and honor. They selflessly put their lives on the line September 11 and the weeks after to save others and performed terrible tasks that most of us could not handle. They are truly heroes and deserve our respect and gratitude for those actions.

I believe that three groups are responsible for these people having lung damage because of the work at Ground Zero. First to blame are the agencies that decided to limit the experts in personal safety, experts such as OSHA, NIOSH, and others to perform only in a 'consultation' mode instead of enforcement. Had OSHA been able to enforce the safety rules that pertain to almost every other worker in this country, virtual elimination of these cases was the most likely result. Sure, there are firefighters and others that suffered personal injuries during those first few days, especially on September 11. Unfortunately, most of those were unavoidable. No one had expected those buildings to collapse or had prepared for it. However, the health damage after that time did not have to occur.

OSHA did a commendable job of getting respirators to the workers, demonstrating how to wear them, and encouraging them to do so. OSHA was even willing to give people with beards respirators, something they would never do in any other scenario. They felt that any protection was better than nothing was and they were willing to take their victories in small increments. OSHA had respirator stations set-up around the site and had four-wheel vehicles that would travel anywhere on the site to bring respirators out to those that needed them. We called them to come out to our areas on dozens of occasions. The only thing they could not do was to make the recovery workers wear them. That was not their call unfortunately.

Here are a few statistics to back up what I am saying about OSHA's efforts. These statistics are available to the public on OSHA's website. (OSHA.GOV)

1) *Conducted an initial assessment of the site within 24 hours of the attack to identify hazards and potential health and safety risks involved with the rescue/recovery efforts. OSHA had a staff in their World Trade Center office in Building Six. They evacuated along with everyone else, but came back and went to work assessing the situation after the towers collapsed.*

2) *Distributed more than 113,000 respirators from September 13, 2001 through February 6, 2002. Approximately 4,000 were distributed daily during the first weeks after the attack at fixed locations and one mobile unit. Respirator stations were located at the World Trade Center site, FDNY mustering point at World's fair Marina in Queens, and initially at the Staten Island landfill.*

3) *Along with my company, they initiated private-sector support for a respiratory protection program, generating donations of resources and equipment from Mine Safety Appliance (MSA), 3M, and other companies.*

4) *Conducted fit testing of negative-pressure respirators for FDNY and assisted contractors with that testing for their employees and other rescue workers.*

5) *Took over 3,600 bulk and air samples for metals, asbestos, silica, and other volatile organic compounds. (I can personally attest to asbestos sampling, as I wore an OSHA sample pump for eight hours myself and they provided the site wide testing results to us every other day).*

6) *Provided around the clock monitoring of the site hand-in-hand with us for a month to identify and alert workers to safety and health hazards. That equates to over 6,000 eight-hour shifts their personnel worked at the World Trade Center.*

The agencies controlling the site should never have allowed this situation to exist once they were organized and obtained supplies, which was in the first few days. I will admit that this was an extraordinary circumstance and there was not enough time to follow most safety rules when there was a possibility of people being trapped and alive. However, we are not talking about having meetings, training sessions, and long delays. It only took a five-minute training session and pick-up and delivery to the work area was available. In addition, it takes only seconds to put one on. Therefore, any argument that it would slow the rescue efforts is invalid.

The FDNY, NYPD, PAPD, and other agencies and contractors are also responsible for not taking the stand that their employees were going to wear them and enforcing the rules. For any other employer, a citation for willful negligence under federal OSHA standards for ignoring the known danger and condoning these unsafe practices awaited them. They are going to have employees and their families lives ruined because of these preventable illnesses. On top of that additional tragedy from this disaster, it is going to cost billions of dollars to get these people treatment, pay workers' compensation to them, and settle the inevitable lawsuits that are coming. In the cases of federal, states, and city employees, guess who is going to pay for it. You, me, and the citizens of New York will.

Finally, yet importantly on the blame list are the individual firefighters, police officers, construction workers, and others. You knew better, were told repeatedly, and for whatever your reasons made a personal decision to not wear protection. You would put them on when we told you why you needed them and took them off when we walked away. You threw

197

them by the hundreds into the debris pile, most of them never worn, and then
you walked into the smoke, steam and dust and worked all day breathing it
all in. Some of you played the big shot in front of your friends when you
unloaded your attitude onto us, letting us know that 'no one tells me what to
do.'

I knew that after this was over we would hear lots of excuses about
how no one made you wear them, how no one told you this could happen, no
one told you it was bad for your health, and we are hearing these 'it is
someone else's fault' complaints every week now. Lawyers are telling us
someone else is to blame as well and it seems it is always the fault of the ones
with lots of money. The truth is that in spite of being informed of the
dangers and provided with protection, you ignored it. Take some
responsibility for your own actions.

FDNY, you were the worst of the offenders and you knew better than
anyone else did. You train for it and it is an everyday part of your lives.
You have the best equipment money can buy, yet now you have firefighters
with their lungs damaged badly enough from their work at Ground Zero that
they may never work again. It more than likely has shortened their lives.
You have some hard questions to ask and answer of yourselves. You need to
look at yourselves instead of pointing the finger of blame at others.

I am not saying every one of the workers is at fault because that is
certainly not the case. There were many offenders, but not everyone was
ignoring the warnings and advice. I feel sorry for all of the rescuers who
have lung problems from trying to rescue victims those first few days after
the attack when it was difficult to get a respirator onto everyone. You should
receive any medical and financial assistance you need to maintain the quality
of life you had before. I am sorry so may others have injured their lungs now
as well. It was so unnecessary and avoidable. You and I know that many of
you simply would not listen to the many groups that were telling you to
wear them for your own good. OSHA, NIOSH, NYEPA, FEMA, Red
Cross, and many more of these agencies tried.

29

Two Million Bullets

October 24

The firefighters and recovery teams located and removed several more victims' remains today. I do not know exactly how many, but there was a lot of activity in my area as well as the others. I witnessed a few victims carried out. Those seemed to be civilians based on the lack of ceremony. There were dozens and dozens of people standing for hours on the debris pile, many were right in the middle of the smoke from the fires below. I do not understand why they feel it necessary to gather these crowds of 30 to 60 or more to stand there for hours. I also do not know how they can breathe in the smoke for so long. Many of them never wear a respirator, some only part of the time. I cannot take it more than a minute or so when the wind shifts the smoke plume in my direction. I have to put on my respirator quickly to keep from choking.

I have resolved to keep myself safe and deal with the issues from a safe distance until I leave in a few days. I have repeatedly tried to fix these ongoing situations with people in danger and to no avail most of the time. With that said, I cannot justify taking any more chances with my life. I tried to stick to that resolution today and take it safe and easy. Nevertheless, I still could not stand by and let some things continue without attempting to stop it at least. The best laid plans of mice and men...

A few of our crew spent a lot of time in Matt Carney's area today, the Tully work zone near WTC Buildings Five and Six. We were looking for small arms ammunition of all things. This search resulted from an unexpected incident in that area yesterday. An ironworker was cutting a piece of steel with an acetylene torch when he heard a loud bang and felt something strike his cheek. Further investigation revealed that a piece of shrapnel from a live bullet he had set off with the hot torch struck him. Fortunately, it was not a serious injury. Now that this has happened, the contractor tells us that ammunition has been going off for a week or more and there are 1,700,000 live rounds scattered in that area, somewhere. We heard earlier that the ammo, which belongs to the US Customs service, had been in WTC Six. We did not know that it might have spread this far from that building. Our search did not turn up any bullets lying on top of the ground, but one of our crewmembers did find a melted glob of them in another area nearby. This is a perfect example of the unknown dangers that lurk around us all of the time here. Lord knows what else is in here that we do not know about yet. We can only hope this was an isolated incident. We stopped the contractor from using the torch in that area. Matt had them start hauling the steel beams a hundred yards further away from the ammunition before resuming the torch cutting operation.

We did have some fun teasing Matt over it though. We were taking turns informing him what a lousy safety representative he is for being the only one of us to have a subcontractor shot. He took the ribbing in stride, though we really harassed him at times. At least we are still able to keep some of our sense of humor. If we lose that, I am afraid we are all going to end up in psychotherapy.

This afternoon, New York City had another major catastrophe in Manhattan when some multi-story scaffolding collapsed. We knew something big had happened because the firefighters began running from everyplace to their vehicles and sped off the site by the dozens. It got a little dangerous as they left because they were driving excessively fast down the site roads, particularly West Street. There are hundreds of people on the site at any given time and as most of us are pedestrians, these roads are our walkways. I had to hurry myself to get out of the way of an ambulance during this emergency exodus. It turned out to be a very serious accident. We heard five people perished and a dozen or more were seriously injured.

The fact that the FDNY had to send so many responders from the site during this incident and a few others brings up some questions we have often discussed among ourselves about why so many firefighters and their vehicles have to be at the site all of the time. There are firefighters by the hundreds and at least fifty vehicles at the site at any given time during the day. They just seem to be standing by most of the time, sitting along the roads at their temporary stations or standing out on the debris pile. It is an everyday occurrence to observe 60 to 70 firefighters standing in the smoke and dust for several hours as they just watch other crews search for bodies. It seems to us that most of them risk exposure to the danger of injury, not to mention breathing in God knows what along with the smoke and dust, all for no apparent reason other than to be here. It seems so unnecessary to have this many people and vehicles here if they are not actively involved in the recovery.

The FDNY has so many vehicles parked on the site that in many areas and streets it has become difficult for other vehicles to maneuver through them. The corner of West and Liberty Streets is a virtual FDNY parking lot of fire engines, rescue vehicles, and cars. Those fire trucks take up a lot of space that is very limited because of the debris on the streets and all of the heavy equipment and trucks needed to clean it up. In addition to all of the parked vehicles, it seems there is a steady parade of FDNY officials in cars driving up and down the passable roads. They usually have passengers, so they are either toting dignitaries around or giving tours. The congestion on West Street makes it necessary that I look in every direction at least twice before I try to cross it. Our crew discussed on several occasions the need to reduce the amount of FDNY personnel in the work area. We understand that many of them feel a need to be here because of their lost comrades, however for **safety reasons**, the FDNY needs to start reducing the amount of personnel here.

However, not all of the vehicles belong to the FDNY. The NYPD has many parked and driving back and forth as well. They need to eliminate some of those, too. There is not an obvious reason that I know of for all of these vehicles to be here in the way.

As far as personnel numbers on the site, the difference I see is that the police officers all seem to be busy guarding a building or checkpoint. They do not appear to just be here on standby.

This afternoon I stood and watched as the construction crew pulled a very large section of a steel column out of the rubble of WTC Tower Two. The grappler wrapped its jaws around the column and pulled back and forth until it broke free of the other debris in the pile. Once free, the operator swung it over and set it onto one of the flat bed semi-trucks. After all of this time buried under the debris, it still has a deep and distinctive cherry red glow and is still hotter than Hades on the Fourth of July. Once the grappler deposited it onto the truck trailer, one of the ironworkers began spraying it down with a fire hose. As soon as the water made contact with the steel, steam began billowing and jetting in every direction. It was incredible in its intensity and made a loud, eerie hissing sound. After a few minutes of drenching the steel with the water, it was still so hot that even standing ten feet away I could feel the heat on my face. When the water stream was directed to another spot on the beam, the area just sprayed would dry up almost instantaneously, leaving only slight wisps of rising steam. When the drops of water would hit a hot spot again, they would instantly begin to dance around until disappearing in a super-heated puff of steam. It took over ten minutes to cool that beam down enough to allow the ironworkers to safely chain it down on the truck for transport. It is six weeks after the attack and the temperature of the material underneath the surface of the debris pile is still very close to its melting point. The intensity and tenacity of the fires below is still incredible after all of this time.

The rest of the shift was mostly uneventful. I spent a lot of time talking to people I have met and carefully inspecting my areas. I went into the 90 West and World Financial Center Buildings to check on my crews, however I took it slow and easy. I stayed away from areas that were still obviously dangerous inside. I took a few discrete photos here and there. I took several photos of the cross in the middle of West Street for my Mom. She told me that she had cried the first time she had seen it shown on TV and asked me to get a picture of it for her.

I believe I saw Bill Gates walking down Liberty Street towards Battery Park today. The man was talking with a few people that appeared important and as I was not positive it was Bill Gates, I did not attempt to get an autograph. He sure looked like Bill Gates though and I would have loved to ask him to sign a blank check for me. I am sure he has probably heard that joke more often than he can stand.

Weather wise it was sunny, warm, and a beautiful day. It is hard to believe the weather is this nice so close to November. I have not worn my jacket for most of the week and was actually too warm one day even though I was only wearing a short-sleeved shirt.

After work today I went out for my usual walk and trip to the store. When I walked into Times Square, I saw a group of people gathered around the front windows of the ABC Studio. I have found that whenever a crowd gathers here you can be sure that something interesting is taking place. Whether it is a celebrity, someone performing, using plastic buckets as a set of drums, or some idiot arrested, it is usually noteworthy. I walked across the street to check it out and found out the crowd was watching Barbara Walters do the 20/20 television show. We could hear and see her while she was taping the show. She was sitting on the 20/20 set, which was only about thirty feet from the windows. I watched for a few minutes until she announced a commercial break in the show. During the break, she told all of us gathered around hello and thanks for coming. I did not stick around to see if she came out after the show was over. I wandered around a few blocks in a different direction tonight to see if there was anything else of interest. Nothing caught my attention as being out of the ordinary so I bought something to eat and went back to the room to make my telephone call to Janice and watch a little TV until I went to sleep. Although I have tomorrow off, I am exhausted and will probably be asleep early.

Afterthoughts

*As it turned out, we were not the only people thinking about all the firefighters on the site. On November 1, less than a week after we left, Mayor Giuliani issued an order to greatly reduce the crews of firefighters and police officers that could be on site per shift for **safety reasons**. Although Mayor Giuliani had their best interests in mind, he underestimated the FDNY reaction that led to one of the sites most ugly moments as they staged an angry protest the next day at Ground Zero. Fueled by raw emotion, they marched onto the site in defiance of police orders and subsequently committed assault and battery on several NYPD officers. Several firefighters ended up arrested and led off to jail. As we watched it all on the evening news, I commented to my wife that many people at the site had seen this coming a mile away.*

After a few more days of protests and talks between the mayor and city officials, the number that could be on site was increased. The city dropped the criminal charges and things seemed to settle down.

It is admirable how the FDNY wanted to bring their entire missing crews home for a proper burial. Their goal was to help the families and their own department to get some comfort in knowing that they had done everything they could to accomplish that awful task. I have said that many times in this book. Nevertheless, I have also said that it is not admirable to needlessly place people at risk to do so. You cannot let emotions drive you to make unwise decisions and take foolhardy risks. Mayor Giuliani wisely listened to the experts and recognized that this was the case here and attempted to do the right thing by correcting it. Unfortunately, the ever-

present emotions and politics at the site again dictated the outcome as it had throughout my time there. Common sense and safety once again returned to the bottom of the priorities list.

As far as that unruly march, protest, and fistfight at the site, I only have one comment about it. Fame and admiration are fleeting in our world today. Today's heroes can become tomorrow's zeroes so easily. FDNY you stand as heroes to the entire civilized world and your actions on September 11 and the days of rescue following, more than earned you that title. The November 2 debacle blackened your eye, however you seem to have healed with little scarring. A multitude of your ranks that are now standing up in public denouncing the actions of their city during this tragic and unforeseen act of war and threatening to bankrupt her coffers may be more injury than even heroes of your status can endure. FDNY, you now have all of America on your side; do not allow that to change because of greed. Duty and honor was your motto on that tragic day, it should be from here on out.

Those incredible fires underneath the debris continued to burn unabated until December, on the 100th day until finally extinguished.

30

What a Place

October 25

I set the alarm and got up early for breakfast with Randy, Mark Spitzer, and one of the other guys on the night shift. We walked a few blocks down the street to a bar that they have frequented a few times. At 8:00 in the morning, this place was crowded and busy serving breakfast as well as drinks, with a lot more alcohol consumed than eggs and bacon. I ordered breakfast while they went with the beer. As they had just completed their twelve hours of night shift duty, this was their unwind time. We hung out and talked for an hour or so about the job and how tired we were all of the time. It is clear that they are just as fed up as the rest of us on the day shift with the way things are going. They have the same problems with the firefighters and subcontractors as we do. For some reason, they seem to have more problems with the police than we have experienced.

Night shift sounds very interesting, however it seems spooky as well. I am not sure if I would like working in the shadows of the lights. I guess it has its pros and cons. I do not know which would be better, the dangers lurking hidden in the dark or seeing it all in living color as I do everyday. Almost all of the power is cut off in the surrounding buildings, so temporary, diesel-powered light plants illuminates everything they do. They have not entered as many of the buildings that I have due to the lack of lighting. I told them to go into the 90 West Building if they can, it is incredible inside. We swapped a few stories, paid our bills, and they headed for their rooms for needed sleep while I headed off into downtown Manhattan.

I wandered around and looked at the sight again. I found a souvenir shop and bought two of our girls some T-shirts. For a few hours, I just walked around the immediate neighborhood. What a neighborhood it is, too; Times Square, Broadway, Radio City Music Hall, the Garment District, Rockefeller Center, Trump Tower, Fifth Avenue, and more.

As I returned to Times Square, I noticed a small crowd had formed along the curb close to the corner where my hotel is located. There was a small crate sitting in the street where they were gathered and as I have said before, a crowd usually means something interesting. My instincts were right again. No sooner than my curiosity had gotten the best of me, Bill Gates walked up and climbed onto the crate. I guess he needed the crate so the crowd could see him as well for filming while he introduced his new product, Windows XP. I took two pictures and then continued on my way. Well, that was Mr. Gates at the site yesterday. I should have asked him for his autograph then.

I stopped to eat lunch at the Olive Garden in Times Square. I just took my time and watched the hordes of people pass by in the course of their day. What a unique city. Almost every type of people that you can imagine walked past my window observation point. Some with spiked hair, purple hair, tattoos from one end to the other, and some with their nose, eyebrows, or belly buttons pierced. There were straight, gay and lesbian couples walking hand in hand. A few people seemed to be in between genders as one person that walked by my window looked for the entire world like a petite female in a mini skirt, only as she passed my window, it became obvious that *he* had a very bad case of five o'clock shadow. People of every nationality, color, sexual orientation, and religious denomination were walking peacefully side by side. What I found noteworthy is that all of them were going about their daily lives and business without causing trouble with anyone else.

I am not a prejudiced person by nature and upbringing except for scammers, child molesters, and people who cause harm to others for no apparent reason, to name a few. I believe that you should live in a manner that makes you happy as long as it does not hurt others, you pay your own way, and you do not try to force your lifestyle or beliefs on others. As far as I am concerned, matters about color, ethnic origin, sexual orientation, religion, or anything else that seems to get narrow-minded people upset are irrelevant as long as you are a good person. From what I have experienced here to this point, New Yorkers, at least in Manhattan, seem to think like that as well.

New York is definitely the melting pot, as it is called, of all those human differences and anything else you can think of and all seem to get along just fine with each other. I have not seen anyone harassed or bothered because of his or her differences from anyone else. I like it here and I feel comfortable almost every place I go. The only time I get a little nervous is when I am not positive where I am or the few times that I saw fights or the aftermath of some crimes that took place. Even then, it had nothing to do with race, religion, etc., only that those involved were either violent or criminals. Unfortunately, criminals, idiots, and punks come in every color and race. I think some of these people with so much hatred toward one group or another should spend some time on the same streets that I have the last few weeks. I am sure it is not like this in all places of New York City, however Manhattan seems to have it together.

After lunch, it looked like rain so I went back to the hotel for a nap instead of taking a ferry past the Statue of Liberty as I had planned. I slept like a rock for a few hours and had I not had to pick up my laundry before they closed I probably would have slept until morning. The laundry is down the street from the hotel and reminds me of one you would see on the Jerry Seinfeld show. It is in a row of brownstone houses, restaurants, and other small shops that have become so familiar to me from various television shows. A nice oriental couple owns it and they do a great job at a cheap price.

Cleaned and folded, our clothes are finished in a few hours. Best laundry service I ever used.

The laundry service at the hotel is good, too. The only drawback is the price, which is way out of my affordability range. It costs eight dollars to get a pair of jeans washed, three dollars for a T-shirt, and two dollars for a pair of socks! My bill the first week was over $95.00. The company was paying for it, nevertheless, that was enough of that. I could have bought brand new work socks for less than the two bucks a pair they were charging to wash them. As it is, I am wearing a hole in them within a week because of all the walking I do everyday. The convenience of not having to haul it back and forth is nice, but not at that price.

After dropping my laundry back at the room, I walked around for a while more. I thought about going to the site with the night crew and pulling a 24-hour shift. I really wanted to experience the site at night and to hang out with the crewmembers I do not see more than a few minutes each day. Especially Randy and Mark. I do not know Mark very well, but I like him already. He is smart, funny, and good at his job. Randy thinks highly of him and that is good enough for me, since I trust his judgment. In years gone past, I would have jumped at the chance to spend some extra time exploring somewhere as significant as this place. However, I do not have the energy and the desire has left me. I decided that I would not make it for the 24 hours no matter how hard I tried. I decided to watch TV and then go to bed early instead. It would be my luck that in the morning Stew would inform us that the plans have changed and we are staying longer. I would be a walking zombie until my next day off when I could catch up on my sleep. Hell, I think I might be mistaken for a zombie now as it is.

31

Anniversary of Mixed Emotions

October 26

I tossed and turned all night, it seemed, and awoke well before the alarm was set to go off. My restlessness must have been the anticipation of today, my one-month Ground Zero anniversary and if all goes as planned, my last day working at the site. Usually my exhaustion overrides any lingering thoughts or problems I may have and I sleep so sound that a tornado would not wake me. I am physically still exhausted, however my mind is right back into hyperactive drive, same as every morning since the day I first walked onto the site. It is amazing how your mind adapts to your particular situation. Although I normally sleep only 4-6 hours each night and am an early riser, I generally need coffee and several minutes to kick start my brain into action. Here it is opposite. I have to coax my body to move off the bed and into action so it can catch up to its onboard computer.

The ride down to the site this morning seemed to take longer and was more quiet than usual. I think we were all lost in our own thoughts about whether we were actually leaving or not. My thoughts ranged from how much I looked forward to seeing Janice for the first time in a month, to wanting to finish what I came here for. We need a trip home or at least a few days off to see our families; it is a physical and mental necessity as far as I am concerned. However, I am sad about leaving because I think there are so many more accomplishments we could make. I feel that we could succeed at getting a safety culture established and complete the work safely if just given the chance.

Once we parked and walked to the Command Center, Stew gathered the night shift and our crew together for what turned out to be our last morning meeting. Stew began by thanking all of us for dropping what we were doing, putting our lives on hold, and heading to New York when he called for our help. He said that we have all done a great job and should be proud of what we have accomplished. He went on to say that we had all been an important part of one of the worst tragedies to ever strike America and had experienced some extremely difficult things, but we had held up well and continued our mission without complaint. However, he added that some of those difficult experiences may bother us further on down the road and we may need to talk to someone. Our company is offering counseling for any of us who may think that they need it. He encouraged us to take advantage of it because there were so many emotional and terrible experiences here. I think that I am all right mentally for the time being and will be able to work through any lingering issues myself. There is no doubt that I will never be the same man as I was before I came. A reorganization of my emotions, beliefs, and entire mental makeup has occurred.

The original plan that called for Randy and a few others to stay for an additional week has changed. According to Stew, everyone is finished today and leaving this weekend. This is the end of the night shift, no work even tonight. There goes any chance I had of spending any time with Randy and Mark on the night shift. Our instructions are to leave New York tomorrow or Sunday at the latest. The flight they instructed me to book earlier this week leaves tomorrow around noon.

My plan today was to keep myself safe and just walk around the perimeter, watching the work from a distance and saying my good-byes. However, I did not stick to that plan for very long. The urge to go out into the middle of it and look around one last time was too strong. I felt that this was my last chance to experience history, no matter how bad it is. I also wanted to make sure I always would remember the sights, sounds, feel, and everything else that goes with this place. I walked all over Ground Zero, the twisted, burning mass of devastation and death. The sights still stagger the imagination, even after so many hours and days of standing right in the epicenter of tragedy. I walked out into the middle of the WTC Tower Two debris field and stood for several minutes just soaking up all I could.

I spent most of the day walking around and looking at everything, no matter how many times I have seen it already. I visited some of the places that have significance for me in one-way or another. Some of these places have damage that is just so incredible and I notice something new each time. Other spots of interest to me are where something happened out of the ordinary. I had sworn to my coworkers and supervisor this week that I was not going to put myself in any position of risk these final days, however there are some things that seemed to justify my taking those risks to see them again. As I was working my way into one of those dangerous places I just could not resist seeing one more time, my supervisor noticed me and called on the radio to remind me to be careful. He knew what I was doing because he has been doing the same today.

One of the areas I spent a lot of time in this afternoon was around World Trade Center Buildings Four and Five. The construction crews had built a ramp down into the area between these two buildings a few weeks ago to allow trucks and machines to get in and remove some of the street level concrete deck and plaza area that are heavily damaged. This ramp goes down into the underground mall which has some stores completely buried in debris, but others still visible. One of these is a clothing store that had lost its façade and had part of the roof torn off in the attack. Looking into this store for the first time weeks ago, I had noticed what looked to be a couple of bodies lying on the floor and initially it shook me up pretty good. I had maneuvered around for a closer look and realized they were only store mannequins and my racing heart settled down some. The mannequins were clothed and covered with debris and dust. It was very hard for me to distinguish whether they were real people or not. I am sure that a rescue worker that first day would have had to go in there to be positive. This area, as most of the areas that have been searched, has information painted nearby in fluorescent paint to keep others from searching again. It is common to see ' searched on 9/12, 1300 hours' for example, painted over a window or doorway. However, not all of these areas appear to be marked in that manner and I am never sure what I may find when I walk into an area.

There are other stores in the mall and all suffered heavy damages. The inventory is scattered across the floors for the most part, but some is still in place on shelves and counters. Advertising posters are on the walls and one even has an open sign hanging on the remnants of a door. It amazes me to see the complete destruction of everything in some cases and in others, a row of bottles on a shelf or a single mannequin out of a dozen remain standing upright in the middle of it. There are many scenes like those throughout the area. As far as I know, all of the people that were on these floors of the WTC complex at the time of the attack managed to escape safely. These locations being the closest to the exits and subway tunnels for escape, as I understand it. However, no one really knew where the victims were located when the towers fell and there was a concentrated effort to search these lower floors because if people had attempted to escape through here during the collapse, they would have had the best chance for survival. There are areas down here that have not collapsed and some not damaged at all beyond the ever-present dust. There are restaurants, banks (vaults would be a good place to take refuge), and other shops on those lower floors. For anyone trapped in here, restaurants meant a source of food and fluids. Access to those would have greatly extended their survival time. As the world knows now, there was not anyone found alive after September 12.

The recovery crews are still entering and searching these underground areas and stairwells whenever they are able to gain access to them. These types of searches have continued daily during my entire time here. It is a common sight to see a dozen firefighters climbing down a ladder into a small opening to a lower floor. They are equipped with high-powered flashlights, radios, and other tools. Of course, they are looking for the dead and assessing structural damages now. I have not had the opportunity to go on one of these trips underground with them, but some of our engineers have accompanied them. The engineers have told us how eerie it is underneath with nothing other than flashlights to guide them through a maze of tunnels and around piles of debris. They said that the damage extends several stories underground in some places and there are cars, a subway train, and many other things deep below the debris pile, invisible to those of us above ground.

In my conversations with the rescue crews I have heard more than once that their biggest fear besides their own safety is to finally get access to an area like these and find the bodies of people who have obviously died while waiting to be rescued. It is bad enough having to recover the bodies of those killed outright, but to know that they managed to stay alive, were waiting for you to rescue them, and died before you could get there would be devastating. It would emotionally crush everyone on site, the families, and the nation. It would be more than we could handle.

In the area between World Trade Center Building Five, is a concrete plaza that had led into the main plaza or common area in the middle of all the WTC Buildings. This main plaza is where the gold ball sculpture is located. While I was looking this area over again and saw the concrete slabs lying on the ground, I recalled the incident that happened last week. As I mentioned above, this plaza covered part of the underground mall. Severely damaged, some of it already removed, and other areas barricaded to keep people out. One of these barricaded sections was along the south side of WTC Building Five. This section was a severely undermined, unstable, and dangerous concrete deck. In addition, WTC Five had large pieces of steel beams and debris hanging from the roof directly over this area. Our group and others continually informed everyone in the morning and afternoon meetings to stay out of this area. Unfortunately, this was also one of the best locations to see most of the site work activities taking place and was a magnet for visitors, officials, and most everyone else. These people ignored the warnings, barricades, danger, and walked out to the edge of this deck at every opportunity. Our safety representatives assigned to this area were continually attempting to chase these people out of there, most of the time to no avail.

One evening last week, some officers of the NYPD, ignoring the barricades and warning signs, led one of their 'tours' out onto the edge of the deck and stood there watching the work. There were about ten people and one of our crew advised them of the danger and asked them to please leave. As was usually the case, they ignored him like the barricades and stayed where they were. Finally, after apparently seeing all of what they wanted to, they left the area. Fifteen minutes later, the portion of the plaza they had been standing on collapsed due to its own weight and condition and fell twenty feet or more below into the mall area. This was another tragedy avoided by pure luck and timing. I guess if you do not have enough common sense to listen to the experts, a little luck and timing come in handy.

I looked over all of the remaining WTC Buildings at length. WTC Buildings Five and Six are still standing for the most part, though almost destroyed inside by the fires that resulted from the attack. Part of WTC Building Four had collapsed those first few days. In all of these buildings you can see window blinds flapping in the breeze, partially melted computers sitting on blackened desks, offices just the way they had been when evacuated. Now most every surface has either a black charcoal look or gray dust covering. There are not many windows left in any of the buildings except WTC Building Five. It has a bookstore and donut shop on the first floor that escaped most of the inferno and is not as heavily damaged as the upper floors. Everything sits in these stores and offices just as they were on September 11. It is easy to visualize their employees going about their normal daily business routines and customers sitting relaxed at the tables enjoying their coffee and donuts. Then at 8:46 AM, that first plane slammed into WTC Tower One and any sense of normalcy in their lives changed forever.

At WTC Building Six, you can see what is left of the OSHA offices that faced WTC Tower One. Our OSHA peers that worked in this office on September 11 had pointed them out to us, where they were during the first strike and mesmerized us with their stories of the aftermath. Tales of their horror at watching as the employees on the upper floors of WTC Tower One, with no hope of escaping the raging inferno, jumped and crashed to their deaths onto the streets and surrounding buildings below. They told of us of the evacuation of their building, running for their lives during the collapse, and their fear and uncertainty of their own survival. We listened as they told how they returned when the choking dust cloud had subsided, only to find both WTC Towers reduced to ruin and the other buildings engulfed in flames. They spent untold hours afterward helping the injured to treatment centers and desperately searching for any other survivors.

There were many offices of other agencies and businesses in these buildings and we have heard their occupants tell similar stories. I believe that these people and their unselfish acts of courage have been overlooked in the news reporting of this day as most of it has been focused on the heroics of the FDNY. Untold numbers of ordinary citizens and employees witnessed unspeakable horror, stared death in the face, and pushing fear aside walked right back into Hell to help in any way they possibly could. Many of them lost friends, coworkers, and family as well and have terrible memories that will haunt them to their dying days. So many of them performed extraordinary acts of heroism and saved countless lives.

In my opinion, they are American heroes in every sense of the word. They deserve as much respect, adulation, and thanks as anyone else that was there that day. Let us never forget that it was not their jobs to risk their well being to place themselves in danger, they are not firefighters or police officers, but accountants, waiters, laborers, and everyday ordinary people. They could have run to safety and stayed away like so many others did, and no one could have blamed them. However, they did not run, they stood up in the face of death and did what they could.

We will never know how many heroes there were and how many heroic acts took place that day, as many of the witnesses and heroes did not survive to tell us. Other heroes that did survive will keep their deeds to themselves out of modesty or an unwillingness or inability to return to those painful recesses of their minds and relive the horror. Ordinary people that were caught up in a firestorm and had challenges and life and death choices thrust upon them. They chose to rise to greatness.

There are so many places that I made sure to see again today. Buildings like 90 West Street, the World Financial Center, the Winter Garden, and FDNY Firehouse 10 all have memories or are unique in some way to me. Many are so different since a month ago, now cleaned up, windows boarded, and portions torn down. However, most still hold pieces that send me back to that first time I saw them or to those incidents that my involvement in etched them into my memory.

I have many of those memories with the 90 West Building. Although many hours spent toiling in salvaging this building have passed, barely evident is a dent of accomplishment thus far. Many of the floors, although now shored up to prevent collapse, still are nothing more than burned out remnants of what they were. Wires, piping, and ceiling portions still hang precariously. The floors with gaping holes and some slanted towards now barricaded holes in the walls are still dangerous areas to avoid. The thick dust now trampled down into trails by the comings and goings of the work crews. I have left my footprints all over on a dozen or more of these floors, fleeting evidence of my presence in history.

I stood on the sixth floor and looked through a jagged wall opening, out at the remaining portions of WTC Tower Two. It was an incredible sight, a photograph of ruins framed by a devastated wall. I wandered around in there for an hour, thinking, remembering, and examining it all again. I will think of this building and my experiences here often. The shock of seeing the inside for the first time, exhausting stair climbs to check on my Polish friends, and my explorations of the devastation guided only by the beam of my small flashlight, all such vivid memories. I believe that others and I have cheated death during our time in this old building. There are so many pitfalls and danger lurking in the dark, waiting to make one of us the next victim of this tragedy.

The World Financial Center Buildings have made quite a transformation in these four or five weeks. Removed now are the hundreds of broken windows and plywood now covers the openings. The domes on the towers that frame Liberty Street have been cleaned by the workers that caused me so much anguish as they slid from the tops down to the short rail circling the bottom. Although they were wearing harnesses and tied off to safety lines to prevent them from falling a dozen stories to the street below, it looked like a suicide mission to a safety representative who has a fear of falling. They had either a lot more courage or less sense than I do. Many offices are beginning to regain their old appearance as the removal of debris and dust and the upended filing cabinets and desks are set back into their place progresses. The foyers, once littered with the paper and thick dust that I waded through to climb the powerless escalator now have crews polishing the floors and erasing the evidence left behind by an act of evil. It is quickly returning to its former magnificence, a building worthy of the lofty title of World Financial Center. Yet, reminders of the terrible tragedy that unfolded here are still present. A main floor foyer corner still contains a few stretchers and stack of body bags waiting for the discovery of another victim. The body bags are particularly still haunting, bringing back the uneasy feeling in the pit of my stomach. I have seen many stacks of these bags everyday for weeks now as they are all around my area and the site. I have watched through tear-clouded eyes as honorable men who refuse to surrender to tragedy have filled them with the remains of victims and carried them away to impersonal morgues.

I stopped at Firehouse 10 or commonly called Ten House here. I looked at all the photographs of their lost firefighters and read several letters filling every available spot on its walls. The letters, cards, posters, and drawings come from people all over the world, but mostly school children. Crayon drawings of firefighters, flames, fire trucks, and flags are the most popular subjects. This station has become one of the many memorials that have sprung up throughout the site and it is without a doubt the best. Candles, flowers, crosses, and trinkets adorn a table set out on the sidewalk. They have a guest book for the thousands of people who visit here to sign their name and leave personal messages of grief, thanks, and encouragement. I took this opportunity to do the same. Around the corner of the station stands a metal statue of a firefighter waving an American flag. Donated by a high school, it has found its way here, the most fitting place in the world it could call home. It is a great work of art and a touching gesture. I took my chances of the NYPD confiscating my camera and got a photograph of it.

As I left Ten House, I noticed a lot of firefighter activity in the debris pile of WTC Tower Two. There were over a hundred people, mostly firefighters and search and rescue crews gathered around a few locations. It was obvious that they had found something they thought was significant as the crowd was much larger than usual. I stopped in front of the 90 West Building and watched the activity for a while, wondering if they had found a stairwell, void, or worse. After a few minutes I had my answer as ambulances began arriving and lining up in a row as near as they could get to the makeshift road into the pile where the flurry of activity was taking place. Eventually six ambulances lined up with their back doors facing the debris pile. I thought about continuing on my trip around the site, avoiding what I have watched so many times these weeks here, but I could not. Some voice inside said that it was too important not to watch it one last time. As the crews prepared to bring out the grisly results of their hours of searching and digging, a respectful silence fell over the entire area. I watched intently for what seemed to be a very long time as the recovery crews carried out the stretcher laden with the bodies of victims, one after another. At the start of the road leading out to the ambulances, they set the stretchers side by side in a neat line until there were seven. Six of those stretchers draped with American flags, their edges tucked neatly and lovingly underneath the body bags. Six firefighters and a civilian, found today after weeks of waiting.

While they were staging the stretchers for the trip to the ambulances, the firefighters, police officers, and construction workers formed lines along both sides of the road. I was standing on top of a debris pile and decided to stay where I was rather than walking the 30 yards or so to join in the line. There were dozens of us standing around the perimeter waiting to pay our respects to our fallen citizens.

The first stretcher carried out contained the body of the civilian and the firefighters did something that I think was callous and disrespectful. In my mind, it confirmed what I have heard many people discuss about their behavior these past weeks. This civilian was not placed into a body bag like the firefighter victims, just laid on top of a bag with another one draped over it to hide him or her from view. During the walk down the road, a wind gust caught the top body bag and it rose up, briefly exposing a portion of the charred corpse. The firefighters pulled the bag back over the body and continued to a spot past the lines of people and near the ambulances. Here they set the stretcher on the ground, gathered a few chunks of concrete from the debris and placed them on top of the body to hold the bag down. They left the stretcher there and walked back to the six-firefighter bodies.

Before the procession of the firefighter victims began, an FDNY chaplain led the crowd in a prayer ceremony. As six or eight firefighters began to carry each flag-draped stretcher slowly down the road, the firefighters and police officers snapped to attention and froze in a salute. When all six stretchers had reached the line of six ambulances, they were loaded one by one, each into their own ambulance.

As those ambulances began to drive slowly off the site, my thought returned to the stretcher containing the civilian. I looked to the spot I had seen them place it and sure enough, they had left it sitting on the ground as if he or she were an unwelcome guest at their ceremony. I watched as the crowd dispersed and most of the firefighters either went back to their temporary stations or resumed their search activities. A few stayed in the general vicinity of the body until 45 minutes or so until another ambulance arrived and this civilian was finally allowed the start of his or her trip home.

I have heard many people speak in disgust and anger of this type of behavior these last few weeks, however this is the first time that I have actually witnessed it for myself. Nothing special for a 'civilian', not even taking the time to put them inside the body bag or put them in an ambulance at the same time as the firefighters. However, they went the whole nine yards to make sure their people received the respect they deserved. It is just not right to treat someone that way. Every one of the people lost here is innocent victims and deserve treatment with the same respect and dignity as everyone else buried here, hero or not.

Well, I wanted to experience it all and now I have, no matter how much it pisses me off. I have certainly learned one thing and that is apparently the arrogance problem runs deeper than just the individual firefighters that I have encountered to this point.

After that disturbing episode, I continued on my trip throughout the site. I wandered around the perimeter of the buildings and looked over the damages. Scarring, in one form or another, covers the faces of many of the surrounding buildings. Besides the thousands of boarded up windows there is a range of deep gouges to superficial scratches and small to gaping holes in the sides. Oddly, there is not a pattern or consistency to the damages or what buildings received the brunt of it. Although all have affects in some form or another, one may have major structural damage and the one next to it only minor problems. Every one of them has dust damage throughout their interiors and bushels of paper in, around, or on top of them. Some surrounding buildings with offices and stores are yet untouched by clean-up crews, their content dust preserved as portraits of a historic moment in time.

The streets are much cleaner now, the destroyed vehicles have been loaded up and hauled off, and untold truckloads of paper, steel, and concrete removed to the landfill. However, carved holes from falling debris still mark the asphalt and street signs are still twisted and bent with their poles leaning away from the epicenter of the collapse. Subway signs have holes through them or hang by a single bolt, swaying in the breeze. Blue police barricades are set up on every street, blocking access to the public until someone can check identification to see if they belong inside. You can look in any direction and see those orange fluorescent signs painted on the walls of buildings to direct you to the temporary morgues and first aid stations or stating that a search was completed.

Posters, still taped onto walls, sign poles, and machines, some tattered and fading-still pleads for any information about missing loved ones. The faces in the colored photographs seem to be pleading for more time, as if a divine intervention, a miracle, is still just moments away. They are never going home to those that loved them. Their chance for a miracle has passed, but not for a lack of prayer, hope, and tremendous human effort to create one. God has other plans for them. I have seen them so many times, so many innocent lost souls. I have studied their faces and wondered of their stories, history, and families. Pausing to see them again ends with the return of the painful sadness that was as intense as it was that first day. I have spent many hours today revisiting it all.

During my trip around the site, I stopped and talked with the people I had come to know during my time at Ground Zero. Some I had had many conversations with and saw almost daily, others it may have been an encounter when we did not see eye to eye about their safety. All of them were part of this extraordinary effort and of my experience here and I wanted to say goodbye and tell them to keep safe. Some of these people meant a lot to me during my stay and I will never forget them. We went through a lot together.

Ray, the Bovis safety manager on site, was a great asset and is an excellent safety person. Ray and I talked several times a day and accomplished a lot together. Ray has a very difficult job to manage and he will handle in all in stride and professionally. I have spent more of my time with Ray working out problems than with anyone else on the site.

Mike, the Grace Company safety representative, was also good at his job and it was always an experience to talk with him. Mike is a native New Yorker who has a unique way of looking at life and tells some hilarious stories that always brightened my day. He also can talk the New York language that was a definite advantage. He could get more done with a few swear words and gestures than I could with a thousand words. Mike had his hands full in keeping his crew straight and safe, but he has done a great job and will continue giving it hell everyday.

Mario, who worked for both Grace and Verizon at the site, was a lot of fun. He would change into a hard hat with the logo of whatever company he was working with at that time of the day. It seemed like he was always wearing a different hard hat and I began to suspect he would change into his Verizon hat when he would see me coming to address something that either he or Grace might be doing wrong. He knew that I did not have any say in how Verizon performed their activities. He would say he was not working with the problem company now, then laugh and tell me he would fix it. He always took care of anything I asked him to and was about as friendly as you can get. I caught him doing things that were borderline acceptable safe practices all the time. He always owned up to it and never did them again. He must have worked eighteen hours a day, six or seven days a week for the entire time that I was there.

I looked up so many other good people this last day. The volunteers at the Red Cross and Salvation Army centers that took such good care of me. The guys directing the truck and machine traffic, what an outstanding job they did. Most people would have run from that complicated task, trucks moving in so many directions among hundreds of people walking around. These guys made it look so easy, and they were a pleasure to talk with over these weeks. I caught up with the foreman of the Polish crew and said goodbye. After our initial problems, he turned out to be a valuable asset in keeping his crew safe. I spoke to many individuals of the NYPD, FDNY, Army, and National Guard who looked out for us and were so friendly. The OSHA folks from Manhattan and the New York area who stayed on throughout our time there even though they had been through so much. All of them are wonderful people that answered the call to perform one of the hardest jobs on earth. I tried to talk to them all, shake their hands, and tell them what a great job they are doing.

As my shift was ending for the last time, I just stood beside the graveyard of the WTC Tower Two and reflected on what it all means. This month has been an overwhelming experience for me in so many ways. There is an overabundance of crippling pain, grief, and sadness here. Now etched onto the rescuers' faces are deep furrows and dark circles on the background of pale, tired skin. Their shoulders now slump forward from carrying the burdening weight of grief and despair. Physical changes that were not here a few weeks ago are now the portrait of the damage to their soul. These prematurely aged faces greet the newcomers, the unknowing, and tips them to the presence of something that lies much deeper. Until they spend countless hours beside them, listen to their tales of heroism, loss, and uncertainty; they will never fathom the depth of their profound anguish and sadness. It is to the bone.

The signs of lives extinguished are everywhere. A broken computer mouse peeking from under a beam, dozens of business papers swirling in miniature dust devils down West Street, and a single shoe, it's sole scarred from running desperately, its owner's soul gone here forever. All these sights are reminders that innocent people no different from I began that beautiful September morning unaware that fate awaited. All the while death was approaching for their rendezvous, guided by misguided men with dreams of burying them here. The anguish left is unbearable. I have witnessed its unmerciful grip on the family members of those dead, mourned as it sucked out the remnants of their lives, hopes, and dreams. It has left many of them paralyzed and sobbing on the corner where their life, future, and accomplishment once dwelled.

Sadness seems to ooze from the mountains and valley of debris. It almost seems as if this immense grief is a living, breathing, and palpable force. Through tragic circumstance, it has taken residence here. This unwelcome squatter has replaced the bottomless void left by the death of loved ones, collapse of once vibrant towers and anticipated futures. This soulless opportunist has taken these few acres of Manhattan, slipped into every nook and cranny and will call the sacred place home for untold generations to follow.

Unexpectedly, I have found another force during these weeks I have spent in these ruins. It is a quiet calm yet remarkable power, a spirit undeterred by grief, suffering, and shattered dreams. It seeks not to replace the grief and sorrow but only assist in making it survivable. It puzzled me somewhat during those first days here, its unwavering strength, purity, and effect having caught me off guard. Perhaps I have been too wrapped up in my own life to notice before or it lies dormant in most of us until circumstances call for its awakening. Whatever the case, it has touched and changed me in ways that I would never have imagined. It is simple and pure, a heavenly aura if you will, that comes from deep within the soul of man and gently touches those that need it so desperately. This force is the best of mankind itself, as close to what I imagine our Creator intended as I have ever witnessed. I will never forget this compassion and love for as long as I live.

It is almost time to leave and I find myself torn emotionally about leaving a job unfinished. I want to go home to see my wife, nevertheless a part of me says we should come back here and see it through to the end. They need us here, even if most of them do not realize it yet. This is a dangerous and monumental task and they need all the assistance they can muster. I think that most of us have these thoughts in the back of our minds and I have heard both Randy and Stew say the same. A sign of true safety professionals, I guess. However, it is not to be. We gave it our best shot and did some good things in spite of the resistance and attitudes we encountered.

Around 6:00 PM, the call came over our radios from our supervisor. He said "let's go home fellas, we have done everything that we can." It was a bittersweet walk, those four or five blocks to the Command Center. I stopped and looked at the 'cross' for the last time, contemplating its significance here and where some get their unshakable faith in the Creator, the belief that is all part of His plan and He is taking care of us even if we do not understand how or why. Even this unparalleled tragedy does not seem to cast any doubt in their hearts. The erecting of this cross was such an important task to many of the people here. They worked many hours preparing it for placement here in the middle of West Street. People of all religious faiths have gathered here many times to pray for peace, salvation, and things known only to them. Anyway you look at the cross, destruction surrounds it. The most dramatic view to me is the one I took today, looking southeast with the remnants of the WTC Tower Two façade rising behind it. Looking to the northeast, the background is the building where this cross, formed by chance or diving guidance, stood when the rain of roaring debris ceased its fall and deathly silence fell into its place. The building stands as a burned out and collapsing hulk. In the middle of this devastation stood this cross, two pieces of rust-coated steel that were once only part of the support structure of a building, hidden from the view of its occupants by walls of wood and plaster. How it ended up in this shape of a cross and standing upright in the midst of chaos is a question unanswered, however it has become a symbol of hope for people throughout the world. Whether I believe any of the rest of the religious significance or not, one thing I have learned from this cross and now believe to be true; humanity needs to believe in a greater, purer, and loving force because it gives us hope. Without hope, we have nothing.

We loaded up the vans for the last trip back to the Marriott. As we traveled this familiar road, we passed by the many security checkpoints, blew the horn at our unwavering support groups one last time, and left the acres of destruction, death, pain, and all the rest behind. Physically, my thirty days at Ground Zero are over. In my mind, heart, and soul, I will be there forever.

32

Leaving on a 'Jett' Plane

October 27

I am finally going home to see my lady for the first time in a month. I have been waiting for this for weeks now. I was up early as usual and did not have much time to waste before I left for the airport. I made sure I had everything packed up and ready to go before I took one more, quick trip through Times Square for another look. The place is busy even this early on a Saturday. Afterwards, I gathered up my stuff and checked out of the hotel. I caught a cab to the airport and the driver ended up traveling around and through Central Park, which made for an interesting trip. This was one of the places I had wanted to visit while here and never seemed to have the energy when I had days off. The airport was busier than when I came here in September. However, the crowd of travelers is not nearly back up to the level they were before. It appears that people's fear of flying after the attacks is starting to subside. I am still apprehensive about flying myself, but not nearly as much as I was in September. Providing me some sense of security are armed military personnel, stationed inside and out of the terminal.

I boarded my flight thinking that I would catch up my notes in the journal and try to doze off awhile. As soon as I settled into my first class seat, I began watching the passengers as they boarded. They all unknowingly underwent my terrorist scrutiny as they passed by my seat. I did not notice anyone that I felt needed to have an eye kept on them, which is not surprising as I would not know a terrorist if they sat down next to me. Nevertheless, it makes me feel a little more secure. I noticed that almost everyone seemed to perform the same surveillance while walking down the aisle toward his or her designated seats. After everyone boarded and prepared for takeoff, I turned my attention to my journal and began to write down the last few day's events and thoughts. However, I did not write for long as an unexpected encounter with a passenger captured my attention and provided even more material to document. This first leg of my flight was definitely one for the books.

As I sat there trying to remember all of the experiences of the last few days at Ground Zero, I noticed that across the aisle, one row ahead of me sat a lady, small in stature, spiked short hair and wearing jeans and a sweatshirt. She had a tattoo on the back of her neck that looked familiar to me for some reason. She conversed with a man seated next to her and seemed familiar with him, as if traveling together. I thought for a while about where I could have seen that tattooed symbol, however I could not place it, so I returned to my work on the journal. Just before takeoff, a female airline employee came into the plane and asked this lady to sign a paper that looked like a boarding pass. I did not think much of it as I figured it had something to do with a changed flight or baggage. My curiosity was aroused when the girl inquired if she had a new album coming out or had a concert tour in the works. Now that I am paying attention, I try to figure out who she might be. I attempted to return to my writing, however knowing that this lady is someone famous, my thoughts naturally drifted back to her identity. Later, the man sitting next to her laid a picture down onto a newspaper she was reading and she started writing on it. I looked over at what she was signing and saw that it was an advertisement for a concert. It had this lady's photo on it and the name of the band, Joan Jett and the Blackhearts. Son of a gun, I was sitting across the aisle from Joan Jett! Now I know why that tattoo was so familiar.

Well, now I had to get her autograph, but I did not want to be rude. I continued writing in my journal and waited for about an hour until she got up and went to the restroom. As she came back up the aisle, I held up my journal and motioned to her that I would like her to sign it. She came over and when she saw Ground Zero written on the front of the journal, she began asking me questions about it. She ended up kneeling in the aisle and blocking it for five minutes while she talked to me about what I did at the WTC, what I had written in the journal, and looked at it and the autographs inside. Star struck, I did not even think to move over to the unoccupied seat next to me so she could sit down.

We talked awhile about what it was like at the WTC and she said she had not been to the site yet, but wanted to go as she is from New York City. She told me that she has been giving concerts all over the place, twenty since September 11, and had just returned from giving a concert to our troops in Guantanamo Bay, Cuba. Joan gave me a great autograph, thanked me for going to NYC to help out, then leaned over and kissed me on the cheek! What an experience this was.

After she sat back down, her companion and her talked a minute or two before she came back over to ask me whom I thought they should contact to get into the site. I told her that I thought their best bet would be to talk to the police officers at the checkpoints, tell them whom she was and they would probably escort her. I told her how much the people working at the site appreciate it when celebrities visit and pay some attention to them. Joan said that she is going to try to go to the site as soon as she gets back from her concert trip. When she returned to her seat, her companion got a CD out of their carry-on luggage to give to me and he thanked me for helping. Awesome, I love New York!

As we stood across from each other in the plane aisle while waiting to disembark in Cincinnati, I thanked her for being so nice to me. She said that maybe the next time she plays in Knoxville, she would see Janice and me in the crowd. Besides liking her music, we will have to go if she does come to town to see if she will recognize me. Once we got off the plane, I was surprised as Joan went walking through the airport pulling her luggage along behind her just like the rest of us. I did not see her again as I went on my way to catch my connecting flight.

The next leg of my flight was uneventful other than a few bouts of turbulence that played havoc on my penmanship in the journal. One minute you are conversing with a rock star and the next back to reality. This has been one hell of a trip.

On the ground in Knoxville, I found Janice waiting for me at the baggage claim area. God it was great to see her and be back in her arms and in Tennessee. Arriving back at our home was wonderful. I felt as if I had been gone for months and months. A safe, comfortable, and loving feeling just seemed to grab on to me as soon as I walked in to the house. When our dog, Paco, saw me, he attacked and licked me a few hundred times to confirm that I was back where I belonged, back where there is love, caring, and peace.

Notes

I later learned that the gentleman traveling with Joan Jett was Kenny Laguna, a well-known record producer and musician in his own right. I wish I had asked for his autograph, too. They were both very nice to me and it was a thrill to talk to them. Throughout my time in New York, I met and spoke to famous people that I had never imagined. Almost every one of them was friendly, nice, and genuinely appreciative that we had come to New York to assist. Their visits helped us to briefly forget the terrible place and job we were doing. That meant a great deal to us and helped relieve some of the stress.

I hope that Joan and Kenny were able to go onto the site and experience it for themselves. Whether they did get to lift the spirits of the crews at the World Trade Center or not, they deserve a huge American thank you for traveling to Cuba for the sole purpose of entertaining our men and women in the Armed Services. Joan and Kenny, you have made a friend and fan for life.

32

Aftershocks and Afterthoughts

After my return home on October 27, 2001, my plan was to take a week off to rest and spend time with my wife. However, duty called and I ended up working a few half days during that week and went back full time the following Monday. Assigned a different position than I had before I had left for the World Trade Center, I was now a safety supervisor for two construction projects. I really thought I needed more time to get some rest, relaxation, and clear my head. However, going back to work quickly was probably the right thing to help keep me from dwelling on the terrible and emotional images I had witnessed in the last month.

Adjusting back into any normal daily routine, whether at work or home, was not without difficulties. I struggled with what seemed to be a pace that was stuck in slow motion compared to where I had just left. It took several weeks before I began to get my thought processes to slow down to a normal functioning speed. At home, although I was in comfortable and loving surroundings, I felt a little out of place, edgy, and restless. I was so happy to be back there with Janice and our peaceful life, however it was difficult to relax and enjoy it as I had just a month ago.

I had problems concentrating at work and frequently went for walks in an attempt to get back into focus. Meetings were the absolute worst and I had to attend several in those first few weeks' back. These meetings really were no different than they always have been, people sitting around discussing work and making decisions. The problem was with me. I had been assessing intense situations and making snap decisions several times a day, decisions where taking the time to have a discussion of the pros and cons might be the difference between life and death. Several times, as the meeting conversations seemed to drag on and on, I just wanted to jump up

232

and scream 'will someone make a damned decision already!' Fortunately, I never snapped and I think I kept all that inner turmoil hidden from my coworkers.

Another item that I seemed to have a problem tolerating was a few people making a big fuss over the smallest of safety problems- not that these items were not important in their own way. They just did not rise to the level of life or death and merit the amount of tension and time others believed they demanded. Someone that is not wearing his or her hard hat correctly seemed so trivial in comparison to the dangers I had just been through in New York. It took quite a long time before I could decompress, refocus, and adjust.

After several weeks of irritability and impatience, I figured out that those, along with the short attention span, the restlessness, and frequent emotional episodes, were all symptoms of Post Traumatic Stress Disorder or PTSD. When anyone experiences extremely stressful or horrific events their brain deals with those images or experiences in a variety of ways. Depending on previous experiences, emotional make-up, time exposed, and severity of the situation, the after effects will vary for each individual. On the low impact end of the spectrum, some are able to walk away with little effect and in severe cases others may end up in a lifetime of emotional difficulties that will virtually render them unable to function as before. Nightmares, inability to remain employed for long terms, relationship problems, and even suicides are common results of PTSD. Short term and minor difficulties such as I experienced are a form of Post Traumatic Stress, but as I fortunately returned to normal in a short time, did not rise to the 'Disorder' level. The severe, long lasting cases are the ones normally classified as true PTSD. There will definitely be many cases of PTSD resulting from the WTC disaster, primarily from firefighters, police officers, and those involved in body recovery.

Besides those short-term stress issues, I continue to discover that I have changed in many other ways. Some of these differences are completely new for me, and others are just a shift in the intensity of how I now feel about certain subjects. Before I left for New York, my wife and I had discussed her fear that I would return a different person from the one she had married. Our discussion was in the context of the negative personality changes that could result from an experience like this. Changes such as alcohol or drug abuse, turning distant and uncommunicative, anger, depression, nightmares, or a whole list of mental problems could surface. I am sure that there are many of the rescue and recovery workers and their families dealing with issues like these now and will for years to come. In my case, whether significant or not, changes occurred and I think that overall they were positive and an improvement in my psychological make-up. Up to this point, almost two years later, I have fortunately escaped any serious, long-term emotional issues related to my time at Ground Zero.

I now find that like most other Americans, I am much more apprehensive about the future of America and the world now. We have lost our security, our comfort in believing that the bad portions of world strife happen elsewhere, not on American soil. I do not worry about myself so much as I do for our children, grandchildren, and young people everywhere. I often wonder if they will be able to grow and have a great life as I have had, free, comfortable, safe, and full of love and laughter. On the other hand, is this just the beginning of a life of hardship, pain, and suffering for them? Of course, no one knows the riddles of the future and it has become obvious that humankind cannot seem to learn from our past mistakes. I can only hope that the world comes to its senses and that no one has to experience something like this tragedy again. I do not have the answers on how we can change this globe we are riding into a safe, loving, peaceful paradise like it was meant to be.

I fear there are always going to be Osama bin Ladens, Saddam Husseins and Adolph Hitlers in our world. Power, madness, greed, and pure evil have existed since the first recordings of history. It has been in every country, society, and village, including America. I do not have any conclusive answers on how to rid us of it. I do believe it is not outside our grasp to become united humankind that will not allow borders, different cultures, races, and religions to blur the facts. It affects us all and together we must stop these lunatics. Together, we can prevent a repeat of the kids of atrocities they have inflicted upon us. It is time to stand as one and say we are not putting up with the lunacy any more. You are not going to continue raining mayhem, chaos, and death upon the world. It ends here and now and we will use any means necessary to ensure that it does.

Politics is something that I did not pay that much attention to before. My attention was limited to listening to the issues and the particular candidates positions and voting for the one that I agreed with the most. After the elections, I ignored most of the workings of government. Now I find myself scrutinizing the politician's comments, promises, and ideas. I have not liked what I have seen or heard. Actually, I am frequently disgusted at what I perceive to be as a gaggle of adults willing to destroy the reputations and lives of anyone on the other side for their own personal gain.

It always seems that the politicians feel the need to call a news conference and trash the other side's competency on an issue, no matter whether they could have done it better or not. All that seems to be of importance to them is that they make you aware that the other guy is not perfect and give you the illusion that they, on the other hand, would do a better job of running things. Democrats and Republicans alike are spending most of their time wasting our money on investigating each other. You cannot turn on the news anymore without hearing how one of them has overlooked some clue to the tragedy or the other side is hiding something.

Somehow we have acquired the expectation that our elected officials and government agencies are supposed to know or foresee every possible threat or problem throughout the world and make sure it does not affect Americans in any way. They should know when a mentally unstable religious fanatic is going to try to pull off something somewhere, at sometime, somehow, and stop them before they are able. Well, I would like to know where they find these all-knowing people because we could use them in many other places. It would be nice to have this ability in our cities and villages to stop crimes before they can even take place. What a safe country we would have if the police showed up at the corner store five minutes before the drug addict with the intention of robbing it did.

Did these intelligence agencies miss some of the clues that could have tipped them off that a horrendous event was in the making? Absolutely they did. However, we must be able to understand a few things before we allow these politicians to ruin careers and throw the intelligence baby out with the bath water.

1. The 9/11 type terrorists are truly fanatics in every sense of the word. Nothing will keep them from their missions other than their own death. They are willing to live, breathe, die, and sacrifice their own people for their misguided cause.

2. They are also of an exclusive ethnic group and religion, Arabic and Muslim. The Middle East does not have the diverse ethnic composition as America does. Here it is commonplace to have white, black, oriental, and others intermingling with each other in most every aspect of life. It is not that way in the Middle East where anyone other than Arab sticks out like a sore thumb. Although we captured a few white Americans during the Afghanistan war, they were not in any important positions of the terrorist organizations nor privy to their inner workings. These factors make it extremely difficult to infiltrate these groups with an informant. To have a chance of success in this area, one of their leading members would have to change sides.

3. These terrorists are so secretive that their own families and friends did not know that they even belonged to Al-Qaida, let alone they were going to perform a suicide mission. One of the September 11 terrorists had discussed their upcoming

wedding with his fiancée at length a day or two before. Another had spoken with his father about a car his parents had just bought for him. He related how eager and excited he was to see it in a few days. They never gave their loved ones a single clue that this was their final conversation or their plans.

4. There are literally thousands of bits of information finding their way into our intelligence community every single day. Some of this data could be factual; others deliberate misinformation, and others so vague as to require a wild guess at an interpretation at best. Where do we get the resources to translate, decipher, and analyze all of this information with a fine-toothed comb and quickly besides?

How can we reasonably expect the CIA, NSA, and FBI to know exactly if, when, where, why, and how every dangerous group in the world is going to strike? In reality, we cannot, no matter how many of our politicians seem to think otherwise.

We should always look at our mistakes and weaknesses and learn from them. However, we should make the necessary corrections and move forward, not waste valuable time with this infighting. United we stand, divided we fall. This phrase is how old now? You would think that most of these politicians would have grasped the concept by now.

I believe 20/20 hindsight is not the qualification we need in the people we choose to run our country. Anyone of us can look back and say you should have done this, you missed that, or I would have did it this way. By the way, what in the hell is wrong with you for not being perfect? We elect these leaders to have the vision to lead us into the future, not lurk in the shadows waiting to bayonet the wounded during the heat of the battle. Enough is enough.

I did not care much for this attitude before, but now I absolutely loathe the people who are coming out of the woodwork whining that they should get money because they had a tragedy, too. Statements such as "it is just not fair that Americans should give those victims money and not me" are disgusting. One middle aged lady whose parents were killed in the Oklahoma City bombing had the audacity to go on television and cry that it was so unfair the people in New York got money and she did not. She said that her parents had helped support her and now her poor teenaged son had to get a part-time job after school so he could have some extra spending money. Do not take this wrong, I sympathize with their loss of their loved ones, but excuse me? Is there something wrong with a teenager having a part-time job and earning his or her own money? I would also like to know when it became your parent's job to support you for the rest of your life. I suppose I wasted my time working various part-time jobs from the age of twelve all the way through to high school. It apparently was the wrong approach to life. I should have been convincing my parents that they owed it to me to take care of me for life. What is wrong with you people? Is it always about the money? Are you incapable of making your own way in life? Do you honestly feel that someone should pay you for every bad thing that happens in life?

Now, some of the surviving family members of the World Trade Center victims are fighting over who gets how much money and whom they get to sue. I have not heard any of them say that they are grateful to the American people for holding fundraisers, children collecting pennies, corporations giving money and supplies, and the millions of people who reached into their pockets and gave what they could to help them. None of them had to give a dime to anyone. They did it because they wanted to help these people in their time of desperate need. They gave from their hearts and some of these victims have forgotten that fact. Rather than going on national TV and thanking the American people for their generosity, companion, and assistance, they use the media to complain that their share of the pie is not big enough. These people have cast a taint over one of the most beautiful things I have ever witnessed, something so special that I will remember and speak of it with awe and pride until my dying day. Therefore, you survivors go ahead and fight tooth and nail for those few dollars more that you think the American people owe you. Just know that they will never buy you the gifts you so selfishly are overlooking, the pure gifts of love, charity, and compassion that were given to you by strangers for no reason other than they wanted to help ease your burden in this time of tragedy.

The inevitable lawsuits are growing in number all of the time. They allege it is the airlines fault, the government should pay for not being clairvoyant, even the New York Port Authority is being sued because they did not protect people walking down the sidewalks near the WTC from the danger of the debris falling on them after a plane slammed into their building. They actually stated that the Port Authority should have foreseen this potential problem and protected them from it! It goes on and will continue for decades to come. We hear repeatedly from these people that it is not about the money, it is finding out who is responsible. If that is true, why do they not stand up and say to keep the millions of dollars, an admission of responsibility and an apology will do? Because it is about the money and they are not bullshitting anyone otherwise. They see their tragedy in dollar signs and believe that 30 pieces of silver will make them feel better. It is disgusting and is getting worse all the time.

Some of the other changes in me are not so noticeable as they have more to do with my inner self. Answering the question of could I actually walk into hell day after day, do my job, and help people instead of just believing I could was priceless. I never thought those types of questions would be answered for me. It has raised my self worth as a man and parent and filled a part of me that was missing before. I guess that I always knew that this question was hanging out there in my subconscious. I just did not realize that answering it would mean so much to me.

I find myself being a little more tolerant of others. I say thank you a lot more often and am quicker to open my wallet for charity. I am making it a point of saying 'I love you' to my family and letting

them know how I feel about them. I have renewed some
relationships that fell by the wayside during the pursuits of life and
finding that the things which really matter in this world are love,
happiness, laughter and caring for one another. I have always known
that deep down, but like most of us, I needed reminding of it.

It is evident that I will never be the same person that I was
before. I do not know how anyone that went to Ground Zero could
ever walk out of there without a different mental and moral
composition. Despite the fact that there were so many unpleasant
experiences that I am unable to bury, as I would like, I came away
from that place with so much more soul than I brought with me.
Seeing Americans come together by the thousands to do whatever
task needed no matter how bad, and supporting each other every step
of the way was incredible. I experienced personal inner growth
because of my being a part of this extraordinary event. These
magnificent experiences far outweigh the bad that went hand-in-
hand.

I now find that my emotions run right near the surface. They
have always been here, but I was able to keep most of them
concealed. I do not seem to be able to suppress them anymore. Many
things seem to touch my soft spots so easily now. I believe it is a good
thing, although some of it hurts. Wearing my 'heart on my sleeve'
now is foreign to me and there was a time not so long ago that I
would have been embarrassed had a tear rolled down my cheek in
public. So many times at Ground Zero, I witnessed men cry like
babies in front of hundreds of coworkers and strangers. They were
men that were so much stronger than I was. I am not ashamed to
admit that I frequently cried right along with them. Hiding my
emotions behind a tough, emotionless, and stoic façade no longer
seems the 'manly' thing to do and it no longer matters to me. Some
memories still bring out that emotion in me almost two years later. I
still try to allow only small pieces at a time to find their way to the
surface. Old habits are hard to break I guess, but it is more likely my
defense mechanism. Deep down I am still fearful that dropping my

guard may let the tears begin. I know how to cry now; it is being able to stop once I start that worries me.

Anyone of us could have easily come away from there a basket case. I feel blessed that I was strong enough to keep my sanity. It would have been so easy to emotionally disintegrate witnessing what we did day after day. I will never forget some of those awful sights and experiences, but I can say that I am stronger each day because of them.

I spent 30 days at Ground Zero and although I regret why we all had to go there, I will never regret going. It was the most significant thing I have ever done.

Notes

After our return from the World Trade Center, Randy Bailey, Mark Spitzer, and I studied and passed ten hours of examinations to become Certified Safety Professionals (CSPs). This designation is the measure of excellence in the safety business. All three of us considered ourselves to be 'get down in the mud' construction hands at heart and the CSP designation is such a respectable title it conjures up thoughts of scientists, Ph D's, and three-piece suits. Not one to miss the irony of it, Mark dubbed us the only 'three knuckle dragging CSPs in the world.' A title I wear proudly.

As of this writing, Mark Spitzer has just returned to Oak Ridge from a long and dangerous assignment involving the reconstruction of Iraq. I am thankful he is back on American soil and out of harm's way. I admire his courage for stepping up and taking a tough assignment again.

Keep our troops and citizens that are in harm's way in these dangerous places in the world, in your thoughts and prayers. Without courageous people like them, not only would America not be the free society it is, neither would countless others.

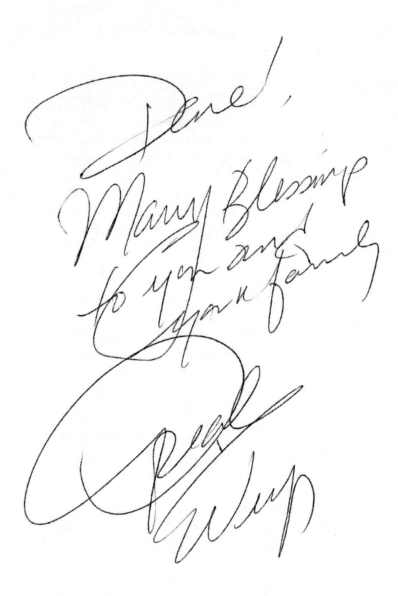

Oprah Winfrey's Autograph

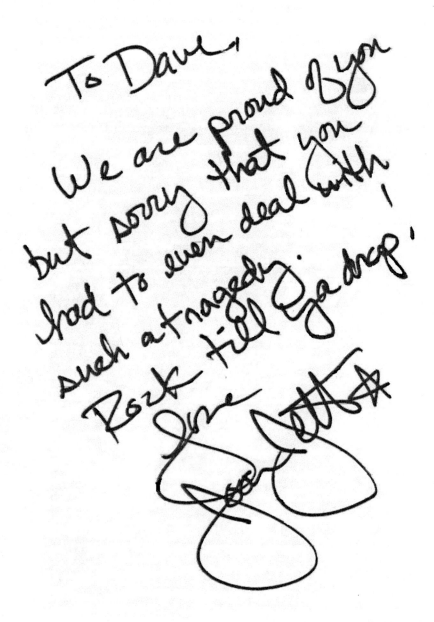

To Dave,
We are proud of you
but sorry that you
had to even deal with
such a tragedy.
Rock till ya drop!
Joan Jett

Joan Jett's Autograph

Photo: Courtesy Bill Stanley

From left to right: Randy Bailey, author David Ausmus, & Mark Spitzer

The unrelenting fires continued to burn for 100 days.

Photo: Unknown

These were the conditions every day during my time at the site.

Photo: Unknown

Photo courtesy of U.S. Coast Guard

Overhead photo of WTC Tower # 1. Note the facade leaning against WTC Building # 6.

WTC # 3, The Marriott Hotel connected to Tower # 2

Photo: Unknown

Photo: Author

Work on WTC Tower # 2

A view from the roof of World Financial Center # 1 building. The facade of WTC Tower # 2 is on the right and Tower #1 is on the left.

Photo: Author

Photo: Author

WTC Tower # 1 debris field. In the background is Building # 5.

Collateral damage to the American Express Building
across West Street from WTC Tower # 1.

Photo: Author

WTC Building # 4. A portion of this building had collapsed on September 11.

Photo: Courtesy of U.S. Coast Guard

WTC Building # 6. This building housed many government agencies, including OSHA .

The front of the World Financial Center building # 1 on the corner of West and Liberty Streets.

Photo: Unknown

Close up of WTC Building # 6

Photo: Unknown

A few of the hundreds of damaged vehicles.

Photo: Unknown

The remains of destroyed vehicles being removed from the site.

Photo: Unknown

Photo: Unknown

Disturbing signs like this one were located all around the site.

The grim reality of this heinous attack. Unfortunately,
this was a painful and frequent sight.

These solemn processions brought the work to a halt while we paid our respects.
Dead heroes being carried home by living heroes

Photo: Unknown

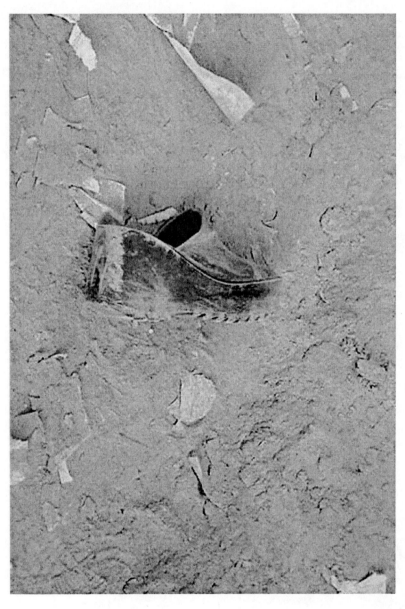

One of the hundreds of shoes scattered
throughout the debris piles and streets.

A view of the congestion on West Street. Photo taken from the pedestrian walkway at the corner of West & Liberty Streets.

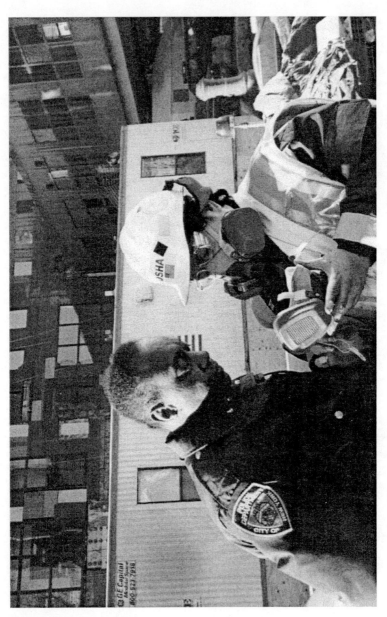

Photo: Courtesy of OSHA

OSHA officer instructing an NYPD officer in proper respirator use. OSHA performed hundreds of these sessions. The current claims by some that respirators were not provided is untrue.

MISSING FLIGHT RECORDERS
(BLACK BOXES)

ALLIED SIGNAL
COCKPIT VOICE RECORDER

MODEL # 980-6020-001

ATTENTION: If above units or components, including loose circuit boards or 3.5" magnetic tape reels, are found, document location, secure immediately and provide to the FBI. Items may be blackened, charred or rusted in appearance with no discernable lettering.

These posters were given to everyone when the first reported to the Command Center. They were posted around the site also.

HQ SECURITY PERSONNEL
10/8/01 .

HAS ID

APPLICANT'S PEDIGREE SHEET

Candidate is to print data called for by the following captions

Investigator Shall insure completeness of all entries, and secure photo in space provided.

List # ___317___   Exam # ___2000___

HAMDANI   MOHAMMAD   _S_
Surname   First Name   M.I.

34-31 204st   BAYSIDE NY 11361
               Street Address

_____   Zip # ___11361___

Home Phone # ___718-225-8569___

Sex: __MALE__ Country of Birth __PAKISTAN__

Race: White ☐   Black ☐   Other ☐

(If Hispanic, state origin as Puerto Rico, Cuba, Spain, etc.)

Age: __20__   Date of Birth __12__ __28__ __1977__
                              Mo   Day   Yr

Height: _5_ ft. _11_ in.   Weight __190__

Build: __LARGE__   Complexion __TAN__

Scars, Marks, Tattoos: _____

Civ. Occupation: __STUDENT__

MOHAMMAD.S. HAMDANI
EXAM #2000   LIST 317
INV. DIAZ

NYPD
POLICE CADET
MISSING SINCE
ATTACKS

JOINT TERRORIST
TASK FORCE
SEEKING HIM

HAS CHEMISTRY
BACKGROUND !!

The wanted poster that was pasted up all over the site. This poster was unjustified and an insult to this man and his family. (See next photo page) No agency or individual that I am aware of ever claimed responsibility for making or distributing this poster.

Rumors dispelled at hero's funeral

■ A young Muslim who died helping at the World Trade Center was later called a terrorism suspect.

By Larry McShane
Associated Press

NEW YORK — For six months after Sept. 11, the family of Salman Hamdani had to endure the rumors that he was a fugitive terrorist, or that he was in federal custody. Yesterday he was remembered for what he truly was: a hero who died in the rubble of the World Trade Center.

The 23-year-old Muslim, his remains in a flag-draped coffin at a Manhattan mosque, was praised at his long-delayed funeral for a selfless and fatal choice: heading to the attack site to help his fellow Americans.

"We don't know how many people he helped, how many lives he saved," Police Commissioner Raymond Kelly told several hundred mourners at the Islamic Cultural Center of New York. "But if you look at his life, you know he was determined to make a difference — and he did. He was indeed a hero."

Hamdani, a Pakistani-born laboratory research assistant who also had training as a medical technician, was missing for more than six months after the terrorist attack that killed more than 2,800 people. His remains — along with his medical bag, containing an ID — were recovered near the north tower. Hamdani was not positively identified until March 20.

Hamdani, who came to the United States when just a year old, was known to co-workers at Rockefeller University as Sal. The Queens College graduate majored in biochemistry and hoped to become a doctor.

Mourners carry the coffin of Salman Hamdani from the mosque at New York's Islamic Cultural Center. A funeral was held yesterday for the 23-year-old Muslim, who died helping others after the attack on the World Trade Center.

He was already an American citizen.

On Sept. 11, Hamdani left his home in Queens in the morning and apparently saw the disaster in lower Manhattan unfold from the elevated train tracks. He immediately headed toward the scene.

In the weeks after his disappearance, a newspaper linked him to the terrorist attack, and a flier with his picture was circulated among city police officers, saying an FBI-Police Department joint terrorist task force wanted to speak with him. The fliers were unauthorized, and their source was unclear, police later said. But the rumors about his involvement in the attack spread.

Yesterday, his mother, Talat, blasted the news reports, saying: "If your name was David, the story would have been very different."

At the funeral, scores of police cadets sat on the floor, their shoes removed in accordance with Muslim custom. Hamdani's parents, two brothers and other family members sat in front of the casket. His father and other relatives wore red, white and blue scarves featuring the American flag.

The real story of Mr. Salman Hamdani. An American hero if there ever was one. He had medical technician training so he rushed to the scene as a concerned citizen to help those in need. He sacrificed his life on September 11 assisting his fellow Americans.

THE CITY OF NEW YORK
OFFICE OF THE MAYOR
NEW YORK, N.Y. 10007

October 12, 2001

Dear Family:

On behalf of the entire City of New York, I want to express my deep respect and admiration for the wonderful strength and courage you and your family have shown in the face of the tragedies of September 11, 2001. Your resolve and determination continue to inspire me, your fellow Americans and all people of goodwill throughout the world.

On Sunday, October 28 at 2 p.m. there will be a memorial service for the victims of the World Trade Center attacks. I invite you to join me for a loving tribute to the memory of your loved one and all those we lost. Immediately following the service memorial urns will be presented to the next of kin at the New York City Family Assistance Center at Pier 94. Please RSVP at (646) 710-6245 between the hours of 8 a.m. and 8 p.m. by October 18 so that your credentials can be mailed to you. Five credentials are being made available for each family.

I look forward to being with you on October 28.

Sincerely,

Rudolph W. Giuliani
Mayor

Letter from NYC Mayor Rudolf Giuliani to the families of the victims.

FEDERAL, STATE, LOCAL AGENCIES AND OTHER CONTRACTORS SAFETY OBSERVATIONS DISCREPIENCY REPORT

SHIFT: 7:00pm October 24 to 7:00am October 25, 2001

Observation Number	Agency	Work Sector	Comment Category	Observation
01	PAPD	Amec	Vehicle safety	Seven officers not wearing PPE transported in the bed of silver Ford Ranger XLT pick up truck # 32 between WTC1 & WTC2
02	NYPD	Amec	PPE	Two officers in off road vehicle on ramp @ WTC1 not wearing hardhats and safety glasses
03	NYPD	Amec	PPE	Four officers not wearing respirators on debris pile
04	FDNY	Amec	PPE	Three firefighters eating and drinking on the debris pile
05	FDNY	Amec	PPE	Eight firefighters without respirator on debris pile
06	Surveyors	Amec	PPE	Two exposed to 15 ft. fall @ unprotected edge of crane mat
07	Engineers (DDC sub)	Amec	PPE	Weidlinger engineer repeatedly asked (3times) by ▬ o comply with basic PPE other than a hardhat, employee refused, he states "he will take care of DDC", employee has "Site Safety" on the front of his white hardhat. ▬ spoke with a DDC Construction Supt. regarding incident.
08	PAPD	Bovis	PPE	Two officers escorting visitors on the debris pile without respirators
09	NYPD	Bovis	PPE	Five officers without respirators on the debris pile
10	NYDOT	Bovis	PPE	Drivers out of trucks on debris pile without respirators
11	NYPD	Tully	PPE	Three officers at Liberty and Greenwich Sts. without head or

Typical report on site problems (page 1)

				eye protection
12	NYPD	Tully	PPE	Two officers and girlfriend in work area at Liberty and Greenwich Sts. without head or eye protection
13	FDNY	Tully	PPE	Three firefighters and two Chiefs on debris pile without respirators
14	MTA	Tully	PPE	Two officers on debris pile without any PPE
15	FDNY	Tully	PPE	Ten firefighters on debris pile without respirators
16	NYPD	Tully	PPE	Four officers on debris pile without respirators
17	NYPD FDNY	Tully	PPE	Two officers and one firefighter in work area without head protection
18	FDNY	Turner	PPE	Four firefighters in work areas without head or eye protection
19				
20				

Page 2 of the report.

**New York City Department of Health
Responds to the World Trade Center Disaster**

ADVISORY: Health of Rescue Personnel

What risks do human body parts found inside of exploded and collapsed buildings pose to rescue workers?
There is no threat of a general outbreak of infectious disease among workers at the site. You may be at risk for infection if you cut yourself with an object contaminated with blood, body fluids or tissue, or if these materials touch your eyes, nose or mouth or areas of broken skin. Bad odors that come from decomposing bodies, although unpleasant, are not harmful.

What should I do if I'm injured or splashed?
Immediately report to your supervisor any injuries or splashes to eyes, nose, mouth or broken skin by blood or body fluids so that appropriate medical evaluation and care can be provided. Infections can be prevented if you follow appropriate precautions.

What precautions should rescue workers take?
Do not touch bodies or body parts directly. Rescue workers who expect they might have direct contact with human remains should do the following:

- Wear heavy-duty waterproof gloves to protect against injury from sharp objects.
- Use eye protection and respirators equipped with OVAG cartridges to protect eyes, nose, and mouth from splash exposures and noxious odors.
- Wear protective garments to protect skin and clothes.
- Immediately wash hands with soap and water after removing gloves.
- Alcohol-based hygiene products are a useful substitute only when hands are not visibly soiled.

How can my overall health be affected from exposure to decomposing remains?
Seeing decomposing remains can cause emotional trauma, grief, anger and sadness. Immediately after the disaster, it will be normal for you to feel:

- Numbness
- Flashbacks and nightmares
- Anger
- Sadness

- Denial or shock
- Grief reactions to loss
- Despair
- Hopelessness

What should a rescue worker do if he or she experiences emotional distress?
Several studies following the Oklahoma City Bombing found that many rescue and relief workers experienced emotional distress. However, many did not believe they needed help and would not seek services despite feeling emotional distress. It is important to get help by talking with family, friends, religious leaders or neighbors if you are feeling:

- Normal emotional responses such as grief, anger, guilt, shame, helplessness, hopelessness, and emotional numbness.
- Confusion, disorientation, indecisiveness, worry, shortened attention span, memory loss, and difficulty concentrating.

Information sheet on precautions and recognizing if our work took too much of an emotional toll.

- Physical reactions such as tension, fatigue, edginess, difficulty sleeping, body aches or pain, nausea, change in appetite, being startled easily, change in sex drive and racing heartbeat.
- Interpersonal problems such as distrust, irritability, conflict, withdrawal, isolation, and feeling rejected or abandoned, being distant, judgmental, or over-controlling.

OR

If you experience Post-Traumatic Stress Disorder, which is less common and could include:

- Feeling as if you or the world is unreal.
- Re-experiencing the event during the day or as nightmares.
- Being frightened of leaving home or losing interest in normal activities.
- Feeling prolonged and increased anxiety, nervousness, or fear of losing control.
- Abusing drugs or alcohol.

If these feelings remain longer than a month, we urge you to seek help from medical or mental health professionals, or disaster service organizations like the American Red Cross. The following Department of Mental Health Hotlines can provide direct access to services.

English Life NET (800) 543-3638
Spanish Life NET (877) 298-3373
Chinese Life NET (877) 990-8585

Do I need to contact law enforcement about any remains found?
Yes, in the setting of a disaster, remains should be brought to the attention of appropriate law enforcement and forensic representatives for identification.

For additional information regarding occupational health issues, please refer to the U.S. Occupational Safety and Health Administration, World Trade Center Information.

Page 2 of the information sheet.

ACCOMPLISHMENTS (Past 24 hours)

1. Application of water to South Tower area and where heat and smoke are escaping in an attempt to extinguish/reduce the heat.
2. Operations continue on debris removal from the North Tower area with intermittent use of handlines to cool debris and for dust control.
3. Intermittent use of handlines in operation for dust control at 7 WTC.
4. Intermittent use of two multiversals in use for cooling and dust control between 5 & 6 WTC.
5. Continue to collect empty compressed gas cylinders.
6. Emphasis continues on slurry wall reinforcement in front of South Tower.
7. Steel and debris removal continues from core of South Tower. Handline use for dust control / cooling.
8. Revised guidelines for access to retrieve valuables have been completed.
9. Spill prevention and response plan has been submitted for review.
10. Contractor continues MTA shoring on Church Street.
11. Started demolition of 3 southwest bays of 6 WTC.
12. Established procedures for coordinated fueling services.
13. Removed 4 truckloads of FDNY equipment and tools.
14. Site Inspection @ #1 Liberty Plaza complete, will occupy Monday 10/22, FD Systems are in service.
15. Procedures for Contractor C of F for the use of cutting/welding torches have been issued.
16. PESH has conducted air sampling (7 firefighters/shift).
17. Received final copy Environmental Health and Safety Plan, it is being reviewed.
18. Procedures for tube trailer movement issued to all contractors.
19. NYCTA conducted entry to Rector St. station for bi-weekly inspection.
20. Removed 12 55 gal. drums of kerosene from West Command.

PLANNED ACTIONS (Next 24 hours)

1. Steel cutting operations and subsequent removal of debris by rigging and heavy equipment will continue. Utilize ironworkers to accomplish this mission. Utilize FDNY SOC and PD ESU personnel to assist and supplement this function. Utilize all available cutting set-ups on a continual basis.
2. FD SOC personnel and PD ESU personnel will continue to conduct void searches as required when heavy steel is removed.
3. All Emergency personnel operating on the South Tower in selected areas will be in bunker pants as needed.
4. Continue to place and use large caliber water streams for continuous fire extinguishment operations on 1 and 2 WTC as required. Place and use protective hand lines elsewhere as needed.
5. Continue to review operational/engineering plan to facilitate removal of the West façade walls still standing in the South Tower area. FDNY, DDC and site construction manager will review plan and evaluate results of deconstruction process.
6. Continue GPS mapping and documentation of recovery operations and structural features.
7. NIJ continues to operate five camera points for use in locating the flight recorders.
8. ARMY continues laser mapping to detect any movement/shifting of piles. OEM coordinating.
9. Fire companies to wet down debris fields and dirt roads when requested by DDC.
10. DSNY will continue to water dusty streets and remove garbage.
11. Partial removal of west wall 2 WTC continues. (See attached Exclusion Zone diagram)
12. Continue demolition of 3 southwest bays of 6 WTC.
13. Fire Prevention will begin confiscating 1 & 5 gal plastic gas cans.
14. DOB Derrick & Crane Unit site safety inspection of operations, movement, placement & maintenance. (Continuous)

Portions of the daily FDNY Reports.

15. Fire Prevention to meet with DCAS to develop fueling procedures for Agency vehicles and equipment.
16. Issue Contractor Certificates of Fitness for cutting/welding torch use.
17. Cutting/pulling 1st four columns of west façade of South Tower.
18. Entry into Concourse Level Building 5 WTC, to retrieve valuables by Friday.

ANTICIPATED ACTIONS (72 hours)

1. Continue in the planned actions and operating instructions.
2. As other crane(s) are set up and / or relocated, continue in the accelerated debris removal and void search operations. Concentration of operations will follow prioritized order as conditions permit:
   Backfilling of slurry wall
   North Tower (1 WTC)
   North and West sides of Marriott
   South Tower (2 WTC)
3. Perimeter security will continue and improve.
4. Review by Mayor's Office of the WTC Long Range Site Plan.
5. NYARNG/USFS will retrieve unattended hand for consolidation.
6. Clear sites for the erection of warming tents at East Command, Vessey Sector and Liberty Sector.

SPECIAL INSTRUCTIONS

1. FDNY Sector Chiefs will approve all searches.
2. Follow identified procedures to handle requests for retrieval of valuables from damaged structures.
3. Review posted information regarding Minimum Protective Equipment Requirements, Site Safety, Evacuation Signals, Site Hazards, Blood Borne Pathogens and Hazard Markings on Buildings.
4. For non-exempt personnel, only white, non-photo credentials will allow access into the site (Security checkpoints have a list of exempt agencies).
5. FDNY personnel arriving by bus from the Flushing Marina Staging Area will be issued color-coded bands for authorized entry into the site. The colors for this operational period are as follows:

10/19	0700-1100	PEACH
10/19	1100-2300	GRAY
10/19-20	2300-0700	YELLOW

   The band must be prominently displayed to allow entry onto the site.
6. GPS is to be used to plot locations of all victims, remains, fire equipment and apparatus. If the GPS is not operational, hand held GPS will manually record grid locations **grid map dated 09/20 or later.** GPS units are available through the Sector Chiefs, who shall contact the GPS Team via channel 5.
7. When public safety personnel, apparatus and/or equipment are found, please protect the area and notify the appropriate agency for appropriate documentation and removal. If **weapons or ammunition** are found, secure the area and immediately notify law enforcement authorities.
8. There are two small residential type safes in the canine area on B-1 of 2 WTC, which contain explosive materials used for training dogs. The pile of debris is now ten feet above grade but as pile is reduced to grade level operations in this location must be coordinated with PAPD and NYPD.
9. When any SCBA or compressed gas cylinders are found the Sector Chief will notify the ICP for Fire Prevention notification.
10. Enclosures on North and South projections on West Street are locked. The keys will be located with the FDNY Command Post, NYPD Officer at enclosure and OEM.
11. A single unit with one fire officer and 2 firefighters is dedicated to initial response to fires and emergencies within the restricted area dispatched through Manhattan CO.
12. NYPD will have K-9's available at 1 and 2 WTC's, the Marriott Hotel and the Plaza for use when excavators are not operating.

Portions of the daily FDNY Reports.

15. Fire Prevention to meet with DCAS to develop fueling procedures for Agency vehicles and equipment.
16. Issue Contractor Certificates of Fitness for cutting/welding torch use.
17. Cutting/pulling 1st four columns of west façade of South Tower.
18. Entry into Concourse Level Building 5 WTC, to retrieve valuables by Friday.

ANTICIPATED ACTIONS   (72 hours)

1. Continue in the planned actions and operating instructions.
2. As other crane(s) are set up and / or relocated, continue in the accelerated debris removal and void search operations. Concentration of operations will follow prioritized order as conditions permit:
   Backfilling of slurry wall
   North Tower (1 WTC)
   North and West sides of Marriott
   South Tower (2 WTC)
3. Perimeter security will continue and improve.
4. Review by Mayor's Office of the WTC Long Range Site Plan.
5. NYARNG/USFS will retrieve unattended hand for consolidation.
6. Clear sites for the erection of warming tents at East Command, Vessey Sector and Liberty Sector.

SPECIAL INSTRUCTIONS

1. FDNY Sector Chiefs will approve all searches.
2. Follow identified procedures to handle requests for retrieval of valuables from damaged structures.
3. Review posted information regarding Minimum Protective Equipment Requirements, Site Safety, Evacuation Signals, Site Hazards, Blood Borne Pathogens and Hazard Markings on Buildings.
4. For non-exempt personnel, only white, non-photo credentials will allow access into the site (Security checkpoints have a list of exempt agencies).
5. FDNY personnel arriving by bus from the Flushing Marina Staging Area will be issued color-coded bands for authorized entry into the site. The colors for this operational period are as follows:

10/19	0700-1100	PEACH
10/19	1100-2300	GRAY
10/19-20	2300-0700	YELLOW

   The band must be prominently displayed to allow entry onto the site.
6. GPS is to be used to plot locations of all victims, remains, fire equipment and apparatus. If the GPS is not operational, hand held GPS will manually record grid locations grid map dated 09/20 or later. GPS units are available through the Sector Chiefs, who shall contact the GPS Team via channel 5.
7. When public safety personnel, apparatus and/or equipment are found, please protect the area and notify the appropriate agency for appropriate documentation and removal. If weapons or ammunition are found, secure the area and immediately notify law enforcement authorities.
8. There are two small residential type safes in the canine area on B-1 of 2 WTC, which contain explosive materials used for training dogs. The pile of debris is now ten feet above grade but as pile is reduced to grade level operations in this location must be coordinated with PAPD and NYPD.
9. When any SCBA or compressed gas cylinders are found the Sector Chief will notify the ICP for Fire Prevention notification.
10. Enclosures on North and South projections on West Street are locked. The keys will be located with the FDNY Command Post, NYPD Officer at enclosure and OEM.
11. A single unit with one fire officer and 2 firefighters is dedicated to initial response to fires and emergencies within the restricted area dispatched through Manhattan CO.
12. NYPD will have K-9's available at 1 and 2 WTC's, the Marriott Hotel and the Plaza for use when excavators are not operating.

Portions of the daily FDNY Reports.

SPECIAL INSTRUCTIONS - Continued

13. **No open flames or warming fires.** Use the warming tents if necessary.
14. **No parking along Church between Liberty and Vesey.**
15. Prior to any vehicles being removed/towed from bldgs. FDNY Ops chief must insure a foam handline is provided.
16. Prior to any steel cutting @ 3 WFC(Amex) a charged handline will be stretched to a location TBD.
17. The exclusion zone for Banker's Trust will be maintained & enforced during cutting operations
16. Exclusion zone for 2 WTC continues until all pulling is completed @ 2 WTC. All personnel are to remain outside the exclusion zone (See Diagram)

DEPARTMENT OF DESIGN AND CONSTRUCTION UPDATE

ACCOMPLISHMENTS (Past 24 hours)

PLANNED ACTIONS (24 hours)

1. Continuing construction of south to east access road to Plaza.
2. Continue to backfill void North of slurry wall & South of 2 WTC from Greenwich to West Street to be completed by end of the week.
3. Well points being installed on Liberty Street and also West Street by Moretrench Drilling.
4. Continue to shore floors at 3 WFC to be accomplished by the end of the week.
5. Removal of 2 WTC south and west façades to continue.
6. Contractor will continue to construct retaining wall for BMT on west side of Church Street.
7. Debris removal in plaza area adjacent to 5 WTC.
8. Core drilling and installation of tiebacks for slurry wall south of 2 WTC.
9. Continue debris removal from 1 and 2 WTC footprints.
10. Removal of Bankers Trust debris.

ANTICIPATED ACTIONS (72 hours)

1. Well points, core drilling and tiebacks being installed on Liberty and West Streets to be continued.
2. Construction of north to south retaining wall for BMT on west side of Church Street.
3. DDC will provide an overall site project plan on 10/22/01.
4. Debris removal north of Marriott (Vista) hotel.
5. Demolition of southwest bays of 6 WTC.
6. Continue south to east access road to plaza.
7. Continue slurry wall backfilling on Liberty Street.
8. Continue shoring in 3 WFC.
9. Continue removals of 2 WTC west and south facades.
10. Removal of debris north of Bankers Trust.
11. Removal of debris on plaza and concourses.
12. Continue removals from 1 and 2 WTC footprints.
13. Demolition of southwest bays of 6 WTC for crane access to north façade of 1 WTC continues

There is an OEM representative located at the OEM trailer (Murray and West - 212 941-5337) to contact DDC to handle contractor problems.
To contact the contractors on site, DDC has a person stationed at 10/10 to assist. .
OEM is also the contact for OSHA.

Portions of the daily FDNY Reports.

DR-1391-NY New York City
Facility Locations - October 18

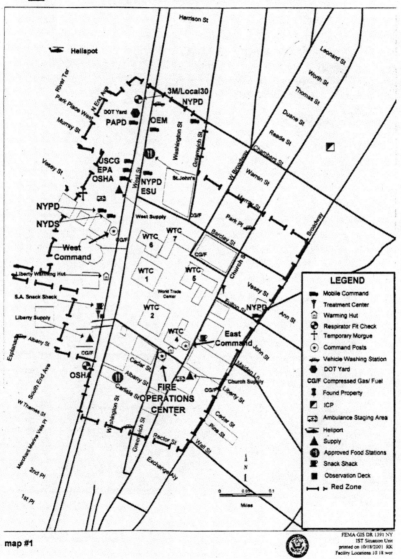

map #1

FEMA GIS DR 1391 NY
IST Situation Unit
printed on 10/18/2001 RK
Facility Locations 10 18 wor

FDNY Map of the site.

Photo: Author

The 'Teddy Bear Wall, the saddest place I have ever been. Memory of a wife's letter to her fallen husband still makes me cry to this day, almost two years later.

Photo: Unknown

Close up of the 'Teddy Bear Wall'.

The police officer's memorial across from the
'Teddy Bear Wall' in Battery Park.

Photo: Author

Photo: Author

Firefighter statue outside of FDNY Firehouse 10
on the corner of Liberty and Church Streets.

New York Senator Hillary Clinton poses with an unidentified firefighter in front of a pedestrian walkway across the street from WTC Tower # 2. Visible over the firefighter's left shoulder hangs the American Flag that I recovered from under fallen rubble days after this photo was taken.

Another view of the flag I recovered from underneath collapsed rubble
inside this walkway on October 1, 2001.

Photo: Author

Photo: Author

The photo of the 'Cross at Ground Zero' I took for my Mom.

My friends from Quincy Junior High School. Seated from left to right: teacher Bonnie Brueggeman, Justin Childress, Tony Young, Kevin Leindecker, & teacher's aide Janet Stephenson. Standing in back L to R: Norman Peterson, Melinda Pritchard, Ryan Clair, Matt Albert, Ronnie Syrcle (who's letter I read), Ammanda Stepp, & Drrick Wilson.

Information on photographs.

I have noted some photos as unknown because I have received literally hundreds from friends, contractors, or have found them on the Internet with either no one or more than one person or entity claiming them as their own. If I have reproduced your photograph in this book, and did not attribute it to you, I sincerely apologize. I can assure you that I made every effort to find the true owner(s). If a photograph is indeed yours, please contact the publisher at the address listed and I will either remove it or list it as belonging to you in any future editions.

The cover photograph:
Used with the permission and courtesy of FEMA.
Michael Rieger took the photo.

ISBN 141201000-4

9 781412 010009